H Senior Humor

A TREASURY OF SENIOR HUMOR

D0469483

Edited by

James E. Myers

THE LINCOLN-HERNDON PRESS, INC.
818 S. Dirksen Parkway
Springfield, Illinois 62703

A Treasury of Senior Humor

Copyright © 1992 by Lincoln-Herndon Press, Inc.
All rights reserved. This book or parts thereof, may not be reproduced in any form without permission.

Published by
Lincoln-Herndon Press, Inc.
818 S. Dirksen Parkway
Springfield, Illinois 62703
(217) 522-2732

Printed in the United States of America

LIBRARY OF CONGRESS CATALOGUING-IN-PUBLICATION DATA

ISBN 0-942936-20-5: $10.95
Library of Congress Catalogue Card Number 91-61819
Fifth Printing

Typography by
Affordable Laser Typesetting
Springfield, Illinois

TABLE OF CONTENTS

INTRODUCTION

A TREASURY OF SENIOR HUMOR offers the jokes, tall tales, funny stories and hilarious cartoons that identify what it means to have lived sixty and more years in this wonderful U.S.A. And perhaps the very best analysis of just who and what and why senior citizens are what they are is given in an analysis by Wesley N. Haines (AKA Reggie the Retiree) in his book, *"LAUGHS AND LIMERICKS ON AGING,"* 1983.

"We were here before the 'pill' and the population explosion. We were here before television, penicillin, polio shots, antibiotics and frisbees; before frozen food, nylon, dacron, Xerox, Kinsey, radar, fluorescent lights, credit cards and ball point pens. For us 'time-sharing' meant togetherness, not computers; a chip meant a piece of wood; hardware meant *hard wear,* and software wasn't even a word. Co-eds never wore slacks. We were here before pantyhose and drip-dry clothes, before ice-makers and dishwashers, clothes-dryers, freezers and electric blankets; before Hawaii and Alaska became states; before men wore long hair and earrings . . . and women wore tuxedos. We were here before Leonard Bernstein, yogurt, Ann Landers, plastic, the 40-hour week and the minimum wage. We were married first and then lived together. How quaint can one be?

"Closets were for clothes, not for coming out of; rabbits were small bunnies - not Volkswagons. We were before Grandma Moses and Frank Sinatra and 'cup-size' bras. Girls wore Peter Pan collars and thought cleavage was something butchers did. We were before Batman, Rudolph The Red-Nosed Reindeer, and Snoopy. DDT, vitamin pills, disposable diapers, Jeeps, the Jefferson Memorial, pizza, Cheerios, instant coffee, de-caffeinated anything, and McDonalds were all unheard of. We thought 'fast food' was what you ate during Lent. We were before Boy George, J. D. Salinger and Chiquita Banana; before radios, tape recorders, electric typewriters, word processors, Muzak, electronic music, disco-dancing and that's not all bad!

"In our day, cigarette smoking was fashionable, grass was for mowing, Coke was a refreshing drink and 'pot' was something you cooked in. If we'd been asked to explain, CIA, Ms., NATO, UFO, JFK, ERA and IUD, we would have said 'alphabet soup'."

And he is correct! We Golden Agers have lived through marvelous and frightening times. What an astonishing period were those last two generations of thirty years each! Those were the years that saw the most terrible depression of all times, then World War II, then the Korean War, Vietnam and the atom bomb. But through most of those years, Americans had prosperity unrivaled in any previous time. Most remarkable has been the change in life expectancy from forty-five years in 1900, to seventy-six years in 1990. Also worth remembering is that in 1920, two-thirds of American men over sixty-five years of age were still working; whereas by 1950, less than twenty-five percent were at work. But thirty-eight years later - 1988 - only 2.9% of men were still at work. Social security, pensions and all the other blessings given us were the cause of this tremendous change.

Curiously, all these benefits, social security, pensions, medicare and medicaid - all government help of any sort given to the aged - were once contemptuously referred to as "socialism!"

It is a true blessing that Americans take such good care of their elderly. It seems fair to say that Americans truly observe that Fifth Commandment: HONOR THY FATHER AND THY MOTHER THAT THY DAYS MAY BE LONG IN THE LAND.

It is another notable fact that through all those past sixty awful and wonderful years, encompassing two generations, Americans have found laughter to be in fact, as well as in "folk-say," the best medicine. That condition never changes and never will. As William James said, "We don't laugh because we are happy, we are happy because we laugh."

Most of us know that laughter is one of the best anti-depressants for the elderly. Laughter eases emotional pain and the unavoidable stress of growing old. And we must exercise our risibilities, our ability to find laughter in painful situations. When we Golden Agers do that we are exemplary! And fun. We bring smiles and laughter when we joke about our erratic and demanding bladder, failing eyesight, diminished hearing, creaky joints, lessened sex drive, undependable memory. Add to all that, our wrinkles, bald and grey heads and, yes, let us admit it, our sometimes noisy flatulence!

If it is true that "aches and pains are the way your body educates you," well, our elderly certainly are the most learned segment of our entire population!

But in spite of it all, our seniors have shown us that to grow old does not require the elderly to be a burden of gloom, a pall on society. Those humorous sparks that our seniors throw out assure us of that. There is also a bit of a "to-hell-with-it-all" attitude that says, "I've seen it all, buddy, and it is to laugh!" Theirs is the point of view that tells us that we all head for the same fate and that finding humor along the way is like thumbing your nose at our inevitable end. It is as if we said, "Nobody, but nobody gets out of this life alive." Golden agers have taught us that humor is to life what shock absorbers are to an automobile.

It is the hope of the editor, himself an "old codger," that readers young and old will find jokes, stories, cartoons with a special quality of joyfulness, even feistiness and a kind of defiance that says "come hell or high water, by golly, I'll make the best of it." With senior humor comes a deeper understanding of what it means to grow old in our beneficent America, to be a senior citizen, a golden ager or, to use a country term, an old coot.

So...throughout the days of your years, keep a little laughter up your sleeve because, as most of us know, LAUGHTER IS THE BEST MEDICINE.

Perhaps the wisest, most useful statement advising us to laugh, because laughter does us good, is what Josh Billings (1818-1885) had to say. Incidentally, Abraham Lincoln is said to have remarked about old Josh, his favorite humorist, "Next to William Shakespeare, Josh Billings is the greatest judge of human nature the world has ever seen."

"There ain't much phun in medisin, but there's a lot of medisin in phun."

So let us all salute our senior citizens who have done so much good - and still do - for our unparalleled American society. Long may they live - and laugh.

1

OLD MAIDS

Definition of an old maid:
1.   A gal without a gent to her name.
2.   A lady who knows all the answers, but isn't asked the questions.
3.   An evaporated peach.
4.   An unfound treasure.
5.   A lady-in-waiting.
6.   A lady in her ancedotage.

An elderly maiden lady had worked all her life at an accounting job. Upon retirement, she decided to move to the country, to a small farm, and to raise chickens. So she bought ten acres, built a chicken house and poultry run, then went to the hatchery to buy baby chicks. "I want," she told the hatchery salesman, "one hundred baby hens and one hundred baby roosters."

"OK, MAUDIE... BUT I'M DRIVING THIS TIME."

An old maiden lady made pajamas for a man and gave them to the Salvation Army. "I made them myself," she said proudly.

The Salvation Army attendant noticed there was no opening, no fly, in front of the pajamas. She explained the deficiency to the old maiden lady, who said, "Couldn't you give them to a bachelor?"

An old maid moved to Rochelle,
And went round ringing a bell,
    She was asked why she rang it,
    She replied, "Gol' dang it,
This old town is quieter than Hell."

Old Miss Stokes rarely left her comfortable old house. And behind the house, in the backyard, she kept a lovely vegetable garden. What was her surprise and dismay to look out the window, one morning, and there was an enormous grey animal pulling up her cabbages. She rushed to the phone and called the police. The sergeant on duty responded, "Miss Stokes, kindly tell me what harm the animal is doing?"

"Harm? Why he's pulling up my cabbages with his tail."

"I can understand your concern...but, he's using his **tail** to pull your cabbages? Miss Stokes, what does the animal do with the cabbages once he pulls them out with his...his...tail?"

"He...he...oh, officer! If I told you, you'd never believe it!"

An old maid is a woman in the prim of life.

There was an old maid of Shanghai
Who was so excessively shy,
When undressing at night
She turned out the light
For fear of the All Seeing Eye.

2

An old maid kept walking about, in and out of the house, constantly speaking one word: "embargo." Her friends and neighbors grew quite worried about this loony habit of hers until they finally figured out that her speech was not crazy at all, not if you spelled the word backward.

The desperate age: Too young for medicare and too old for men to care.

An old maid whose name was Bella
Fell in love with a bow-legged fella,
    This malformed sap,
    Let her sit in his lap,
And, of course, she fell into the cella.

"Yes, I can see some improvement: You're getting worse at a slower rate."

*Reprinted by permission, **The American Legion Magazine***

3

The elderly spinster and her friend were arguing the value of marriage, and of men. "What do I want a husband for? What would I do with a man? I've already got a dog that snores, a cat that stays out all night, a parrot that grumbles, a chimney that smokes! And every time I get out of this chair, I get a pain in my...you-know-what."

A corpulent old maid from Oak Knolls,
Had an idea droller than droll;
    At a halloween ball,
    Wearing nothing at all,
She mooned as a Parker House Roll.

The old lady was so bashful, she would go into a closet to change her mind.

"Frankly, Robert, I find it hard to put complete confidence in someone I once had to flunk out of ninth-grade math."

Reprinted by permission, **The American Legion Magazine**

There was an old maid from Siam,
Who said to her lover from Priam,
  "If you kiss me, of course,
  You'll have to use force,
But, gosh knows, you're stronger than I am."

Advice to the aging: Always remember that a raisin is a grape that worried too much and got wrinkles.

Here's an old story told during World War II. It seems that two guys, one huge and the other quite small, boarded a train and the big guy announced that they were about to rob all the men of their money and kiss all the women. The small guy said to the big one, "Aw, c'mon, Pete. All we want is money. Why not let the women alone!"

But there was an old maid on board, and she said, "Say, little man, you just shut your mouth! That big fellow is robbing this train."

"YOU MUST TRY THEM EDITH, THEY'ER ABSOLUTELY THE
JUICIEST GRAPEFRUIT YOU'LL HAVE EVER EATEN..."

Effie Roundtree was a faithful black maid who had worked for Beth Smith for a year. But one day she reported and announced that she could only work until noon because she had to take her young son to the doctor.

"But, Effie, I didn't know you were married. I thought you were an old maid like me."

"I ain't married. And I am an old maid. But I ain't the fussy kind."

There was a lonesome, lorn spinster,
Whose luck had for years been against her,
    When a man came to burgle,
    She shrieked with a gurgle,
"Stop thief while I call in a min'ster."

Poor Shirley was in her sixties and had never been married. "The only man who considers me a 'ten' is the shoe salesman," she moaned.

An old gal born in Vancouver,
Once got a man by maneuver,
    She jumped on his knee
    With laughter, with glee,
And nothing on earth could remove her.

There was an old maid of Florence,
Who for kissing professed great abhorrence,
    But after she'd kissed,
    And found what she'd missed,
She cried and the tears flowed in torrents.

The old girl, never married, was asked which qualities in a man she liked best...brains, money or appearance. She thought a moment, then replied, "Appearance...and the sooner the better."

That same old girl went to her bedroom one night, and discovered a thief under her bed. She slammed the door, ran downstairs to the phone and called the police. "Please, oh please! Send a cop to 618 South Maiden Lane. But send him in the morning."

Minnie Pearl used to say, "I haven't been kissed in so long I don't recall if you suck in your breath or let it out."

Most old folks don't mind suffering in silence as long as everyone else knows about it.

There was an old maid named Ethel
Who wore underwear made of metal.
    When asked, "Does it hurt?"
    She replied, "It keeps dirt
From the stalk and the leaves and the petal."

The old maid finally had received a proposal for marriage but he had little money to offer so she told him that he must earn ten thousand dollars first.

After a lapse of several weeks, the old boy called again and told her that he still wanted to marry her, that he had a job and had saved money.

"And how much have you saved?" she asked.

"One hundred dollars," he replied.

"Well," she replied, "that's close enough."

There was an old maid of Lynn,
Who said all this kissin' was syn.
But suddenly a beau tried to see if 'twas seau,
And she said: "Please, oh do it agyn."

An old maid is one who failed to strike while the iron was hot.

There was an old lady named Wilde,
Who had kept herself quite undefiled.
    She feared men of all ages,
    All diseases contagious,
And the bother of having a child.

Was she heavy? Beefy? Well, I guess! She resembled an hour glass in which most of the sand had filtered down into the Southern zone!

Old maid calling on the telephone: "Is this the fire department?"

Voice: "Yes, ma'am. What can we do for you?"

Old maid: "A man is trying to get in my window."

Voice: "Lady, you need the police department. Call 1-222...."

Old maid: "No, I want you! The fire department. I'm on the second floor and this man needs a ladder. So please hurry over...."

The above story reminds us of another, similar tale. This time there _was_ a fire. Twenty firemen rushed over and put out the fire. The old maid thanked them profusely, then said: "Now nineteen of you can go back to the station."

There was an old maid of Oneida,
Who screamed at the sight of a speida;
    She would kick at a lamb,
    And run wild from a ramb,
But fearlessly tackle hard ceida!

There was an old maid from Duquesne,
Who with rigor of mortis did fuent;
    She came to with a shout,
    Saying: "Please let me out,
This coffin will drive me insuesne!"

In Peoria, Illinois, there lived a lovely old lady, never married, who surprised the community by announcing that she was going to get married that spring. An old friend, hearing the news, came to call on her and, in the conversation, suggested that she should not marry the younger man, much younger at that, but should choose an old mate, someone closer to her own age.

"Don't be silly," she replied to his suggestion, "Who needs an old geezer, for goodness sakes! What I need is someone to charge my batteries, not run 'em down."

"I figure this has got to be her last year . . . I think they have mandatory retirement at age 100."

The smart folks in life learn to keep their mouths shut and draw their own confusions.

They say there is an old maid in Chicago, a gal not overburdened with the smarts, who changed her name from **Flossie** to **Credit** because she heard there was gonna be a squeeze on **Credit**.

Romantic old man:
    If you were a flower
    And I were a bee
    My dear, you would learn
    How I worship thee.
Old girlfriend:
    I could tell you best
    What I think of thee
    If I were a dog
    And you were a tree.

Never, never use the term "old maid." It is more appropriate and considerate to speak of them as "God's unchosen roses."

chon
Day

"So when she said *that* to me, I merely shrugged slightly, smiled in a condescending manner, said I was awfully sorry she felt that way about me, and hauled off and hit her with my handbag."

*Reprinted with permission of **The Saturday Evening Post***

2

PHYSICIANS, NURSES AND SUCH

Should you have the notion that concern for our bad eating habits was not a concern of our forefathers, well, take a peek at this revelation of quite similar concerns some sixty-five years ago (more than two generations back).

THE VITAMIN CRISIS OF 1937

I think it was in the latter part of December 1936 that the *New York Times* published a sensational article to the effect that a crisis was impending in the science of nutrition. Scientists were giving up hope of discovering any more new vitamins because the resources of the English alphabet were exhausted.

The use of double and triple letters could only postpone the evil day. Long ago the scientists had isolated Vitamin AA, occurring in several species of Madagascar yam and valuable for treating cases of prolonged lapse of memory. Vitamin CF, isolated by Pengoe of Helsingfors in the Baltic fried sole, was found effective against ballot-box stuffing.

Much was heard after 1934 about Vitamin AAA as found in Kansas, Iowa, Minnesota, Nebraska and the Dakotas. Even greater vogue, though not so long-lived, was enjoyed by Vitamin NRA as isolated by the United States Supreme Court. I scarcely have time to mention other popular varieties, like Vitamin WEAF and Vitamin WABC, occurring practically twenty-four hours in the day.

But, as I have said, despite all the efforts and ingenuity of the scientists, the alphabet famine was in full blast by the early days of the new year, 1937. For nearly a fortnight the world was without a single new vitamin. Men went on eating hamburger steak with relish and profit but without a scintilla of scientific

11

authority. Then literally overnight the emergency vanished, and the scientific world breathed again.

Like all great discoveries, it came about in the simplest manner imaginable. One of our leading nutritionists, on his way home shortly before midnight, was knocked down by an automobile on Fifth Avenue. He was only slight jarred, and though the offending car sped away without stopping, he had sufficient time to note the license number. Immediately the answer to the vitamin crisis flashed upon him.

The very next day this distinguished scientist announced the discovery of Vitamin 2N36-48, occurring in macaroni and certain species of Sicilian violets. Inasmuch as there are nearly 2,000,000 registered automobiles in New York State, it will be seen that the supply of vitamins for a great many years to come is assured.

Oscar M. Ridge,
Doubleday, Doran & Co.,
Garden City, NY, 1937

Everyone at the nursing home had joined the special hospitalization plan except a fellow named Maynard. Since the deal required 100 percent participation, the plan could not operate without Maynard.

Everyone talked to him, pleaded, argued, pressured him but nothing worked. He would not sign.

Finally, one old boy, a former professional wrestler until he grew too old for it, came up to Maynard and said, "Man, if you don't sign that hospitalization plan, I'll break every bone in your body, then reduce the bones to toothpicks!" So Maynard nods, takes out his pen and signs the paper.

A bit later, the home manager came to him and asked, "How come it took you so long to make up your mind?"

"I finally found somebody who could explain it to me."

Show me a man with his head held high and I'll show you a man who is having trouble adjusting his bifocals.

Old age is that time when a fellow thinks that in just a week or two he'll feel as good as ever.

For three generations, the Becker Family had been farmers, all except Peter Becker, who, after working with the family business for ten years, abandoned it and went to medical school, subsequently becoming a gynecologist.

One day, into his office waddled the elderly wife of a neighboring farmer, a lady he had not seen in fifteen years. They had a nice, preliminary conversation after which the doctor asked her to step into the examination room, disrobe and get on the examination table. When the obese old lady finally maneuvered herself on the table, the doctor stood before her and, from the force of habit, said, "Open your mouth please and say 'moo.'"

No one ever truly knew the truth as to the reason for it, whether it was bad hearing or just plain stupidity, but when Joe Smith went to the physician for an examination and was told to strip to the waist, he took off his pants.

"Mr. Gordon, I want you to drink a cup of hot water every morning," the doctor ordered. "Hot water. Do you understand? A man your age needs help for his elimination."

"Of course, Doctor. That'll be easy. I've been doing it for years. Only my wife calls it coffee."

An elderly lady went to see her physician about a certain problem she was having. After an examination, the doctor told her that she needed a sigmoidoscope, a search of the S-shaped section of the lower intestine. He began the examination, telling her to let him know if she felt pain. Well, the doctor's efforts brought forth a tremendous amount of gas on her stomach that she expelled with a very loud "noise"! "Madam!" the doctor exclaimed, "A simple 'yes' or 'no' will suffice."

"Why so depressed?"
"Doc told me I was sound as a dollar."

It's sure too bad that Susie ain't feelin' well. She's such a nice lady. But she got a bad case of the furniture disease.
"Furniture disease? What's that?"
"Her chest has fallen plumb down into her drawers."

"I'm sorry, Mrs. Rafferty, but medical science has not come up with an operation to get the lead out."

Mary Jo Short was a feisty old gal who delayed her hospital visit as long as she could. Inevitably, she had to go and finally submit to the indignity of being fed through a tube in her rectum. Yet she was hungry. So she pleaded with the nurse to get her a roast beef sandwich...even offered her a bribe of twenty dollars to get it. To no avail, the nurse saying, "Miss Short, you are getting quite enough nourishment by means of rectal feeding. Not to worry."

This really bugged Mary Jo who said, "Tell you what I'd like, Nurse. Tomorrow I want you to bring two extra tubes so that I can invite both you and the doctor to join me for lunch!"

A wealthy merchant of seventy-four married a twenty-year-old fashion model. They had a wonderful honeymoon in Miami but, unfortunately, the old boy suffered a coronary and was hospitalized. When his young wife came to see him, the old man said, "Sweetheart, your future has been taken care of regardless of what happens to me. You will have an income of two hundred and fifty thousand dollars a year, my home in Palm Springs, my farm in Iowa, my Mercedes. You'll never need to worry about money."

"Oh, sweetheart, please don't talk that way!" his young wife exclaimed. "You've been so good to me already. If you go, I'll be devastated. Oh, there must be something I can do to help you. Please...tell me what I can do?"

"Well," the old man gasped, "you can quit pinching the inlet tube to my oxygen supply for starters."

A Minnesota woman died at eighty-five years and bequeathed to her doctor of long standing, a steamer trunk. He took the large trunk home and opened it to discover that it contained, unused, every prescription that he had given her throughout the entire time of her dependence on him for medical help!

Mrs. Jones was a married lady who had always lived a rather sheltered life in a small town, surrounded by her children and loving husband. She went, for the first time, to visit a gynecologist who was young and, of course, the shy lady patient was quite embarrassed to go through all his tests in the examination room. Later, seated in the doctor's office upon conclusion of the many tests and examinations, the old lady asked: "Tell me, young man, does your mother know how you make a living?"

Millard Fetzer was told to take more exercise, a must since his retirement. So old Fetzer did what he could...he quit buying cigarettes and now rolls his own for the exercise!

Jimmy had been a rounder all sixty years of his adult life. At the doctors, he was advised, "Jimmy, we can add fifteen more years to your life, if you'll just quit your old routine of wine, women and song."

Jimmy thought for a few moments, then said, "Tell you what, Doc, I'll settle for five more years and just give up singing."

The estimate has been made that MEDICARE in 1995 will pay only for aspirin. In the year 2000, it will pay only for bandaids. And things will be so bad for it in 2002, it'll only pay for "*get well*" cards!

When you need a physician, you esteem him a god;

When he has brought you out of danger, you consider   him a king.

When you have been cured, he becomes human like yourself;

When he sends you a bill, you think him a devil.

Kedodoah ben Abraham Bedersi (c. 1270-1340), French poet and philosopher

Mrs. Bauman went to see the family doctor about her husband. "For our first twenty years, he was just fine, Doctor, not nervous and jumpy at all. Then for the next ten years, he's been irritable, jumpy and fidgety. But the last five years he's been awful jumpy and nervous as a short-tailed horse in fly time. Can't sit still and I don't know what to do for him. Can you help?"

"What your man needs is a little rest, Mrs. Bauman. Here's a sleeping powder."

"Oh thank you, Doctor. A million thanks to you. And when do I give him the medicine?"

"Not *him*, Mrs. Bauman, *you* take it."

A con man, a real flim-flam artist, is selling his own elixir of life that he guarantees will add years, even centuries to the life of those who take it. "And I'm your prime example of the truth of what I say," the flim-flam artist goes on, "Just look at me. I'm 285 years old."

A gullible onlooker turns to the man beside him and asks, "Is he really and truly that old?"

The man beside him, his shill, replies: "How should I know? I've only known him 120 years."

Maybe the old-time doctor didn't know what was wrong with you, but he didn't charge you $40 to send you to somebody who did.

A couple in their seventies were married, first time for both. They wanted a child but seemed not to be able to create one. So they went to see their doctor and asked him to make suggestions. "Is there anything you can do to help us?" the would-be father asked. "We want so very much to create a child."

The doctor examined them and said: "Let me put it this way. You are heir-minded, but not heir-conditioned."

Never argue with your doctor - he has inside information.

The sixth American President of the United States, John Quincy Adams, was eighty-years-old and a visitor asked him how he was feeling. President Adams replied: "I inhabit a weak, frail, decayed tenement, battered by the winds and broken in upon by the storm. From all I can hear, the landlord does not intend repairs."

An elderly fellow was taken to the hospital for an examination of his circulatory system. When he got home, he was asked what had happened and he replied, "They worked this gadget into my artery and up into my heart and then they sucked out thirty years of chocolate cake."

"When he got up this morning he took an aspirin and some vitamins, then he took pills for his ulcer and pills for iron. Then after some cough medicine he took drugs for a cold, and when he lit a cigarette there was some kind of explosion."

*Reprinted with permission of **The Saturday Evening Post***

Mrs. Jacobs called the doctor's office and was met with this response: "This is Dr. Samuel's office. What would you like to talk about?"

Mrs. Jacobs was disturbed by this response and replied sarcastically, "I want to order a hamburger with fries, for goodness sake! Just why would I call a doctor if I didn't feel sick? I need an appointment."

"Fine. I can make an appointment for you...let me see...one week from next Friday."

"Good. Just dandy. I'll have my mortician drop me off!"

The doctor had made a thorough examination of old Joe Defrates, a coal miner...at times. "Your husband has a truly bad case of voluntary inertia, ma'am" the doctor reported to Mrs. Defrates.

"Well, what d'ya know. And all this time I been sayin' that he was just plain lazy."

Mamie Delong went to the doctor because she hadn't been feeling well for some time. "Can you help me, Doctor?" she pleaded.

"Mrs. Delong, doctors are not miracle men," the physician said. "When one gets older, one's body simply, slowly wears out and all kinds of ailments move in. So please, dear lady, don't ask me to make you younger."

"Doctor, I'm not asking you to make me younger. I want you to make me older!"

Edgar Routman was seventy years old when he went to see a psychiatrist for the first time. "Yes, Mr. Routman, what seems to be wrong with you?" the doctor asked.

"It's people. I start to talk to them but they turn away laughing and walk off."

"OK...OK. Let's start at the beginning."

"Very good. As I was saying, 'In the beginning...I created the heavens and the earth. And the earth was without form, and void...'"

The social worker was visiting old Mrs. Brown. It seems that Mr. Brown was always sick and the social worker had been sent to see why. "He always thinks he's sick," Mrs. Brown told the social worker. "Always. That's all he thinks about...his sicknesses."

"You should pay no attention to what he thinks. What actually is, and what he thinks it is, are two different things." Mrs. Brown nodded and the social worker left.

A few weeks later, the social worker paid another visit to the Browns. "Well, Mrs. Brown, did you follow my instructions and pay no attention to what Mr. Brown thinks?"

"Yes, I certainly did."

"And how is Mr. Brown now?"

"He thinks he's dead."

Isaac Newton had been a rounder, a real boozer all his life. But now that he had grown old, he thought it best to visit the doctor. Naturally, the physician advised him to quit what he loved most...wine, women and song. "Will I live to be a hundred if I do without all those things, Doc?" he asked.

"No, probably not, but it'll certainly seem like it."

Joe Franz suffered from hardening of the arteries and prostate trouble. They operated on him for his prostate and, when Joe awakened, he looked up at the white-robed figure beside his bed and asked, "Doc, tell me, Doc, was my operation a success?"

"You got the wrong man, sonny boy," the figure said. "I'm St. Peter."

A lovely young woman, a recent bride brought her seventy-five-year-old husband to their doctor. It seems that the old boy was losing his getup...and get-off. So the doctor proceeded to examine him after which the husband asked: "Well, Doc, am I OK? Maybe a little bit overweight?"

The Doctor looked at the young wife, then replied: "No, not so much overweight as overmatched."

Old Betty Miller says that although she has diabetes, asthma, high blood pressure and a few other ailments, it's a good life! Betty also says that her view of life is like a tea kettle that sings...though it's up to its nose in hot water.

The old man staggered into the doctor's office, leaning heavily on the arm of his son. Slowly he made his way into the examination room where the doctor appeared and asked the old fellow how he felt. "It's just like this, Doc, I'm still kickin', all right, but I ain't raising any dust."

"I HAVE GOOD NEWS AND BAD NEWS. THE GOOD NEWS, YOU'RE NOT A HYPOCHONDRIAC..."

Many of us remember the early times when it was supposed to be a proven fact that monkey glands (yes, you remember them?) were supposed to rejuvenate the old and make them like young, once again. Well, old Joe Edgar decided to try it. What could he lose? And he did.

After the operation and return to normal consciousness, old Joe began to weep bitterly. The nurse assured him that all was well, that the operation was a success and there was no need to cry. "Any pain will soon disappear," she assured him.

"Whose crying from pain," old Joe sobbed. "I'm just afraid I'll be late for school."

Constipation is a chronic problem with many aged folks. One old guy said he had Chinese constipation. Asked the symptoms, he replied, "Hung Chow."

Another old fellow defined his problem with constipation as, "To have and to hold."

Sarah's mother hadn't been feeling well and this, coupled with a bad fall, sent her to the doctor for an examination. When she returned, Sarah asked her what the doctor had said was wrong with her.

"He said I had a Flucky."

"A Flucky? What's that?"

"I ain't sure. Didn't ask. But he said I had it."

So Sarah called the doctor and asked him the meaning of her mother's illness. "She said that you said she had a flucky."

"A what?" the doctor exclaimed. "I don't know what she told you but there is nothing wrong with your mother - 'you got off lucky' is all I said."

An old dentist who lives in Duluth,
Has wedded a widow named Ruth.
    She's so sentimental,
    Concerning things dental,
She calls her dear Second her Twoth.

How's this for a final endorsement...an epitaph for a *dentist.*

STRANGER APPROACH THIS PLACE WITH GRAVITY.
(DOC BROWN IS FILLING HIS LAST CAVITY.)

Doctor Eddie Edwards had been practicing dentistry for forty years. His nurse had been with him nearly that long. And she deserved the job since she protected him no matter what the situation. For example, the dentist had a full day of appointments and it was the very day he wanted and needed to play golf. What to do about all those appointments? Sally, his nurse, called everyone of them and said their appointments would have to be changed because the doctor had *eighteen cavities* he simply had to fill that very day!

Overheard in a badly crowded nursing home: "I'm so derned full of penicillin that if I sneeze in this crowded joint, I'll sure as hell cure somebody."

Mrs. Jenkins, long a widow and not feeling so good lately, dropped into a doctor's office for an examination. "I just haven't been feeling good, Doctor," she said, "and I'd like you to give me a thorough examination, please."

"Madam, at first glance you appear to be in good health. But just right off hand let me tell you a couple of things...first, your slip is showing; second, you need glasses. The sign on my door reads, 'Doctor Peter Howard - Veterinarian.'"

A senior citizen went into his neighborhood drug store and asked for two dozen quinine pills.

"Shall I put them in a box for you, sir?" the druggist asked.

"No, just hand 'em to me loose. I want to roll them home."

As we get older, we tend to get a bit melancholy, somewhat depressed. Just remember that Thomas Edison kept on his desk a little sign that read, "When down in the mouth, remember that old Jonah came out all right."

It does seem that as a man gets older, nature has him programmed for the benefit of the medical profession.

Mrs. Complaynor had been to see her doctor several times. The last time he told her that she obviously had not been following his instructions to walk two miles a day. He knew this because he could find no improvement in her condition.

"Doctor," she said, "if you'd quit checking my pulse, blood pressure and the like and take a look at my heels, you'd see how wrong you are."

Eddie Edwards was retired and loved to sit in front of his house and watch the young girls walk by on their daily exercise rounds. Then he developed heart trouble and had to have a pacemaker. He still enjoys sitting in front of his house and watching the girls, only now, whenever an especially pretty one goes by, his pacemaker makes the garage door go up.

As John Barrymore grew old, physicians greatly restricted his activities. And it irked him enormously. Finally, one day while quite bedfast, he turned his head to the nurse and said, "I'd like to do some reading, please." "Fine," the nurse replied. "Just what kind of reading would you like...magazine? Book?"

"With the way you good people have limited my activities," he replied, "Why don't you just bring me a postage stamp."

An apple a day keeps the doctor away, but an onion a day keeps everybody away.

Old man Fenstermaker, ninety years young, was a patient in the hospital and required constant nursing care because every minute or so, while sitting up in bed, or in a chair, he'd begin to lean to one side, slowly, slowly, leaning farther and farther until the nurse would prop him up straight, once again.

When his son returned to the city and came on a visit to the hospital, the young man asked his old dad how things were going for him. At first the son could not hear the weakly spoken words but when he leaned over close to the old man's mouth, he heard the father say, "Food's good. Bed and bathroom's fine. But that goddam nurse over there won't let me fart."

There is a standing unstated rule in small Indiana towns that when two people over seventy-five get married, the guests don't throw rice, they throw vitamin tablets.

An old man, very hard-of-hearing, went to see his doctor about his difficulty. The doctor asked him questions:

"Do you smoke?"

"Yes."

"A lot?"

"You bet...all day long."

"Drink?"

"Sure. Anytime I can get it and that's most of the time."

"What about sleep...stay up late? And the ladies, how about them?"

"Dang right, I don't pass up any chance to have fun. No sir!"

"Well, dear sir, you'll just have to cut all that out."

"Just to hear better? Hell no!"

A hieroglyphic has been defined as being almost identical with a prescription written by a physician that is then translated into dollar signs by a pharmacist.

A dentist whose last name was Schloss
Fell in love with an old lady named Foss
    But in such grave abhorrence
    He held her name Florence
That he called her his sweet Dental Floss.

Old Joe Kelly was known as the tightest skinflint in his town. But he was feeling poorly and the local physician sent him to a specialist in the big city. After numerous tests and endless examinations, old Joe received a bill for $5,000. So he sent the big town physician a check for twenty-five dollars. The doctor called him and asked why he did not send the full amount billed or, at least, a decent down payment. "Mr. Kelly," the doctor went on, "as it is, I only billed you for about 50% of the actual cost. If you couldn't afford to pay even that small amount, why did you come to see me?"

"Doctor," old Joe replied, "when it comes to my health, money ain't no object."

Dr. Mayo met an ancient lady who claimed it was her 108th birthday. The famed surgeon was skeptical but, as ever, cordial. "Well, congratulations," he said, "I hope I'll see you on your 109th birthday."

"You will," the old gal cackled contentedly.

"I will?" he asked.

"Sure," she said. "Very few people die between 108 and 109. Look it up."

Mrs. Warner Johnson, Tilton

Rusty Nayle defines a miracle drug as one that doesn't cost an arm and a leg.

An old lady was given her first glass of beer. She sipped it for a time, then remarked, "Why for goodness sakes, this tastes just like the medicine that my husband has been taking every day for forty years."

A medical intern had just finished a long and inclusive physical examination of a crotchety old man. "Tell me, sir," the young intern asked, "Do you suffer from arthritis?"

"Hell, yes!" rasped the old guy, scowling at the young doctor, "What the hell else do you suppose I can do with it?"

The doctor knocked at the hospital door before entering the room. Told to enter, he did so and had the old lady remove all of her clothing after which he gave her a complete examination...from top to bottom, from front to back. When he had finished, the old lady asked, "Doctor, may I ask a question?"

"Of course. Ask on."

"Why did you knock?"

Although his son was an eminent physician, old Mr. Diamond continued to complain of severe pain in his left leg. His son tried various treatments and medication but the pain persisted. The old man was becoming impatient.

"Son," the old man said, in desperation, "You're a doctor. It cost me a fortune to make you one. There has got to be something you can give your own father to make this pain go away in my leg."

"Now, Papa, you listen to me," said his son. "Even doctors have limitations. You got to understand that with age, comes deterioration! Please try to remember that your leg is eighty-six years old."

"I'll keep it in mind," murmured the old man. "But do you think my other leg is maybe ten years younger?"

*Sixth over Sexteen - **J. M. Elgart***

George was telling his buddy, Eddie Flow, about a recent diagnosis of his high blood pressure. "They told me to quit eating red meat," he said.

"Well, did you quit?"

"Sure. You think I'm a dummy? I haven't had a drop of ketchup on my hamburgers since!"

The physician laid down the law to his elderly patient. "George, you been messin' around all your life. No more of that for you. Wine and women are out. But you can sing...in moderation."

There's an eighty-year-old doctor in Middletown, Illinois, who has delivered so many babies that half the town looks on him about like a parent. He charges either $75 or $150 to deliver the baby, and he was once asked how he decided on the price..the high or the low price for delivery.

"Nothing to it," he grinned, "If the father responds to my 'Congratulations, you've just been given a lovely baby,' by asking whether the baby is a boy or a girl, I charge him $150. But if his first question is 'How's my wife,' I only charge him seventy-five."

A man can consider himself old when he's told to slow down by a doctor - rather than a policeman!

"Jimmy, you sure look good for a man your age."

"Thanks, I feel a lot better. For a time, there, I was feelin' awful. I thought I was a fox terrier. So I went to see a psychiatrist."

"I didn't know that, Jimmy. Gee, that's too bad. How do you feel now?"

"Swell. Like a million dollars. Just feel my nose."

The dry skin that comes with old age teaches us that the severity of an itch is inversely proportional to the reach.

———————

Old Pete Ross tried a new doctor and you know what? He was cured of $1500 in twenty minutes.

———————

An elderly teacher named Keyes,
Was weighed down by B.A.'s and Lit.D.'s,
    She fainted from strain,
    Doc said it was quite plain.
You are killing yourself by...degrees!

———————

DAVE CARPENTER...

"By-golly Mr. Clayton, I think we got your blood pressure back up . . . "

Another time, Edna was watching a movie of surgeons in the operating room as they performed an operation. "Now I understand," she murmured.

"Understand what?" her companion asked.

"I understand why, with the prices they charge, they have to wear masks!"

A dentist had an old lady patient who was very hard to handle. As soon as she sat in his dental chair, she panicked and would clamp her mouth shut so firmly that he couldn't get it open to work on her teeth.

One afternoon, on about the third try to treat the old lady, he figured out a way to get the job done. He excused himself from the old lady, went back to the reception desk and, as soon as he was ready to work on her teeth, the assistant was to move up behind the old girl and jab her in the rear with a long pin. Well, the nurse did that and, by golly, the old girl opened her mouth to holler and that opening, maintained with a pry to keep it that way, got the job done.

Finished with the ministrations, the dentist said, "Well, now, that wasn't bad at all, was it?"

"Nope. Not so bad. But I'll tell you this, Doctor, I never expected to feel the pain way down there."

Grandpa Nick says that the School of Experience has given him a new class yell: "Ouch! Ouch! Ouch!"

The physician walked into the hospital room of 89-year-old Jake Fisher. He was surprised to see the nurse hold Jake by both wrists. "You don't have to do that nurse," the doctor exclaimed, "to check his pulse."

"I know that, sir," the nurse replied, "I'm checking his *impulse.*"

Charlie Marr was up in years and rarely went out for dinner. But this one night his wife didn't feel at all like cooking, so they went to a restaurant, had a good meal and started to leave when Charlie thought he ought first to visit the men's room.

Finished, he started out the door of the rest room when he was seized with a terrible pain in his lower back. Even worse was the gnawing sensation at the rear of his neck. Now he could hardly walk! He and the Mrs. did manage to make it to their car and she drove straight to the hospital.

At the hospital they were sent to the emergency room where the doctor helped him onto the examination table, told him to close his eyes and relax. Carefully, the doctor's hands went over Charlie's body. There was a sudden metallic sound that went "Snip." "Get to your feet, Mr. Marr," the doctor said. "You'll be fine, now."

Very carefully Charlie began to move. The pain was gone! "Doctor, you're great! What was wrong with me?"

"Not much at all," the doctor replied. "You just had your tie caught in your zipper!"

32

3

INFIRMITIES

Some of us, as we grow old, lose a little of that heady stuff they call brains. Call it absent-mindedness, soft-headedness, a pint short of a full quart, or even a brick short of a load. As we get older, we tend to lose our younger smarts...not all of us...but some of us are in that "light-in-the-head" category. Here are a few case histories to illustrate the condition.

The old man was attacked by three muggers. He ran like crazy but, finally, they caught him. They searched him thoroughly and found only 50 cents. "You dumb old jerk," cried one of the robbers. "How come you ran like that when you had only 50 cents to your name?"

"Oh gosh. I thought you were after the 100 dollars I had in my shoe."

Then there was old Jim Jehosaphat who had never before been to a movie. His religious faith forbade it. But when he had grown old, he thought that he did not want to pass on without experiencing just what a movie was all about. So he went to the ticket window and put out his money, took the ticket, went inside, came out and bought another ticket. Same thing. Again, he went inside and, shortly after, returned to the ticket window to buy again. Aft this had gone on a few times, the girl at the window said, "Sir, why do you keep buying so many tickets?"

"Perhaps you ought to talk to the guy inside there, beside the door," Jim replied, "he keeps tearing up my tickets."

Old age is twenty years older than you are.

One sure way of breaking a man of the habit of biting his nails is to hide his teeth.

Then there was old Stan who was having foot trouble. He was too old to drive so his son took him to the podiatrist who treated his problem and advised him to be sure to put on a fresh pair of socks each day, and to return in a week for further treatment.

A week later, Stan hobbled from his son's car up the walk and into the podiatrist's office. As soon as the podiatrist saw him come in, he shook his head, saying, "Sir, you should not be walking around without shoes."

"I couldn't get 'em on over seven pairs of socks, Doc."

"It's 'What?' 'Eh?' and 'How's that?' around here till I'm almost nuts."

Reprinted by permission, **The American Legion Magazine**

Then there was Edina Shaker who had lived all her life in the hills of Arkansas. She lived a good but primitive life without modern conveniences...until recently. Finally, she got her first refrigerator and she loved it, along with all the conveniences that electricity brought to her mountain home. But she had one complaint about the refrigerator. "It ain't that we're out of ice," she said. "George he cuts it every winter and we pack it in sawdust and it keeps fine, same as always. But with that new 'frig'rator, it takes me too much time to cut our ice into squares just the right size to fit into all them leetle spaces in the ice trays."

And consider the two old caretakers of the Town Hall. They had been told to measure the height of the flagpole atop the hall but had not been able to figure how to do it. A passerby suggested that they take the pole down, lay it on the ground and then measure it. "Don't be foolish," the one caretaker said. "We were told to measure the height, not the length."

An alternate way to record the passing of years into old age is to recall that first, you forget names. Then you forget faces. Then you forget to pull your zipper up, followed by that final, fatal time when you forget to pull your zipper...down!

Talk about stupid! This old boy had been short of money for a long time. He decided to end that dearth of cash by robbing an airplane. So he bought a ticket, entered the plane, waited until it was half-way through the flight, then announced, "This is a stick-up. Everybody give me their money and we'll have no trouble. Just sit quiet and I'll pass down the aisle and get your dough. I've got a .45 automatic here that'll dust off anyone who makes trouble."

The old boy collected enough money to keep him for the rest of his life, put on a parachute, opened the door and jumped...into the toilet.

"What a disaster...you a barber and bald. How come?"

"Grass doesn't grow on a busy street, that's how come!"

"Oh, I get it...because it can't get through the concrete, eh?"

My hair is white and I'm nearly blind,
The days of my youth are way behind.
My neck's sure stiff and I can't turn my head,
And I try like heck to hear what's said.
My legs, they do tremble and I can't hardly walk,
But, by gosh, I sure can talk.
So this is the message I want y'all to get:
Though it might seem so, I ain't dead yet.

What letter of the alphabet gives a woman who is hard of hearing the most pleasure? The letter a, of course, because it makes her...hear.

Wife: "Dear, I'd love to have some ice cream. Chocolate. About a carton of it."

Husband: "I'll run to the store, now, and get it."

Wife: "Write it down, dear, so you don't forget it."

Husband: "Who needs to write it down! A carton of chocolate ice cream. Right?"

Wife: "I still think you'd better..."

Husband: "Don't be silly. I'll be back in two shakes of a dog's tail. With the chocolate ice cream."

The husband returns and hands his wife...a pound of bacon. Really upset that he'd forgotten, she slaps her thigh and screams at him: "So where's the dozen eggs?"

I adore my bifocals,
My false teeth fit fine.
My hairpiece fits swell,
But I sure miss my mind.

Not many senior citizens will recall that best seller at the turn of the century: *On a Slow Train Through Arkansas.* Thomas W. Jackson was the author and, in 1906, he published another train story called: *Don't Miss It.* The following episode, involving a hard-of-hearing passenger, is a masterpiece, although Mr. Jackson's grammar is a wee bit short of academic!

The name of the next station was Hay. When the engineer blowed the whistle the porter come in the car and hollered, "Hay." An old man said, "I want to know the name of the station." The porter hollered in his ear as loud as he could, and said, "Hay." The old man said, "I want to know the name of the station we are coming into now." The porter hollered in his ear again and said, "Hay. Why in the h--l don't you get an ear trumpet?" That made the old man mad. He went to the conductor and said, "I am going to report that saucy porter." The conductor said, "What's the trouble?" The old man said, "I asked him the name of the station and he wouldn't tell me." The conductor said, "What did he say?" "Why he just said 'Hay'." The conductor said, "That's right." The old man said, "What's right?" The conductor said, "Hay." The old man turned around and said to the brakeman, "Will you tell me the name of this station?" The brakeman said, "Hay." The old man said, "The whole d--- crew is either deaf or crazy."

Forgetfulness is a problem with most folks over sixty-five...and sometimes earlier! Three old ladies were discussing this very problem one day at the senior citizens' center. "My problem is kinda odd. For example, I stop at the bottom of the stairs and can't recall whether I was going up or coming down."

The second old lady said, "I have the same sort of problem. Sometimes I'll open the refrigerator only to find that I don't remember whether I opened it to put something in or take it out."

"Thank goodness, nothing like that happens to me. I guess I'm just lucky. But just to be safe," and she raps three times on the table. Startled, she stands up, saying, "Somebody's knocking at the door. I'd best go see about it."

Most old timers have a gradually increasing loss of memory as they grow older. A notable exception is recorded concerning an aged American Indian. It seems that this brave at eighty-five had a better memory than most men at half his years. A cynical visitor to the reservation decided to test the man's reputation, so he asked him, "Can you tell me what you had for breakfast on June first, eighty-four years ago? When you were one year old?"

The chief did not hesitate. "Two eggs," he said.

"Remarkable. Stunning!" gasped the cynical gent, now a believer.

Six months later, in town, the former cynic met the Indian chieftain on the street of the small town near the reservation. He smiled, held out his hand to the chief and said, "How!"

The chief replied, "Scrambled."

(Dear reader you must admit, THAT was a remarkable, memorable memory).

Old age: When certain parts wear out, spread out, fall out...and...squeak.

Grandpa Homer Jones was kind of deaf but he didn't let that stop him. He was in town one day, just walkin', enjoyin' the sights when a young lady ran into him, hard. She helped him up, brushed him off and kept repeating, "I'm so sorry. I beg your pardon."

"What didya say?" Uncle Homer asked.

"I beg your pardon is what I said."

"Pardon? How come? What'd ya do?"

"Well, I knocked you over."

"What? Say it louder."

"I said I knocked you over."

"Knocked up? Pity. But I didn't do it."

"It was an accident, Sir, I couldn't help it!"

"What?"

"An accident! Accident!"

"Too bad. Take precautions next time."

Old Mabel Peterson is now in a retirement home. She says that your friends may lie to you and your mirror can sure deceive, but nothing is more brutally frank than a flight of stairs.

There is an unsubstantiated report that a huge balloon filled with Texas air and carrying three balloonists landed near a rest home in Arizona where it sustained a severe rip that allowed all that Texas air to escape. Once freed, the Texas air so rejuvenated the elderly patients in the rest home, that fifty old men sprang from their wheelchairs, ran to a nearby swimming pool and dragged fifty young women off by their hair.

It's been said that you know you are growing older when, in the morning, you stand, and hear the usual snap, crackle, pop...and it isn't breakfast cereal.

Two old boys were commiserating about their ailments. One told of his splitting headaches and how difficult it was to get rid of them. His friend said, "Yeah, I used to have them, too. But I got me a young wife, pretty and full of energy and when I get a headache she puts my head on her bosom, hugs it and gives me a derned good kiss. Man, that kills my headache pain right now."

"Is that so?" said the other. "Well whatdya know! I've tried everything else and nothing worked. So I'll try that. Your wife home now?"

"Your teeth are like stars," he said
And pressed her hand so white.
He spoke the truth, for like the stars,
Her teeth came out at night.

Don't worry if you start losing your memory. Just forget it!

It is amazing how some people can go through life and never do a lick of work. Consider the case of Elmer Twist, without doubt the laziest man in Peoria. A stranger came to town and happened to spot a man asleep in a huge oak tree, stretched out on a limb some thirty feet above ground. He asked what the man was doing, asleep in a tree and so far above ground. "Mister," a native explained, "that there is Elmer Twist. He went to sleep on an acorn thirty years ago."

"I said, Do you mind showing me this amazing new hearing aid you've developed?"

A bunch of kids were watching an old man get himself ready for the day. They saw him take three kinds of pills, a drink of water, shave himself, brush his teeth, clean his nails, polish his shoes, then drink a tablespoonful of medicine from two different bottles. "Gosh, mister," one of the kids remarked, "it looks to me like you sure are an awful lot of trouble to yourself!"

Frank Potash was known as the oldest and laziest man in town...and the most superstitious. He never worked in any week that had a Friday in it.

Old Pete Jaegar has quit worrying. He says that worrying is like a rocking chair in that it gives you something to do but you get nowhere doing it.

Consider the young soldier who wrote home to his grandmother that he had grown another foot. So she knitted him a third sock.

"Do you guarantee this hair restorer, absolutely guarantee it?" asked the prospect for a bottle of hair restorer.

"Absolutely. 100% guarantee."

"Can you prove it'll grow hair?"

"Yep! See this hairbrush? Well it was a comb until I spilled some of that there hair restorer on it!"

"Ok, then I'll let you put some of your hair restorer on my head. Go ahead...rub some in."

"You'll be delighted with the results, I promise you," said the barber as he began to put on rubber gloves.

"But why the rubber gloves?" the customer asked.

"My dear sir," explained the barber, "you wouldn't want me to get hair on the palms of my hands, would you?"

If by your hair your sins
    should numbered be,
Angels in heaven would not
    be more pure than thee.

My memory is just dandy. Only three things I can't remember. I can't remember faces; and I can't remember names and...dogonit..what was that third thing?

Old age has been defined as the period in life when you'd just as soon not have a good time as to have to recover from it.

There was an old lady from Natchez
Who sat in some netlewood patches
    Now she lies on her belly
    Feeling weak as grape jelly
And scratches and scratches and scratches.

Mrs. Celia Jones was troubled with gas on her stomach and decided to see her physician about it. "Doctor," she told him, "it is just too painful. I need something to get rid of this gas on my stomach. Now, you should understand, there is no sound and no odor when I expel the gas, but the pain. It is simply dreadful. Can you help me?"

The doctor assured Mrs. Jones that he could. He gave her a vial of pills and instructed her to take two pills daily. Then Mrs. Jones thanked him and left, after being instructed to come back ten days later.

But Mrs. Jones was back in one week! "Doctor," she exclaimed. "When I pass gas...well I mean...when I f-f-fart, ahem, well, the odor is simply terrible! Offensive, and I daren't go out because of the embarrassment. Oh how they stink! There is no sound. Only odor."

"Good! Very good! Now that we have your nose back in order, let's work on your hearing!"

It doesn't much matter, this growing old,
    But the one thing I can't ignore,
Is the affliction of morning's after,
    When I ain't had a night before.

Wrinkles are God's way of saying, "Friend, I'm stepping on your face!"

Two old friends met on the street and soon after their conversation began, the old man said, "Hey, George. Is that a hearing aid you're wearing? That's new, isn't it?"

"Sure is. Just got it. It's the best you can buy. Cost over five hundred bucks."

"Five hundred bucks! Holy smokes. That's got to be a high class hearing aid. What kind is it?"

"Quarter to five."

The Winterhavens

"I don't see how you were able to work for so many years. Since you've retired you can't do a thing."

"How do I know this hair tonic works?" the old gentleman asked the druggist.

"It really does, sir, and I can prove it." He called his assistant over. "George, tell this gentleman about the lady who bought a bottle of this hair restorer for her husband. Tell him how when she grabbed the cork with her teeth to pull it out and accidentally smeared some of the lotion on her lip. And how we had to give her a bottle of hair remover to take off the moustache."

You can talk about baldness all you want, but the record-breaker for bald heads was the head of Ebenezer Talkalot. Why, his head would make a bowling ball look fuzzy.

Old Mrs. Peters took her first plane ride and found that the altitude caused her ears to plug up. She was most uncomfortable and asked the hostess for relief. The hostess gave her a stick of gum and asked her to let her know if that helped.

At the end of the flight, the hostess asked Mrs. Peters if her ears were OK. "Yes. That seemed to help," Mrs. Peters replied. "But could you advise me as to the best way of getting that gum out of my ears, now that we're on the ground?"

You know you are getting old when you hear the phone ring on a Saturday night and you pray it's not for you.

An old fellow was snoozing away contentedly when he was startled awake by the doorbell. He shook his head and staggered off the sofa to make his way to the door. There stood a lovely young woman.

"Oh my goodness," the pretty young thing exclaimed. "I'm at the wrong house."

"Sweetheart, you're at the right house," the old guy assured her. "But you're forty years too late."

44

George says he is getting so old that when Spring comes around, he doesn't remember what his fancy is supposed to lightly turn to. Ice cream? Golf? Hammock?

The American Legion reported on the absent-mindedness of one member. It seems that he phoned his ladyfriend and said, "I know I proposed to you last week...but I'll be derned if I can recall whether you accepted me or not."

His aged ladyfriend handled it very well. She replied, "It was lucky you called because I knew I'd turned someone down but I couldn't recall who it was."

It was the wise custom at the retirement home to pair the old couples and then send them out for dinner and a movie, or other entertainment. This one night, George who was eighty-four, was paired with Edith who was eighty-six.

A few hours later, Edith returned to the home and was she angry! "What happened that you should be so upset, Edith?" the attendant asked her.

"Coming back with that silly old man, I had to slap him three times while we were riding home in the cab."

"Why, that's terrible. And at his age, too. He ought to be ashamed, making passes at you."

"Passes. He didn't make passes. I had to slap him three times to see if he was asleep or dead."

An aged New Yorker was sitting in his ground floor apartment, looking out the window. A pretty girl emerged and walked down the street past him. "Hey, Jeeves!" he yelled to his butler, "Bring me my teeth, I want to whistle."

Old age is when you can do almost anything, but don't. Another way of putting it says that "Old age is upon you when the daily dozen becomes your daily doesn't."

45

A New Yorker is taking a walk in Central Park and, after a few miles, is a bit tired and sits down on a park bench to rest. Soon he is joined by an old man who hobbles up to the bench, eases himself onto it, puffs awhile and then sighs, smiles and says, "Good Morning."

The younger man returns the greeting, exchanges pleasantries, then says, "It's remarkable that a man of your age takes a walk in the park. Just remarkable. My old dad sits home and scarcely leaves the rocking chair. And here you are, vigorous and exercising. To what do you attribute all your energy? You must live a very clean life."

"Nope. Not clean at all. I drink a quart of whiskey a day, never get to bed before two o'clock, handle three cases of beer a week and still smoke three packs of these (and he lights a cigarette) a day."

"Wow! To reach your age after all that dissipation is surely one for the books. How the heck old are you?"

"Twenty-three."

A famous businessman, well into his seventies, made quite a stir when he married his thirty-year-old secretary. They left for an extended honeymoon in South America, and were met, upon their return, by the corporation's public relations man.

The PR man asked his boss, "Tell us, Sir, how was your honeymoon? Was the weather nice?"

The old man sighed and said, "Yes, the weather was lovely. But the humility was discouraging."

"Where's the car, dear?" the old man asked of his wife. "I got to go to the drugstore to get my medicine."

"You've got the car! You drove it to the grocery store."

"I did? That's strange. Oh yes! Now I remember. When I got to the store, I got out of the car and turned to the feller who'd given me a lift and, would you believe it...he wasn't there and I wondered when he'd gone."

An aged farmer was standing by his mail box when a car stopped on the road beside him. "Sir, could you..."

"What's that? Speak up, man."

"Where is Decatur, Sir?" the driver asked loudly.

"You got to speak up, stranger. I'm a mite hard of hearing."

"I'm lost," screamed the driver. "WHERE...IS...DECATUR?"

"Sorry, but we can't use another. We bought one last week," the old man replied.

The driver gave up and drove on to another farmhouse some two miles down the road. He went to the farmhouse, knocked on the door and a lady opened it.

"Excuse me, Ma'am..."

"Continue two miles, turn right and go three miles to Decatur," she snapped. "I heard you yelling down at Joe Spinks' place!"

The new preoccupation (or is it mania) with weight and how to lose it, was wonderfully exemplified during a conversation Mary had with her old friend Susie. Susie's eye was black, she was nursing a lost tooth and she was scratched all over her face.

"It's that husband of mine," she sobbed. "The old fool still has enough strength to beat me...everyday, especially when he's drinking does he push me around and hit me and knock me down...Oh, Mary, I've lost ten pounds."

"Leave him, Susie! Get rid of the old bastard. At once. Why not?"

"Well, I want to lose *twenty pounds,* is why."

Henry was on a date with his college girlfriend, whom he hadn't seen for many years. "Remember those days in the park, Charlie," she reminisced. "when you stood high on the hill, looking out over the lovely countryside, with the wind blowing your hair...and you too danged proud to chase it?"

A wag once described the process of growing old as follows:

You can figure you've reached old age when...

1. You don't need half the room in your house and you do need twice the room in your medicine cabinet.

2. By nine o'clock at night, you've reached a condition that used to come at midnight.

3. The happiest time of your day ends when the morning alarm goes off.

4. You recall on Wednesday, that your wife's birthday was last Monday.

5. You sink your teeth in a porterhouse steak and the damn things stay there.

6. It wears you out to dial long distance. And to comb all ten of your hairs is so exhausting that you don't bother.

7. Lacing and tying your shoes is so much trouble that you buy only slip-ons.

8. You turn out the lights to save money, not to indulge in romance.

9. You don't think about the past because it makes you so danged mad to recall all those temptations you foolishly resisted.

10. Nothing is as good as it used to be. Especially sex.

―――――――――

One time, Zeke walked into the tavern and the bartender told him that he was wearing one brown and one black shoe. Zeke was surprised, saying, "I don't remember buying a pair of shoes like these." When he got home, he looked in the closet, then hurried to the phone and called the bartender. "Damndest thing," Zeke said, "Y'know that pair of shoes I was wearing tonight, one black and one brown?" "I remember," the bartender said. "Well," Zeke told him, "I got another pair just like 'em in my closet here at home!"

Then Zeke said, "Y'know that martini you mix for me, the one that always has an olive in it?"

"Yep! I ought to...I mix 'em for you every night."

"Well, starting tomorrow night, will you put two prunes in, instead of the olive?"

Zeke's only sin is alcohol. He says that dope doesn't interest him at all. "Why," he once told the boys, "I can remember when this thing about using pot was mainly the trouble of locating it under the bed."

The bartender says Zeke is sure getting old. Of late, he's begun to inspect the menu instead of the waitress.

One time Zeke came into the bar and he was crying. "What's the matter, old fellow?" the bartender asked. "I'm gettin' too danged old, that's what's the matter," he replied. "I thought I'd brush my teeth before I came down here...stops bad breath, y'know...so I takes my toothbrush, spread toothpaste on it, felt the bristles and they were wet...I'D ALREADY BRUSHED 'EM ONCE!"

There was an old girl in Havana
Who slipped on the skin of a banana,
    Whoops! Went her feet,
    And she fell on her seat,
In a most unladylike manner.

As Pete Elder gets older and older, he finds it harder and harder...er...ahem...it's harder and harder to make ends meet. What we mean is, it gets harder to have his fingers reach down to his toes.

Old age: Ancecdotage. It is considered by medical science to be the only popular, if fatal disease. (Everybody wants it).

Old man: A male who stopped growing...except in the middle or, to put it another way, has stopped growing vertically but not horizontally.

Another old lady named Hannah,
Slipped on that same derned banana,
    As she lay on her side,
    More stars she espied
Than there are in the Star-Spangled Banner.

Away back in the forties, a salesman handling government bonds was out in the farm country of the middle west. He stopped at an old farmhouse but could arouse nobody so he walked to the barn where he found an old codger forking hay to the cows.

"Howdy, Sir, I'm selling government bonds."

The old farmer looked up, shook his head and put his hand to his ear. "Eh, what say?"

The salesman now spoke a little louder, "You know, Sir, that there's a war going on?"

The old guy scowled a bit, shook his head and started to turn away. The salesman touched his arm and said, "You surely have heard of the trouble at Pearl Harbor?"

Once again, the old fellow shook his head and shrugged.

"Well, gosh, Sir, you've surely heard of Churchill and Roosevelt?"

Still no response, so the salesman turned, went to his car and drove off. When he had finished his chores, the old farmer went to the house where his wife asked, "Before I could get to the door, some feller went to the barn. What'd he want?"

"I never could figure exactly what that feller had to tell me. But if I heard right, he says some feller by the name of Rosyfelt went and got Pearl Harper in trouble over on Church Hill, and...the derned fool wanted me to go his bond."

Nature is provident, especially to elderly folks. Just consider her generosity to us oldies when we reach that sit-around-stage. She provides us with built-in, well-padded (somewhat wrinkled!) cushions.

Social Security has been defined as a method that guarantees you a steak when you have no teeth left to chew it.

An old fellow notices a young boy sitting on the curb just crying his eyes out. So the old guy goes to the kid, sits down, puts his arm around him and asks, "What's the trouble, little feller. Tell me why are you crying?"

"It's 'cause I can't do what the big boys do."

So the old man put his own head in his arms and cried, too.

They say that regular naps prevent old age...especially if you take them while driving.

An old man suffered from tinnitus, a severe ringing in the ears that never stops. He went to his doctor and the old doctor diagnosed it as tonsil trouble and removed the tonsils. The second physician thought it was caused by his teeth and pulled them. But the third physician was grim! He told the old fellow that he had only six months to live.

The old man decided to spend these last few months of his life indulging himself. He would go round the world! So he bought tickets, also bought ten suits, eight pairs of shoes, two dozen silk ties and then went to be measured for several new shirts. The shirt salesman told him that he would need size 16½-inch neck with 33-inch sleeves. "No, that's not right," the old man declared. "I always buy size 15-inch collars with 33-inch sleeves."

"Well, Sir, I measure you as 16½ by 33 and I am sure."

"Nuts!" the old man declared. "I insist on my regular size, 15-inch collar and 33-inch sleeve. That or nothing."

"OK," the salesman said. "But I promise you. If you wear that size, you'll get a ringing in your ears that'll drive you crazy."

"I'm a visible economics textbook," Eddie said. "My blood pressure is in noticeable expansion, my hairline is in obvious recession, my belly is clearly inflated, my sex life is stagnant and, all together, they've put me in one helluva depression."

Old Johnny said that he has reached the last stage of hair conditioning. His first stage was *parted hair.* The second stage was *unparted hair.* And now he's in the last stage, *departed hair.*

When asked why he didn't get a hearing aid, Grandpa Jessup replied, "Don't need it. Why, I already hear now three times as much as I understand!"

An old-timer started, once again, in his old profession of selling life insurance. He didn't much want to but had to. And the following notice was posted on the entrance door to his office.

While in this office, kindly speak in low, soothing terms and do not disagree with me in any manner.

Please be informed that when one reaches my age, noise and non-concurrence cause gastricity and hyperperistalsis, hypersecretion of hydrochloric acid and inflammation of the gastric mucosa and

I...BECOME...NASTY! A...GENUINE...S.O.B.
(Source unknown)

It's a comfort to all bald-headed men to know that marble tops are never put on cheap tables. Unfortunately, it is true that they do put them on antiques.

Barney was a powerfully-built man. On a golf course it was said he could drive up to 500 yards. But Barney, alas, had very poor vision and could rarely locate the ball after he'd hit it.

His best friend advised him: "Take old Petey with you. He loves to walk around the course."

"But he's ninety-two if he's a day."

"So? His eyesight is perfect. Eyes like a hawk. He can spot a pin a mile away."

So Barney asked the delighted Petey to accompany him. He drove off the first tee...a good 450 yards. He turned to Petey and said, "You see it?"

"Right up there. No problem."

So they walked leisurely down the fairway chatting and finally come to the estimated area.

Barney: "Where's the ball?"

Petey: "Oh gosh...I forgot!"

Someone has credited William Shakespeare with definitions of the stages of life. He reduced the stages to three and called them "the three r's": Romance at 19; the rent at 39; and at 69 it's rheumatism!

"Can you tell me how to get to Adams Street?"

"What's that, buddy. I'm a lettle deaf."

"I beg your pardon?"

"You don't say. I'm a leetle deef, too."

"That's sure too bad. Now what was it you wanted?"

"I wanted to know how to get to Adams Street."

"That's easy. Go the way you're heading for two blocks, then turn left. It's the third street down."

"That's Adams Street?"

"What? Oh no, friend, I thought you said Adams Street."

"No, I didn't say that. I said Adams Street."

"Never heard of it. So long. Sorry, stranger."

Isn't it odd that the older some folks get, the nastier they become? And the more trouble they have keeping their teeth in, the more biting they become!

Two old guys met on the street and the one fellow kept repeating, "Eh? What'd you say? Eh?" Exasperated, the other old guy said, "Turn up your danged hearing aid!"

So the old guy reaches to turn it up and he pulls the thing out of his ear.

"What the devil is that thing?" the other old guy asked.

"That's my suppository. Now I know where my hearing aid is."

It Got Up and Went

How do I know my youth is all spent?
My get-up and go has got up and went.
My joints are still and filled with pain.
The pills that I take they give me no gain.
I rub in the ointment like fury I do,
Each pain when it leaves, comes back with two.

But in spite of it all I am able to grin
When I think of the places my get-up has been.
Old age is *golden* I have heard it said,
But sometimes I wonder as I get into bed-
My "ears" on the dresser, my "teeth" in a cup,
My "eyes" on the table until I wake up.
Ere sleep comes each night I say to myself,
"Is there anything else I should lay on the shelf?"
Yet I am happy to know as I close the door,
My friends are the same as in days of yore.

Since I have retired from life's competition
Each day is filled with complete repetition.
I get up every morning and dust off my wits
Go pick up the paper and read the "o-bits."
If my name isn't there I know I'm not dead;
I get a good breakfast and go back to bed.
The reason I know my youth is all spent-
My get-up-and-go has got-up and went.
                    Author Unknown

Just a line to say I'm living
That I am not among the dead.
I'm getting more forgetful
and more mixed up in my head.

Sometimes I can't remember
As I stand at foot of stairs
If I must go up for something
or I've just come down from there.

Before the "Fridge" so often
my poor mind filled with doubt,
Have I just put food away
or come to take something out?

And sometimes when it is left out
with my night cap on my head
I don't know if I am retiring
or just getting out of bed.

So if it's my turn to write you
There's no need for getting sore.
I may think I have written
And don't want to be a bore.

So remember I do love you
and I wish that you were here.
But now it's nearly mail time
I must say good-bye My Dear.

There I stood at the mailbox
with a face so red.
Instead of mailing you my letter
I had opened it instead.

(Source Unknown)

It is a sad, if understandable fact that some senior citizens simply will not face the fact that they are old, that they are, in fact, senior citizens. In view of this melancholy or should we say...exalted truth, the editors have devised a test to concretize, to make *obvious* to the duffers that they really and truly are up and among those folks blessed with years of sixty and more!

1. Does everything you glance at appear to be farther away than it used to be?

2. Do you encounter friends you have known most of your life who have aged so derned much that they don't recognize you?

3. Do you suddenly encounter hills where they have never before been? And does it take you twice as long to climb them as it once did?

4. Is it true that you consider college-age students almost like high school kids in their looks?

5. Do you still try to convince yourself that the gray cast to your hair is due only to overexposure to bright sunlight?

6. Do you tell your friends that you want nothing at all for your birthday except not to be reminded of it?

7. While shaving, do you fail to recognize the strange face that stares out at you from the mirror?

8. Do your friends ask if you've changed to horn-rimmed glasses when the truth is, it's only the dark circles under your eyes?

9. Do your friends admire your western-style haircut but it's only the wide, open spaces of baldness?

10. Does everyone else look so derned young? Do the forty-year old gals seem like teenagers?

11. Have you decided that the only thing you've got working for you is the prune juice?

12. Do you take brisk walks of two miles and discover you've traveled only four blocks - two out and two back?

13. Have you decided that the young generation is terribly shy, uncertain and so soft-spoken that one scarcely hears them?
14. Have you discovered that nights last longer nowadays so that a man must go to the bathroom once or twice before daybreak?

4

SENIOR GALS

Great-Grandpa had a keen sense of humor way back in 1905! He thought this was almighty funny back then. We, 86 years later, think so, too and probably Americans 86 years from today will agree:

I left Grand Central Depot for Buffalo, and I dozed until the brakeman came through the car shouting, "Next station Peekskill."

As he came in, I heard an old lady say: "Mr. Conductor, have we come to Schenectady yet?"

"No," answered the brakeman in a mild tone, "I just said, 'Peekskill,' lady."

"Thank you," she answered in a piping voice.

After a fifteen minute pause, the conductor came in, went his rounds, calling this time, "Fishkill," instead of "Peekskill."

"Conductor, have we come to Schenectady yet?" said the woman again.

"No, didn't I just tell you the next station was Fishkill?" roared the conductor gruffly.

"Well," she said, "I thought it was Schenectady, and I want you to be sure and let me know when we come to Schenectady."

"Look here, Madam," said the conductor in anger, "I will tell you what I'll do, lady."

"What will you do?" said the old lady.

"I will let you off at Schenectady, and if I don't, I'll back the train."

"Now be sure to let me know," said the old lady.

The conductor said, "You have my word."

With this, she slept soundly while the train passed the next ten stations, but she got impatient, and again asked: "Mr. Conductor, have we gotten to Schenectady yet?"

The conductor got red in the face and said: "Madam, I have forgotten to let you know, but I'll keep my word and back the train."

So true to his word, he backed the train to the station, which just happened to be Schenectady.

"Now, madam," he said, "This is Schenectady."

"Thank you," she replied, and stopped as if to pick up her grip, but *instead*, she took from it a bottle and a spoon, and said to the conductor: "I thank you very much for your trouble, but my daughter told me to take my medicine at Schenectady."

On A Slow Train
I & M Ottenheimer, 1905

Be Alert. Lerts live longer.

The old hillbilly's wife stood before the judge. "You have asked for a divorce decree from this court, Madam, is that right?"

"Yep."

"And the grounds for your request is that your husband is too careless about his appearance. Is that correct?"

"That's right, Suh. He ain't appeared at home in goin' on twenty years now."

Mrs. Peters had belonged to a bridge club that played cards every Thursday night. And always, when she got home, her entrance awakened her husband. Well, one Thursday night she got home and decided to undress in the parlor so as not to awaken her sleeping husband. This she did and, with her handbag over her arm, she walked nude into the bedroom to find her husband sitting up in bed awaiting her, reading the paper. He looked up from his reading as she entered, gasped and said, "Holy smokes, Dear, did you lose everything?"

Definition of a youthful figure: A number you get when you ask an older woman her age.

60

Grandma Skilsky tells us that the beauty and wonder of the old-fashioned blacksmith was that when Pa took your horse to be shod, the blacksmith didn't find twenty other things wrong that needed fixin'.

After working at it all day, the old gal staggered out of her garden. "They got that nursery rhyme all wrong," she declared to the neighbor, "it ought to go like this:
Mary, Mary, quite contrary,
How does your garden grow?
Silver bells and cockleshells,
And all them @!X! weeds."

It was graduation time at the New Citizen's Day class at the immigration center. Mrs. Cohen smiled, delighted to learn that she had won the prize for achieving the best grade in her class of new citizens.

"Here is your prize, Mrs. Cohen," the instructor said, handing her a replica of the Liberty Bell.

"Tenks a million," Mrs. Cohen responded. "And I accepts dis prize wit aprec...apprecia...appreciation, even eff it ess crecked."

1st Woman: We're sending my mother-in-law to New York for a vacation.
2nd Woman: Won't the weather disagree with her?
1st Woman: It wouldn't dare!

Mrs. Anita Pree was ninety years old and spry as could be. She was asked: "At what time does a woman stop hoping for love, for romance?" She replied, "I don't know yet!"

Johnny Edgar had been married for more than forty years. But he is beginning to wonder if his wife is getting just a le-e-etle bit tired of him. She's been wrapping his lunch in a roadmap.

The senior citizens club of Springfield, Illinois, made a trip to Chicago to visit the famous Art Institute. In the course of their tour through the Institute, they came into a gallery of quite modern paintings. One particularly abstract painting caught the eye of one old lady who asked the guide, "What on earth is that, young man?"

"That," the guide replied, "is supposed to be a mother and child."

"Well for goodness sake, then," snapped the old girl, "Why isn't it?"

A bit later, they entered the room of modern American paintings. The same old lady stood before a 1933 oil painting of a tramp, an old vagabond dressed in rags, yet looking quite happy.

"Well, for pity sakes," she exclaimed. "He's too broke to buy a presentable suit of clothes, but he can afford to have his picture painted. How do you like them apples!"

1st Woman: I got a necktie for my husband.
2nd Woman: I wish I could get such a trade-in!

There was an Old Fellow of Lafleur
Whose wife was as thin as a skewer.
    Last night, sad to say,
    Poor soul, passed away.
Thru the rods of a drain o'er the sewer.

At a meeting of older citizens, the question was broached as to why God had granted them their ripe old age. One matron raised her hand, then replied: "I suspect that HE wants to test the patience of our relatives."

Reca Jones once remarked that her friends should not worry when she subtracts several years from her true age..."I just add it on to someone else's!" she said. "So nothing is lost."

Old Butch Thatcher got to feelin' bad and thought he would die. So he called his wife, Mabel, to his bedside and confessed: "Mabel, I ain't always been faithful. I apologize here and now. But I want you to know that every time I done wrong, I put a five dollar bill in a little box hid in the cabinet over the kitchen sink. When I'm gone, there's enough there to make you comfortable."

Mabel kissed and thanked him. But Butch recovered! Sadly, Mabel took sick and figured to pass on. So now she called Butch to her bedside and confessed: "Butch, I ain't always been faithful to you neither; but ever'time I done wrong, I put a dried bean in the old trunk in the attic. When I'm gone, you'll find every one of 'em there - 'cept for two quarts I cooked last month when all our relations piled in with us."

An old lady felt herself most superior,
And asked divorce from her husband inferior,
    And the grounds were that once,
    When she'd screamed at him "Dunce!"
He'd said, "Nuts! You horse's posterior."

It was a difficult subject to bring before his aged mother, but John felt that he must. "Mom, you are no longer a spring chicken and you do need to think ahead of what will happen in the future. Why don't we make arrangements about when...you know...when...God forbid, you pass on?"

The mother didn't say anything, just sat there staring ahead. "I mean, Mom, like...how do you want to finally go...to be buried? Cremated?"

There was yet another long pause. Then the mother looked up and said, "Son, why don't you simply surprise me?"

Celeste: "Silas, tomorrow is our fiftieth wedding anniversary. What shall we do?"
Silas: "Let's celibate."

The Winterhavens

"Must you put a sign in every room of the house?!"

The two ladies met for the first time in many years. They got around to age, of course, and one said to the other, "I bet I don't look 55-years-old, do I!" Her companion replied, "No, you sure don't. But I bet you did when you were."

"I don't think that I look my age, sixty, do you, John?"

"Well, no, Sally, not really. But you used to."

The older guys can't seem to get used to these skirts that indicate the manufacturer ran out of piece goods half way through. Pete Edwards spent his life in the fashion design business. He says that the new trend in skirts, six inches above the knee, indicates nudism on the installment plan. But he says he can understand women's fondness for these skirts when he recalls that women love a sale with huge price reductions. Well, skirts today are fifty percent off!

I sat next to the old lady at tea;
It was just as I feared it would be!
Her rumblings abdominal
Were simply abominable
And everyone thought it was me!

For forty years the old girl had been harassed by her husband over her now-and-then overdrawn condition at the bank. Finally, she'd had enough. "Did it ever occur to that pinched brain of yours," she growled, "that I am NOT overdrawn...but that you ARE underdeposited?"

An old lady had always wanted to visit England, the home of her ancestors, before she died. So she went to the Federal Office and asked for a passport.

"You must take the loyalty oath first," the passport clerk said. "Raise your right hand, please."

The old gal raised her right hand.

"Do you swear to defend the Constitution of the United States against all its enemies, domestic or foreign?"

The little old lady's face paled and her voice trembled as she asked, "Who, me?"

"I know he's wealthy! But he's much too old to be eligible," the pretty daughter said.

"Listen, young lady," her mother corrected her, "and don't forget it - he's much too eligible to be old!"

Two matrons were sitting in the park when an old friend, also "up in years," passed by. They nodded, said hello and the walking lady went on her way. "How old do you reckon she is?" one of the seated women asked.

"I can't tell you in exact years," the other said, "but she knew the Big Dipper when it was a mere drinking cup."

There was an old lady from Antigua,
Who said to her spouse, "What a pigua"
    He said, "Oh my love,
    Is't my push, pull or shove,
Or do you refer to my figua."

Mary Higgins said that the one thing she'd learned in life was that a good pair of legs can get a person to first base, even if she isn't a baseball player. She went on to say that well-bred dogs can learn from well-bred girls, not to respond to whistles unless you can interpret them.

The seven ages of women are: infancy, childhood, adolescence, junior miss, young woman, young woman, young woman.

"Careful, honey," the old guy cautioned his wife, "watch your language or you'll bring out the beast in me!"

"Oh yeah?" she said. "So who's afraid of mice?"

Mrs. Peters came weeping to Mrs. Brown. "It's terrible," she sobbed, "We've been married forty years and I discover that he's chasing girls!"

"Don't you worry, honey," Mrs. Brown assured her, "My dog chases cars - but if he ever caught one, he's too danged old to know what to do with it."

"She's difficult you say. Is she outspoken?"
"Not by anyone I know of."

Susan from Texas and Sarah Jane from New York had been WACS together in World War II. Now Susan was visiting Sarah Jane and they were sight-seeing. As they passed the United Nations building, Sarah Jane remarked, "Isn't that a stupendous structure?"

"Not so much! In Texas I got an outhouse bigger than that."

"You need it!" Sarah Jane replied.

A little old lady from the city was nervously walking up and down the aisle of Famous-Barr Department Store. She appeared to be frantically looking for something.

A very bow-legged floor walker came up to her and asked: "Madam, can I be of help to you?"

"You bet you can, young man. I need help in the worst way. I can't find Dr. Johnson's baby powder."

"Walk this way, Madam," he replied. "Just walk this way."

"Oh my goodness, young fellow, if I could walk that way would I need talcum powder?"

Photographer: "Now stop squirming and fidgeting around, Madam, I promise to do you justice."

Dowager: "Justice I don't need. What I need is mercy."

A noble old Roman named Caesar
Told a girl he wanted to kisser;
     But the girl with a blush
     Said the Latin for "Shush
You horrid old thing, let me besir!"

After his speech to the senior citizens at their community center, the speaker turned to shake hands with a woman who had come onto the podium. "I wanted to thank you for taking the time to speak to us old folks," she said. "It's obvious you like seniors."

"Oh yes indeed," the clever speaker replied. "And I like them your age, too."

"This is the most obscene novel I've ever read! Fortunately I have only fifty pages left."

The woman had spent an entire afternoon listening to her decrepit old boyfriend talk about himself. At last she asked him, "Peter, if you had it to do over, would you still fall in love with yourself?"

Young folks philosophize about time, but us old uns tell it like it is, like this: "Time waits for no man...but it sure does stand still for a gal of 60!"

Old Jeb had a wife who was as penurious as he. One day she went into a store and asked for bagels. "They are two for a dollar, Ma'am," the clerk said, holding two out for her to examine. She took both, then handed him one. "I'll take this one, for fifty cents." "Madam, singly, they cost sixty cents." "Fine," she replied, "I'll take the other."

On September 26, 1985, in Springfield, Illinois, Red Skelton appeared on stage at the convention center. He put in a full, exhausting two hours of entertainment, then came on stage and announced that he was 76 years old. "But I expect to live many more years," Red announced, "because I had a grandmother who lived to be 110." The audience gasped and applauded, and Red Skelton held up his hand. "Wait," he said, "you haven't heard it all. I said she lived to be 110. Then she died. But you didn't let me finish, we saved the baby!"

"Do you mean to tell me that you've been married thirty-five years and your mother-in-law has been to visit you only once?"
"Yep! She came the day after the wedding and never left."

I once knew an old flirt from Thurston
Who thought her third husband the worst one.
    For he justly was reckoned
    Far worse than the second,
And the second was worse than the first one.

One of the pleasures of the golden years is that you can look back at all the SOBs you didn't marry.

"Doctor, I'm so constipated. I know that it goes with age, but can you do anything for me?"

"Are you taking anything now?" the doctor asked.

"Oh, yes," she replied. "I take my knitting."

Mrs. Edwards, in her eighties and not very sophisticated, answered a knock at her front door. When she opened it, there stood a policeman who asked, "Ma'am, have you been bothered by a flasher? We got reports that he was operating around here and we wondered if you'd seen him."

Mrs. Edwards replied: "Flasher? I don't know about that; the only feller who's been around lately was some young feller selling raincoat linings."

The traffic officer became highly enraged at an elderly woman who, after he'd flagged her to stay on the sidewalk, strolled calmly out into the street. "Lady," roared the officer, "don't you know what it means when I hold up my hand?"

"I ought to," she snapped. "For the past twenty-five years, I've been a schoolteacher!"

Mrs. Fred Brown had spent most of her life working hard in a small town in Indiana. But a cousin died and left her, the only living relative, a million dollars. It was then she began to prepare for a lifelong dream...to see all of Europe. And she did, returning after six weeks of travel and a wonderful time.

While in Europe, she realized another lifelong ambition...to own a mink coat. But she could not bear to spend more money than was absolutely necessary, so she hid it when she approached the U.S. Customs gate...wrapped it around her middle and under her old cloth coat.

"Are you sure you have nothing to declare?" the customs officer asked.

"Nothing at all."

"Well, Madam," the inspector replied, "Am I to understand that the fur tail hanging from under your coat is your own?"

70

One thing sure...it isn't time that tells on a woman, it's her friends.

A matron showing off to her friends at an Art Gallery began to name the various painters.

"That's a Rembrandt."

"A Velasquez, Madam," corrected the guide.

"Then that's a Goya."

"A Reubens, Madam."

"A Turner..."

"No, Madam, a Constable."

"Well, that's definitely a Picasso."

"No, Madam, it's a mirror."

Mrs. Thatcher had spent her long life in a very small town. One day her young friend invited her to see a ball game. "You know, I've never seen one," Mrs. Thatcher told her. "It just might be lots of fun. Let's go."

Seated in the ballpark, Mrs. Thatcher watched the game for a few innings, then remarked: "Isn't it simply splendid how the man that throws the ball to the man who holds the bat manages to hit his bat most every time, no matter how he holds it?"

The senior gal had delayed her Christmas shopping too long and was now caught in the huge, incautious, seasonal crowds. She was pushed this way and that! Finally she remarked, "A body needs bumpers to get around here." The wag next to her said, "Yep! And you sure got 'em, Ma'am."

Ms. Van Depester walked into her neighborhood grocery store and asked to see a chicken. The butcher, Peter Tomaso, turned to his refrigerator and took out a large bird. Ms. Van Depester shook the bird gingerly, sniffed under the right wing, then sniffed under the left wing, turned the bird over and sniffed under the part that went over the fence last, and announced, "This chicken stinks!"

Pete Tomaso took the bird and said, "Madam, do you think YOU could pass such a test?"

There was an old girl name Lucille,
Who went up in a giant Ferris Wheel.
When half way around
She looked down at the ground,
And it cost her a ten dollar meal.

Lola's husband, Joseph, a merchant was asked why he subscribed to PLAYBOY magazine. "I read PLAYBOY for the same reason that I read NATIONAL GEOGRAPHIC, so's I can see all the sights I'm too danged old to visit."

Mary Jones said that although she didn't mind growing old, it was sometimes frustrating as all get out. Especially was it bad when she came home from the beauty parlor, looked in the mirror, and had that certain sinking feeling that she hadn't been waited on.

Because Mrs. Jones was a most careful shopper, she was outraged to be told that the price of hamburger was $2.50 a pound. "That's highway robbery!" she exclaimed. "Why at Brown and Bigtoe they sell it for two dollars a pound."

"Well, Madam. If I were you, I'd go to Brown and Bigtoe and buy my hamburger there."

"I would, only they're out of it."

"Oh, that's different. Why, when we are out of it, ours is only $1.50 a pound."

Then there was the smart aleck guy who said to a passing matron: "Howdy, darling, anything going tonight?"

She gave him a frigid look and walked on.

"Oh, pardon me," he said, his voice heavy with sarcasm, "I thought you were my mother."

"How could I be!" she retorted icily, "I'm married!"

A number of years ago, at the Drake Hotel in Chicago, a maid was listening to a group of DAR officers calling one another "Girls." Finally, the maid sighed and said, "If them is girls, I sure as heck ain't even been born yet."

A lady entered a room in a Chicago hotel and immediately recognized her Congressman nervously pacing up and down. She asked what he was doing there.

"I'm about to make a speech and I'm rehearsing it."

"You seem so nervous. Does that always happen before you make a speech?"

"Me, nervous? Never! I'm never nervous before a speech."

"Then tell me...why are you in the Ladies Room?"

A reporter had come to the nursing home to interview the oldest resident, Louisa Shuck. "I'm here to do a story on nursing homes," the reporter began the interview, "and I'd like to start things off by asking what the death rate is here."

"Well, without official confirmation," said Mrs. Shuck, "You can put it down as one each."

Two golden-agers were discussing their husbands over tea.

"I do wish that my Elmer would stop biting his nails. He makes me terribly nervous."

"My Billy used to do the same thing," the other old girl replied. "But I broke him of the habit."

"How?"

"I hid his teeth."

Mary Jane Thornapple is mighty tired of people telling her that her stockings are wrinkled. "Why, for goodness sakes," Mary Jane says, "I never, never wear stockings."

The senior ladies of the Sangamo Club were discussing the richest woman in town, and the most conceited. "I can't stand her!" one of the women said. "She thinks she's better than anyone else and doesn't mind saying so. I do believe she thinks she's a saint."

"Well you won't have to dislike her any longer. She went to her maker yesterday."

"You don't say! My goodness, what happened? I didn't know she'd been sick!"

"She wasn't. She went for a walk and got hit by a motorboat."

Edna Schuster was bored to tears with the young man sitting beside her. This kid thought he had to be entertaining all through the meal and Edna was sick of his chatter. When they served the meat, he cut a piece of it, speared it on his fork, held it toward her and said, "Is this pig?"

"On which end of the fork?" Edna asked.

There was an old lady of Munich,
Whose appetite simply was unich.
　　There's nothing like food,
　　She contentedly cooed,
And she let out three tucks in her tunich.

Did I hear you ask if Grandma Mary Jane's face wrinkled? It is true that she's had several face-lifts and other treatments, but they haven't helped. As a matter of fact, she refused to wear long earrings because she knows that when she does she looks like a venetian blind.

A silver-haired seductress was simply up to her ears with the constant advances of an old geezer who seemed to be always around and no way to get rid of him. Finally the old gal said, "George, let us play horse. I'll play the head and you play your usual position."

An elderly, important lady once invited about forty soldiers from the nearby camp to her home. When they arrived, she served them cookies and lemonade. After half an hour, she served them the same things, cookies and lemonade. When the captain suggested they were due back in camp soon, she stood and announced: "Dear soldiers, I have just six cookies left...now what shall I do with them to be fair to you all?"

At once the lieutenant stood and announced: "The first GI that answers THAT gets the guardhouse for a week!"

Two ladies met for the first time in fifty years since high school. Mary began to tell Rose about her children. "My son is a doctor and he's got four kids. My daughter is married to a lawyer, and they have three great kids. But tell me, Rose, how about your kids?"

"Unfortunately, Roger and I don't have children and so we have no grandchildren."

"No children? And no grandkids. So tell me, Rose, what do you do for aggravation?"

When Abel returned to the house one evening, his wife announced that the new cleaning woman they had hired had stolen two towels.

"Yeah," said her disinterested old husband, reclining on the sofa. "Well, that sure wasn't very nice."

"You're darned right it wasn't," the old lady said. "And they were the two best towels we had...the ones we got from the Hilton Hotel while we were on vacation."

Many years ago, an aging actress was asked if there would be a cake at her birthday party. "Of course. What would a birthday party be without a cake?"

"With candles on it?" she was asked.

"That's quite another story. You see this is to be a birthday party...not a candlelight parade."

Charles Dickens put it this way: "She still *aims* at youth but *shot* beyond it...years ago."

Susie was still in love with her husband, after thirty years of marriage, but the dummy divorced her for a much younger girl. After the trial and final separation, she went up to her former husband's lawyer and told him: "If Myron misses a single payment you tell him that I'll...I'll...I'll repossess him!"

A car came to a screeching halt, barely missing an old lady who was crossing the street at an intersection. The driver waited sheepishly while the old girl walked up to his car. He figured he'd get a well-deserved bawling-out.

But the old lady came up to the car, smiled broadly as she pointed to a pair of baby shoes hanging from the rear window. "Young man," she said softly, "Why don't you put your shoes back on?"

Eighty-year-old Mrs. Altrusa Van Dyke was nouveau-riche (her name used to be Mary Jane Smith) having hit it big in her state lottery. So she engaged a young artist to paint her portrait. The fee was five thousand dollars but she wrote a check in advance for six thousand. The artist was amazed. "Why the extra thousand?" he asked.

"I want you to paint me in the nude. OK?"

"Sure. Glad to. But I got to keep my sox on. I need to put my paintbrushes somewhere."

At the age of eighty-six, Celia was the envy of her younger friends. They came to her home one day to visit her excellent garden. As they walked through it, she pointed to a bug on a flower and said, "That is a friend to man, a ladybug."

One of her friends replied, "My goodness, Celia, you sure have got good eyesight!"

THE LITTLE OLD LADY IN LAVENDER SILK

I was seventy-seven, come August,
  I shall shortly be loosing my bloom;
I've experienced zephyr and raw gust
  And (symbolical) flood and simoom.

When you come to this time of abatement,
  To this passing from Summer to Fall,
It is manners to issue a statement
  As to what you got out of it all.

So I'll say though reflection unnerves me
  And pronouncements I dodge as I can,
That I think (if my memory serves me)
  There was nothing more fun than a man!

In my youth, when the crescent was too wan
  To embarrass with beams just above,
By the aid of some local Don Juan
  I fell into the habit of love.

And I learned how to kiss and be merry-an
  Education left better unsung.
My neglect of the waters Pierian
  Was a scandal, when Grandma was young.

Though the shabby unbalanced the splendid,
  And the bitter outmeasured the sweet,
I should certainly do as I then did,
  Were I given the chance to repeat.

For contrition is hollow and wraithful,
  And regret is no part of my plan,
And I think (if my memory's faithful)
  There was nothing more fun than a man!
                    Dorothy Parker.

At the senior center the women were discussing what a chore housework had become. One matron said, "My George and I have worked out an absolutely satisfying way to do housework. We are both completely satisfied with the system."

"Tell us about it. What do you do?" they exclaimed.

"We abstain," she replied.

Mabel was disgusted. "Just look at me," she screamed at her husband, "shabby clothes! Haven't been to the beauty parlor this year! Shoe soles worn through! Why if anyone came to dinner they'd think I was the hired cook."

"Not if they stayed through supper," he replied.

Two aging bachelorettes, Celia and Dorothy, were chatting over coffee one evening. Celia had moved quite recently to a nursing home, and Dorothy asked, "Celia, how do you like it?"

"Just dandy. Nothing to do but talk and eat and watch television. No hard work."

"But there aren't any men there, Celia. I'd think that would be awful."

"Oh, but there are," replied Celia. "There's Lenny Mint and Charlie Horse, and Ben Gay. Can't do much with Ben, Lenny or Charlie, but there's always one you can go to bed with...Arthur Itis."

The reason why some women over fifty have so many aches and pains is because they're over sixty.

A fat old lady from Baltimore,
The same shape behind as before,
    They didn't know where
      to offer a chair
So the dear thing had to sit on the floor.

The lady in Raleigh was having a bad time at the Golden Age bridge club. She trumped her partner's ace, reneged twice, and passed an informatory double. She seemed confused and uncomfortable. Finally she excused herself and went to the powder room.

When she returned, her playing picked up and she and her partner made the rubber. "What happened to you?" asked the partner. "You're really back in the game."

"Took off my girdle," replied the woman calmly.

Johnny was late coming home from his Cub Scout den meeting. Mother was worried about his tardiness and vastly relieved when he arrived. "Johnny!" she yelled at him, "How come you are so late getting home?"

"Couldn't help it, Ma. We were helping a little old lady across the street."

"How nice. But that shouldn't have delayed you this late!"

"Well, Ma, it's like this. She didn't much want to go."

A woman is as young as she feels like telling you she is.

A lady went into a pet store to get a drinking basin for her husband's dog. The clerk asked if she'd like an inscription on the basin, "FOR MY DOG, BROWNIE."

"It doesn't make a bit of difference," the lady replied. "My husband doesn't drink from it and the dog can't read."

A right fussy widow named Pease,
Thought her house was infested with flease.
So she used gasoline and her form was last sean,
Sailing over the tops of the trees.

A famous art dealer is shopping an antique mall when he notices a mangy old cat drinking milk from an interesting saucer placed in front of the booth. At once, the dealer recognizes the saucer as a very valuable and rare antique. So he looks around the place, seeming disinterested, then turns to the elderly lady running the place and asks if he can buy the *cat.*

"Sure sorry, Mister, but I couldn't part with that cat for any amount of money."

"I've grown attached to that cat myself. I'd give as much as a hundred dollars for it. Please oblige me."

So the antique dealer shells out the money, turns to the old dealer and says, "Listen, since I now have this cat, could you throw in the dish because he seems so used to it and all. And I don't have a spare dish at home. Would you let me have it?"

"Nope, can't part with it," the shrewd lady says, "Y'see, it's my lucky saucer. So far this month, I've sold forty-eight cats!"

Johnny Yonkers was extolling the virtues of his wife. He said to his old friend, "That gal of mine is some punkin's. And I expect her to be just the same ten years from today."

"But that's unreasonable."

"You got it! That's the way she is today."

And they do say that easy-crying widows take another husband soonest because there is nothing like wet weather for transplanting! (O. W. Holmes).

Old Jimmy Jones was a pretty noisy eater. He drank his soup and four couples got up to dance. As the saying goes: Soup should be seen and not heard. But on the other hand, there are times when it should not be seen, as when Mary Worth sneezed in her tomato soup and everyone thought she had the measles.

Mrs. Fred Jones had been married for fifty years. A young woman called on her to learn the secret of all those happy, domestic years. Unfortunately, only the black maid was there and when the young lady voiced the reasons for her call, the maid said, "Maybe, Miss, Ah kin help you."

"Please do," the young girl said. "I suspect you've been here many years. Then please do tell me the secret of her successful, long marriage."

"When the missus was fust married, she done took a course in domestic silence and that's the whole story."

Out in Kansas, tornadoes often hit with sudden devastation, and without warning. In one case, a house was completely whisked away leaving only the foundation and first floor. A silver-haired farm lady was seen sitting dazed, in a bathtub, the only remaining part of the house left above the floor. The rescue squad rushed to her aid and found her unhurt. She was just sitting there in the tub, talking to herself. "It was the darndest thing...it was the darndest thing," she kept repeating dazedly.

"What was the darndest thing, Ma'am?" asked one of the rescuers.

"I was visiting my daughter here, taking a bath and all I did was pull the plug and the whole derned house suddenly drained away."

There once was a golden girl named Perkins,
Who loved overmuch those green gerkins;
    She ate a whole quart,
    Which was more than she ought,
For it pickled her internal workin's.

Middle age turns to old age about the time a woman's hair starts turning from gray to black.

They tell the story about ninety-year-old Amanda Perkins who lived all alone in a backwoods cabin, eking out a living on three acres of hardscrabble soil. A social worker came to visit her and said, "Aunt Amanda, I worry about you living out here all alone and not much extra vittles or clothing for you. I think I can arrange for a payment of $300. Would that be all right with you?"

"Sure 'nuff, young man. It'd tickle me pink cause then I'd have somethin' to give the poor."

"The most embarrassing thing that ever happened to me was at Atlantic Beach going on thirty years ago," said the senior lady to her bridge club. "I was out in the water and it was just awful rough and windy and the undertow was terrible. Well, before I knew what was happening, the bottom half of my swim suit was sucked off and I was left there, two hundred yards from the hotel, with no pants."

"What did you do, for goodness sakes," someone exclaimed.

"I did just what any decent, well-trained girl would do...I covered my face with my hands and ran fast as I could for the hotel."

One dark, gloomy evening, 21-year-old Marie Patterson passed a fortunteller's place when she had an overwhelming desire to go inside and see what the future held for her. She was met by an old crone, toothless, wrinkled and baggy-eyed, who seated her across the table. The crone peered deeply into a crystal ball, then fell back in her chair with a groan, moaning, "Death! I see a death! Oh no, oh no! Get out of here. Go! Go!" she moaned, and Marie Patterson ran from the place, her heart overcome with a sense of doom.

Marie is now eighty-six but she has never quite got rid of the impending sense of doom, of catastrophe she got from that fortuneteller on that awesome, distant day.

Mrs. Johnston had been married forty years and she was worried that her husband of all those forty years was growing tired of her. She talked to her best friend about the matter, and her friend suggested that she lead the old boy into love talk. So Mrs. Johnston did just that.

"Do you love me with all your heart, body and soul?"

"Sure."

"And do you think me the most beautiful senior citizen in the city?"

"Yep."

"And my body, so seductive, my hair, so lovely, and my eyes...do you think them soulful as the sea?"

"Yep!"

"Oh, my dear, sweet husband, you do say the sweetest, nicest things."

Fifty-five is the ideal age for a woman...especially if she is sixty-five.

Seventy-five-year-old Sarah Hughes says that if there is one thing she hates, it is a female bore. When asked to explain what she meant by "bore," she explained. "A bore is someone who talks about herself when I want to talk about myself."

There is an ancient proverb that says, "For untold ages women have been famous for untold ages."

Grandpa and Grandma Belks were out celebrating their first male grandchild after twelve girls straight in a row. They met a friend to whom they explained their delight, "And whom does it look like? You or your Mrs.?"

"We don't know. We haven't looked at the face yet."

The spunky farm matron went to visit her illustrious son who had deserted the farm and become very famous and rich in California. She was much impressed with the beautiful mansion he owned in Beverly Hills. After a week of entertainment, parties of all kinds, daily swims in the pool outside, service by the butler and chauffeured drives around Hollywood, her son asked her how she liked the life he led and would she join him, move to California, and have this luxury all the time.

"That's nice of you, Tommy," she said after a bit of thinking. "But y'know I think I like it best where I am. Here, you bathe outside and go to the toilet inside. Home, I go to the toilet outside and bathe inside. Y'know, Tommy, I like it our way best."

———————

Stan says he retired in good shape...and, what he considered himself to be, *a self-made man*. But his wife says he is merely a product of unskilled labor.

———————

A doctor was visited by an elderly woman who complained of chronic constipation. He gave her a box of suppositories and told her to use them all, then to return. He figured it would take her about thirty days and made an appointment at that time. But she returned in a week. "My goodness, dear lady," the physician said, "What on earth are you doing with those suppositories, eating them?"

"What the devil do you think I've been doing with them, Doctor, shoving them up my rectum?"

———————

In the course of a long life, Mary Jenkins says she has learned that it takes a tree about five years to produce nuts...but that's not true of the family tree.

———————

Mary Jane Masters always held firmly to the belief that the most annoying people were those who think they know it all...when it is only she who does!

"He offered to leave his brain to science, but they wanted time to think it over."

Reprinted with permission of *The Saturday Evening Post*

"Isn't it simply divine," gushed the old lady, pointing to her intricately designed birthday cake. "Just look at it and you can see that I've still got my superb sense of design."

"You sure have that," her friend replied, "but from the number of candles, I'd have to conclude that although your ability to design is unquestioned...that ain't so with your arithmetic!"

Perhaps the lady who uttered this one is she who is buried in that Hatfield, Mass. cemetery.

"Always accentuate the positive," shouted the speaker. "Eliminate the negative. Use the word *is* instead of the word *not*."

One woman who attended his lecture said to her friend, "He's right. I'm going to quit making negative statements. I'm going to speak positively from now on."

"Like what?" her friend asked.

"Like I used to say that my husband was *not* fit to live with the hogs. Now I am going to say that he *is* fit to live with them."

There was a duchess from Lynn,
Who was so terribly thin
    That when she agreed
    To drink lemonede
She slipped through the straw and fell in.

An old lady goes into the Bureau of Missing Persons and reports that her husband has not been home in ten days. The sergeant asks for a description of the man and the lady replies, "He's thirty years old, has wavy blonde hair, bright blue eyes, is six feet tall and weighs 140 pounds. He has a lovely dimple in his chin and a wide smile."

A friend who had come with her takes her aside and says, "Patricia! What are you telling him. Your husband is short, bald, fat and sixty."

"I know...but who wants him back."

An old lady having her portrait painted asked the artist to add two diamond rings, an elaborate jeweled necklace, expensive earrings, an elegant diamond and ruby bracelet.

"I can do that, Ma'am," the artist assured. her. "But may I ask why?"

"Well, my husband is running with a young chick and I don't have long to live. I want him to have my picture, of course, but most of all I want to drive that young bitch wild looking for the jewelry."

Living in the past has one thing in its favor...it's a heckuva lot cheaper.

Tillie Davis was sort of inexperienced and smalltown in outlook. So you will understand her pride in the accomplishments of her daughter, who was marrying a professional, a notary public!

They say, "Time heals all." Maybe so. But it sure ain't no beautician.

"Whenever I'm in the dumps, I go get a new dress," a matron confided.

"Oh yes. How interesting," responded her catty friend, "I was wondering where you got them."

If you're over the hill, why not enjoy the view?

Old-fashioned girl: One who used to stay at home when she had nothing to wear.

The Winterhavens

" MAKE YOUR OWN SANDWICH. YOU MAY BE RETIRED BUT THESE ARE MY LEISURE YEARS. "

One thing is certain...that it is better to wear out than rust out.

Two aging members of the fairer sex met after not having seen one another for many years.

"And what has happened to you after all these years, Mary?"

"I got a boyfriend. After all these years I got a boyfriend! And such a man. He gives me everything."

"Fantastic! What does he give you?"

"A mink coat. The very best mink in the world."

"Fantastic!" was her friend's reply.

"And jewelry! I've got a drawer-full of diamond rings, pearl necklaces, brooches. Oh he loves me so very much and he's so good to me."

"Fantastic!"

"But that's not all. He took me to Europe last year. Only the best hotels and accommodations. Boy did we live it up. But I'm doing all the talking. What have you been doing? Tell me about your life over all these years."

"I've been going to charm school."

"Really! And what do they teach you there?"

"How to say 'fantastic' instead of 'bullcrap'!"

Mrs. O'Reilly had been in America only twenty-five years. And she'd never been to an art museum. So her daughter thought it a good idea to take her to the city's finest. With much "ooh-ing and aah-ing" at the splendid art, they finally came to Gainsborough's great painting of *Blue Boy.*

The mother exclaimed, "What a nerve this gent had to copy the picture we've had hanging in our kitchen for twenty-two years!"

After a long life with three marriages, Mary Stuart has come to the conclusion that no woman ever makes a fool out of a man. She merely directs the performance.

Sarah Jane said that she quit wearing jeans at age sixty-five. "Do you think that you'll ever get back to trying them again, Sarah Jane?" a friend asked.

"Maybe," Sarah Jane replied. "When they get around to changing the names on the rear from WRANGLER or LEVI to WIDE LOAD!"

Old Pete says it is amazing how things change. Thirty years ago if you wanted to see a girl in pin curlers, you had to go to a beauty parlor. Now all you need do is go to the local supermarket.

Bertha was never good at spelling. As she grew older, her spelling grew progressively worse. For example, she wrote to her friend Mabel:

Dear Mabel:

My husband John had hiz seventy-fifth birthday last Sunday. Since he luves flowers, I gave him a punch for his birthday.

There was an old gal from Ladue,
Wanted love without further ado,
She walked out the door
With a fig leaf, no more!
And now she's in bed with...the flu!

"DINNER'S READY."

5

SENIOR GUYS

Here's a poem to the millions of men (and some women?) who have spent a lifetime trying (and failing) to pick a ripe melon, be it watermelon, honeydew or cantaloupe, from the piles of delectable fruit on every produce counter.

THAT'S A GIFT

"Observe my bean," the Stranger said,
    "Oh slant the bulge of yonder-brow."
"You have," said I, "a noble head,
    A sterling coco, I'll allow."
"Within that dome," the Stranger cried,
    "Are countless gems of lambent lore,
A flock of wisdom, true and tried,
    A mine of wit, a sapient store.

"Behind my altitudinous brow
    A corrugated thinker sits.
It's in a state of coma now,
    But gosh, it throws sagacious fits!
For it is crammed with all the dope
    Of ev'ry book on ev'ry shelf.
You get my modest view, I hope?
    I hate to talk about myself.

"I know more than art than any Taine,
    More Rome than Gibbon, Greece than Grote,
More law than old Sir Henry Maine,
    More poetry than any pote;
I've delved as deep as Darwin did,
    Beside me Euclid is a sham, and
Socrates a weanling kid,
    I know more words than Percy Hammond!"

"From which remarks I glean," said I,
  "You are shrewd and wise gazook,
A keen and perspicacious guy,
  A shining light, a gumptious gook."
"You're right," he sighed. "My wondrous brain
  Is hep indeed to all the ropes,
But still my heart is full of pain:
  I cannot pick good cantaloupes."
                    Slams of Life, J.P. McEvoy
                    P.F. Volland Co.,
                    Chicago, 1919

'You can't blame Mr. Schnibble, he's retiring
after 35 years as the head librarian."

It is a very hard thing to admit if you are over sixty. Still one must admit that the former overwhelming biological urge isn't much more than a rare and gentle nudge.

———————

Have you heard the story of Johnny Jones, whose old father was dying? Johnny seized the opportunity to propose to his girl, saying, "Marry me, sweetheart, my old man is deathly ill and I'll soon be a millionaire." And do you know what? Three days later, the girl was his stepmother!

Uncle George was a lazy old coot who had never done a lick of physical work in all his life. One day he glimpsed his wife, Bea, carrying a heavy basket of clothes up the basement stairs. "Bea!" he shouted, "This has got to stop. For years you've been carrying the clothing up the stairs in that big, heavy basket. Enough! Today...not tomorrow but today, you go downtown and get yourself a smaller basket and make two trips."

Before he got married, Eddie Foy was an atheist. He did not believe in heaven or hell. But after being married forty years, he's convinced that he was half wrong!

This old guy weighed many an ounce
And used language I hate to pronounce.
When his buddy unkind, pulled his chair out behind,
Just to see, strange to say, if he'd bounce.

An old man was standing around a dance floor loaded with couples swinging and swaying. A young fellow noticed him and said, "Do you like to dance, Sir?" And the old man said, "I don't dance a heckuva lot, son, but I sure do like to hold the ones that do."

Mr. Platt was terribly hen-pecked by his domineering wife. Throughout their forty years of marriage, whenever he entered the house, she made him take off his shoes so that he would not track in dirt. One day she took him by the ear and led him over to his favorite chair. "Look there!" she shouted. "That big spot came off the fishing pants you wore yesterday. Something will have to be done about that. No...more...spots...on...chairs!"

Poor Mr. Platt replied, "Dear, ever since we've lived here I've been taking off my shoes before I came into the house and grease spot or no grease spot, I ain't goin' to go any farther!"

Whether a man retires with a nest egg or a goose egg depends entirely on the kind of chick he marries.

———————

Old Eddie never would give up chasing young women. True to form, he asked the pretty young receptionist if she'd go out with him that night:

"I know your type," she snapped back at him, "You'll have me taking a drink, first. Then you'll ask me to your apartment. Then you'll pour more drinks down me. Sir, I can read you like a book."

"Well then, don't miss chapter five," the old boy cackled. "It's a doozie!"

———————

The old fellow was sitting on the park bench weeping. A kind lady walked over to him. "Is there some way I could be of service to you, my friend?" she asked.

"Oh no. I'm just disgusted with myself, is all."

"Well, tell me about it. It'll do you good to talk about it."

"Well, I'm getting so darned forgetful. A bit ago, I was walking near here and thought I might be late for my doctor's appointment. So I figured on looking at my watch to check the time when I suddenly remembered that I'd left the watch at home. So I walked home fast as I could, hoped I had time enough to get the watch and still make the appointment, reached into my pocket and took out the watch and saw that I had plenty of time, went into the house and my wife asked what I was doing home. I told her I'd forgotten my watch and came home to get it. She said, 'Did you look in your right pocket?' I did and there it was."

The lady walked away saying, "I reckon you do need to cry!"

———————

Old-timer: A man who can remember when the depth of juvenile depravity was to go back of the barn and smoke corn silk.

94

There was an old man from Montrose
Who could tickle himself with his toes
    He could do it so neat,
    He fell in love with his feet,
And christened them Myrtle and Rose.

A wise-guy reporter was talking to a group of old men seated around the cracker barrel in a country store. "Pop," he addressed one of the old geezers, "Can you recall the name of the first girl you ever kissed?"

"Young man," the old duffer replied, "I can't even recall the last one."

They tell the tale of a Northerner transplanted to North Carolina who, one day, visited friends in a small town. They visited the country store that supplied the townspeople, and the visitor noticed an odd-looking loaf that looked like a bologna cut up in thick chunks. He asked what it was and was told that it was a souse meat, a produce made from the remains of the gristle, meat and fat from the head of a pig. The visitor asked, "Does anyone really eat such a nasty mess of stuff as that?"

The old man, owner of the store grinned, pointed his finger at the visitor and said, "You take one slice of that there souse meat that's about half an inch thick, and you soak it in vinegar about twenty minutes, take it out and shake it off. Then you put that there slice of souse meat right on top of your head, Sir, and your tongue'll just plain flap your brains out atrying' to git to it."

Old Joshua is so old, he could have been the Commander-in-Chief for Moses at Jericho!

A wise old man once said that humor is to life what shock absorbers are to an automobile.

A character actor confided to a pal, "I'm almost sixty-five years old, have saved half a million, and have fallen madly in love with a young blonde. Do you think I'd have a better chance of marrying her if I told her I'm only fifty?"

"I think you'd have a better chance," said the pal frankly, "If you told her you're eighty!"

———————————

MY BOYHOOD HERO

The hero of my boyhood days
    (As near as I recall)
Was not Aladdin, Charles the Great,
    Nor Brian Boru nor Paul,
Nor Socrates nor William Tell,
    Nor Hannibal a-tall.

But he who claimed my fealty
    And undivided cheers,
Whose form I see as I retrace
    The trail of vanished years,
Was a boy I used to know in school,
    Who'd learned to wag his ears.

I never longed when I was young
    To own a massive brain,
Nor lead a million men to war
    Nor sail the Spanish main,
Nor roam the world from pole to pole
    For honor or for gain.

No wistful wishes such as these
    Excited me to tears,
One thing alone I yearned to find
    Within my span of years -
I only prayed that I some day
    Would learn to move my ears.

P.S.- I have.
    Slams of Life, J. P. McEvoy
    P.F. Volland Co., Chicago, 1919

There is an old fellow who lives in Bellize,
Who's terribly clever and witty and wise.
    He really did think
    He'd save gallons of ink.
By never dotting his "i's."

The old farmer was standing and looking around the department when a pretty young salesgirl came up and asked, "Is there something I can offer you, Sir?"

The old boy looked around and remarked, "Reckon not. I ain't never in my life seen so many things I could do without."

Clarence got real interested in his wife's study of reincarnation. Since they'd been married forty-five years, he could understand her interest and eventually he, too, took it up himself.

One day, one of his buddies asked how his study of life after death was coming along. "Fine," Clarence told him. "But I haven't figured out what I want to be when I come back."

"Well did you ever think about coming back as a dog?" his buddy asked.

"No, but why a dog?"

"Well, as you know, they get petted a lot, and get fed regularly, looked after by a vet and all sorts of good stuff. They're really well-treated."

"Gosh, I dunno," Clarence said. Then, after a moment's reflection, he observed, "In my case it just wouldn't work. Y'see, if I was to come back as a dog, my wife would still be on my back all the time, just like now. She'd come back as a flea."

Grumpy George said, "If the Lord intended that man to fly, He'd have made it a whole lot easier to get to the airport."

A rich old man advertised for a male nurse. When an applicant arrived, the old fellow cautioned him, saying, "It's not going to be an easy job, young man. I have a wooden leg, a toupee, an artificial arm, false teeth, and a glass eye. Think you can cope with that?"

"You bet. Piece of cake," the applicant replied. "Y'see, I used to work on the assembly line at Lockheed."

There was an old man with a beard,
Who said, "It's just as I feared;
    Two owls and a hen,
    Four larks and a wren,
Have all built their nest in my beard!"

"I don't suppose you've noticed if
Miss Vanbrugh is here this evening."

ONE MOMENT, SIR by Marione R. Nickles

Reprinted with permission of **Penguin Books USA, Inc.**

A visitor to a health spa in southern California asked, "Is it really as healthy out here as they say?"

"You bet it is!" the old native replied. "Why when I first came here, I couldn't speak a word, had hardly a hair on my head and couldn't walk three steps...hadn't the strength. And they had to lift me out of bed."

"Great!" exclaimed the tourist. "And just how long have you lived here, Sir?"

"Hell, man, I was born here."

An old timer is one who remembers when money stayed around long enough for germs to grow on it.

Old Joe had a gal by the name of May,
He was happy when he got her,
But he shucked her for a dame named June,
'Cause we all know June is hotter.

An old man, a tramp who wandered the country over, needed some food. So he stopped by the door of an inn about which hung the sign, "St. George and The Dragon." He knocked on the door and the manager came out, a very proper young lady, who upon seeing his worn-out clothes, down-at-the-heel shoes, unshaven face, and uncut hair, slammed the door in his face and cried, "Get lost! You bum!" The old boy waited a few minutes, rang the bell, and when the nasty girl opened it, and said, "Ma'am, could I now please talk to St. George?"

Jim Edwards says a buck sure doesn't go as far as it used to when he was a kid in the twenties. But then, he adds, "But it sure does go faster."

Henny Youngman was discussing contemporary bathing suits (or are they swatches?). He said he'd seen more cotton on top of an aspirin bottle.

There was a sale at Macy's department store, and an elderly native New Yorker decided to get his wife a nightgown for their fiftieth anniversary. In the store, he was kicked and pushed and shoved by frantic women. He remained quiet for as long as he could, then bowed his head and pushed hard and effectively and plowed ahead through the crowd. "Hey, you!" an angry female voice yelled, "Try acting like a gentleman!"

"That's what I've been doing for half an hour," he retorted. "From now on, I'm gonna act like a lady!"

Two old-timers met and decided to have a drink together. "How are things going with you, Frank," one old boy asked.

"Pretty good. Except my wife's mad at me and ain't talkin' to me this week and y'know what?"

"Sure don't. What?"

"I ain't in no mood to interrupt her."

Zeke Zellers and his wife had lived in the North Carolina mountains for forty-five years. And they'd never had one...single...child. A friend asked him one day, "Zeke, how come you and Effie never had no kids?"

Zeke pondered the question for a few minutes, then said, "I'll tell you just how it was. Two or three nights before we was to git married, I kinda made a suggestion about us goin' to bed together and makin' love and all, and she made such a terrible to-do about it that I ain't had the nerve to bring it up agin."

Two old guys had spent almost every evening in the only tavern in Middletown. But one day the owner announced that he was closing due to remodeling. When improvements were finished, the two old fellows entered the shining, renovated tavern and noticed that there were no spittoons. Since both chewed, that was truly a change. "I'm sure gonna miss them spittoons," one fellow said. "You always did," said the other.

100

It's an amazing thing, a genuine phenomenon how agile, strong and active some men are at eighty and over. Consider the case of Sam Dorman, who still works as a lumberjack at aged eighty-three. A few months ago, Sam applied to the foreman of a lumbering gang. "You're a lumberjack?" the foreman asked him. "At your age, you want to join our gang?"

"Yep! I sure as hell am a lumberjack...all my life."

"See that tree over there? Take this axe and let's see you cut her down."

Old Sam felled it before you could say Jack Robinson.

"Wow! So try this one over here," the foreman said.

With one blow, Sam sent it crashing to the ground.

"Fantastic. Never seen nothin' like it in my life," the foreman exclaimed. "Where did you learn your trade?"

"I worked for many years in the Sahara Park."

"You mean the Sahara Desert, don't you?"

"<u>Now</u> it's a desert!" Sam replied.

Eddie Brown had been a country schoolteacher all of his life. When asked the extent of his schooling, he said that he'd had exactly three years of it. When they seemed astonished that a man could teach school and yet have so little schooling, he explained. "They ain't hardly a boy or girl in my neck of the woods who can count up to twenty without taking off his shoes. Well, I learned to count up to fifty with my shoes on and that was when they hired me to teach school and I been at it ever since."

A man has reached senior citizen status when he doesn't care where his wife goes so long as she doesn't make him come along.

"Howdy, George. I see you got back all right. Tell me, how'd you find the weather in Arizona?"

"How'd I find it? Heck fire, man, I just went outside and there it was."

Elmer Fusil was ninety years old and worried. So he went to his doctor and said, "Doctor, I got to have your advice. Something is wrong because every derned time I kiss my wife I break out in either a terrific sweat or I get cold as an iceberg. What in heck is wrong with me?"

"Tell me a few things and let's see what this is all about. When do you kiss her?"

"Well, on our anniversary, of course, in July. And on her birthday, in December."

An elderly gent had a very successful business but was tired and wanted to retire. The trouble was that he has no son to take over, only a lovely young daughter who had no interest, whatsoever, in his business. It happens that he met a young man while on his daily walk in the park. They became friends, walked daily together in the park, and one thing leads to another until the old boy invited the young fellow home to meet his daughter. Of course, they fell in love and the old guy was delighted.

After the marriage, the old man invited the young fellow to his office. "I want you to come into my business and, eventually, take my place. Let me start you out as treasurer."

"But, Pop, I don't know anything about accounting, math, books, that sort of thing."

"OK, then you can take over the sales."

"That'd be a mistake, Pop, because I never sold anything in my life."

"So I'll make you Chairman of the Board, my job, and you'll run the company."

"Heck, Pop, I don't know a danged thing about business. That'd be a mistake."

"Well, then you name it. What do you want to do in this company?"

And the son-in-law said, "I got it! Why don't you buy me out?"

There was an old man named Peach,
Who mislaid his pearly false teeth.
Laid 'em down in a chair,
Plumb forgot they were there,
Then sat down and get bit from beneath!

How old are you Pete?
About as old as my hair and a mite older than my teeth!

An old timer can remember way back when the only time a fellow ran out of gas was on purpose.

A sad thing happened to Joe Smith, a retired farmer who had moved to Minneapolis. It seemed that he froze to death. The poor guy went to the drive-in to see "CLOSED FOR THE WINTER!" You will understand Joe better when you know he once had his bathroom carpeted. In fact, he was so very pleased with the result that he had it carpeted all the way to the house.

A tourist stopped off at the general store of a very small Arkansas village. He bought a cigar and lit it only to be told by the old merchant, "Hey, mister, ain't no smokin' allowed in here. See that sign?"

"You sell cigars, then how come folks can't smoke 'em?" the tourist asked.

"We do sell 'em," the aged storekeeper agreed, "And we also sell condoms."

Jack Downey, a wise old-timer out of the last century, remarked, "I am now going on eighty years, and yet, except for getting tuckered out easier than I used to, I believe I feel just about as smart as when I was a little boy."

If you think old soldiers just fade away, try getting into your old Army uniform.

The whole town of Gumption turned out for Grandpa Bill Crook's hundredth birthday. During festivities, an old friend said to Grandpa's grandson, "You must be mighty proud of your grand ol' grandpappy."

"Don't see why," the lad remarked. "All he ever done was grow old and it sho 'nuff taken him a long time to do that!"

There was a disgusting old man
Who used to eat catch-as-catch can.
  He covered his vest
  With the remains of the best
of the gravy, the chicken, and ham.

Eddie was the perennial hot character in Greenview Manor Rest Home. He was forever trying to make love to the girls there and no one figured he'd ever succeeded. But this time he took after Lizzie Pruitt, who was a prude from 'way back. "Get away from me, Eddie Fogarty," she said. "And I mean right now or I'll give you a piece of my mind."

Eddie pulled back and said, "Hold it! Hold it! I'll run and get my tweezers."

All things may come to those who wait;
But when they do, they're out of date.

Old Freddie loved to attend antique auctions. He never bought much but it was fun to watch the bidding. But one afternoon, Freddie outdid himself. The auctioneer announced, "One of our patrons has just lost his wallet containing $1000. He offers a reward of $300 to the person who finds and returns it."

Freddie yelled: "I offer $325!"

Bob was kinda dumb, but a good old guy. He dearly loved cigars as much as his wife hated them. Finally, she told him he had to quit - or else - and she could help him do it.

"Just how?" he sneered.

"Every time you crave a cigar," she told him, "You get yourself a Baby Ruth candy bar instead. It'll work."

"OK," he agreed. "I'll do it."

The first evening of his self-sacrifice, he returned home, saying, "I can't do it. It won't work!"

"Why not?" she demanded. "Did you try the Baby Ruth?"

"Yes. But I can't keep the damned thing lit!"

He's so old it looks like one clean shirt would do him.

Seventy-year-old violinist Mischa Elman: "When I made my debut as a twelve year old in Berlin, people used to say, 'Isn't he wonderful for his age?' Now they're beginning to say the same thing again!"

**"There's Throckmorton
reminiscing again!"**

MEN ONLY
Copyright © 1936 by *Maxwell Droke, Publisher*

Jamie Thompkins had been a professional gambler all his life until he retired. Then he took his life's savings and went to the other side of the table. He figured he knew all the angles and couldn't lose. But he did. He lost all he'd saved! Desolate, he borrowed a dime to use in the pay toilet in the restroom. Wonder of wonders, the door was open. He put his last dime in his pocket, went on in and about his business.

Back in the gambling hall, he played that last borrowed dime. He hit the jackpot, then went on to parlay that win into a million dollars.

He became a consultant, lectured groups of would-be gamblers on how to win. Always, he told the story of his lucky dime and that if he ever found the guy who had benefitted him, he'd give him half his fortune.

One time, after he'd lectured all over the country, a man shouted, "I'm the guy! I'm the one who gave you the dime for the toilet!"

But the gambler hollered back, "I'm looking for the fellow who left the toilet door open!"

The old mountaineer came to town with his new, young wife. The wife carried a lovely week-old baby.

The storekeeper greeted them and said, "Come right in, Lemuel. Mighty glad to see ya. Is that young'un yore's, Lem?"

"I reckon so. Leastways, it wuz caught in my trap."

Edgar James has reached such an advanced age that each time that he reads a magazine and comes to a to-be-continued-next-month story, he skips it.

A tourist's car broke down in the hill country of Virginia, near a tiny town. He was given shelter for the night and was amazed at how quiet things were. "Kinda quiet here," he remarked to one of the residents, "How long has this town been dead like this?"

"Not long," replied the old resident. "You're the first buzzard to drop in."

The old guy boarded the bus bound for Chicago. The driver said, "That'll be ten dollars, please."

"I'll give you seven."

"Don't argue. The price of a ticket to Chicago is ten dollars."

"Make it seven fifty."

"Pay the price or get off."

"No. It's seven fifty."

The exasperated bus driver took the old man's suitcase and threw it off the bus. "Now get off," he shouted.

The old man quickly got off the bus, dived for his suitcase, opened it, then turned and shouted, "Well, you didn't have to take it out on my poor grandson, you bum!"

There was an old farmer named Poster
Had an Alderney cow, and he lost her.
   So the country he scours,
   For three or four hours,
Then in his own yard he came across(t) er.

The winner of the seniors' marathon was surrounded by young admirers who kept firing questions concerning his unusual physical stamina. "It's because my Pa was a good runner and general all-around athlete."

"How old is your father?"

"He's eighty-five and one heluva man. He was going to compete here today, but he had to go to my Great Grandpa's wedding."

"Your Great Grandpa's wedding? How old is he?"

"He's a hundred and ten."

"And he's gettin' married? At a hundred and ten! Why would a man that age want to get married?"

"He doesn't want to...he's got to!"

Memory is what tells a man his wedding anniversary was yesterday.

The aged woman walked into the drugstore and looked about for someone her age to wait on her. She found him, went to him and asked, "Have you got Life Boy?"

The old boy was not a clerk but a customer. He looked at her, smiled and replied, "Set the pace, woman, set the pace."

You know you are approaching seventy when "getting a little action" indicates only that the prune juice is working.

Two old guys were fishing off the sandy beach used mostly for swimming. They hadn't paid much attention to the swim-suited passersby until four absolutely stunning young girls came swinging past them on their way to the water. "What do them dolls think they're doing, roiling up the water and scaring the fish," one of the old boys asked.

"I reckon they're trollin' with live bait," his buddy replied.

Arnie Simons got his walker and slowly made his way over to the home of Eddie Edwards, just down the block. Arnie told Eddie he'd like to have the umbrella he'd loaned Eddie just last week. Eddie said he was mighty sorry but that he had loaned it to a friend. "Do you need it?" he asked Arnie.

"Not for myself," Arnie told him, "but the guy I borrowed it from, Charlie Winkel, says that the owner wants it back."

"By the way," Arnie went on, "Did you hear about that awful explosion over at Charlie Winkel's house?"

"Nope. That's terrible. What happened?"

"Their damned gas burner exploded and blew 'em right through the front door into the street. Didn't hurt 'em but sure scared hell out of 'em."

"I'll bet it did. I guess it's the first time the two of 'em have gone out together in thirty years. But they had 'em such a nice home and all."

"Sure did. Many's the time I've seen Charlie sittin' on their porch listenin' to the summer breezes as they sighed through the mortgage. One thing sure, the house may have exploded but the damned mortgage won't."

"Yep. But it's a mighty bossy household, like the dog bosses the cat, the Mrs. bosses the dog and Charlie, he says what he damned well pleases to the geraniums."

"On top of everything else, Charles come down with the laryngitis last week. He says it's great having the old woman tell him to speak up 'stead of shut up!"

The Doc told him the best thing for laryngitis was ice cream. So he goes to Bregers, sits and whispers to the waitress, "Chocolate ice cream." She whispers back, thinkin' it's a game, "Ain't got none." Charlie says, "You got laryngitis?" And the gal whispers back, "Nope. Only vanilla, strawberry and orange."

The older a man gets, the farther he had to walk to school as a boy.

Joe and Susie Ettlebrick were celebrating their 50th wedding anniversary at a party for their family and friends. During the affair, Susie noticed that Joe wiped a tear from his eye and she remarked, "Dear Joe, I never knew you to be so sentimental as you are tonight."

"It's not that I'm sentimental, so much, Susie, as that I just recalled that day when your father caught us in the back seat of my Stutz Bearcat and told me he'd send me to jail for fifty years if I didn't marry you within the week. That tear was because I suddenly realized that today I'd have been a free man!"

Pete Edgar denies marrying old Mary Bietsch because of all the money her last husband left her. He swears up and down that he'd have married her regardless of who left her the money.

My mother-in-law always calls me son...but she never finishes the sentence.

In Springfield, Illinois, Golden Ager Cliff Hathaway confided to a friend that he was sick and tired of the younger generation, adding, "y'know" to the end of every sentence and, often to the beginning. So Cliff made up a poem he recites to every young twerp who uses that "y'know" in conversation. Here it is:

When every other word you say,
Is "y'know" you sure don't sell me;
My impulse is to say, "Y'know,
No! I don't know...Tell me!"

An old widower is tired of living alone and decides to marry again. A dating bureau fixes him up with a girl about his age and he takes her to dinner at the town's finest restaurant.

The waiter appears and haughtily requests that they place their order. Well the old girl orders on and on and when the old boy mentally totals up what her food is going to cost, he is mighty uneasy.

She continues to order! "After the lamp chops, I'd like the lobster and shrimp along with crepes suzette. And I'll finish it off with six varieties of your best cheese."

The old girl then turns to the pale-faced, shaken old guy, her date, and asks, "And what do you suggest that I order to wash it down with?"

"My dear, I can think of nothing so fitting as the Ohio River."

110

Old George was asked what he had learned from life. He replied that if he had his life to live over, he'd make some mistakes sooner.

Washington Irving: "Whenever a man's friends begin to compliment him about looking young, he may be sure that they think he's growing old."

Old Patrick O'Brien had retired and moved to a small home in upstate New York. He was delighted with the change and decided that he'd devote the balance of his years to science. So, for his first project, he worked out a program of study that would take three years to complete. He would sit in his rocking chair and face toward the prevailing wind. Then he would rock back and forth with the wind, then against the wind, then he would rock back and forth with the grain of wood in the floor...and against the grain, record all results to see which move was the easiest.

Old Man: "I'm reading a very sad book. It is so-o-o sad."
Young Lady: "Really? What's the title?"
Old Man: "Lady Chatterly's Lover."
Young Lady: "Why, Sir, that's a red hot number. For many years it was banned from bookstores and libraries. Why, that book is sexy as the devil."
Old Man: "At my age, it's sad!"

On an elevated train, a very large lady, enormously fat, seated herself next to an elderly man during the rush hour. The place was packed and she lost no time informing him, "If you were a gentleman, you'd stand and let one of these ladies sit down!"

"And if you were a lady," the old fellow replied, "You'd stand and let five or six of them sit down!"

Many years ago, an aged Senator from Vermont made an impassioned speech to his colleagues. At his most exciting moment, his upper teeth flew out and fell on the floor in front of him. He reached down, brushed his teeth off a bit, then returned them to his mouth. He waited until the laughter had subsided.

"Gentlemen of the Vermont State Legislature," he said, "You have just witnessed testimony of the most pristine and true kind. You have just seen the only false thing to come out of my mouth today."

They say that old Foster Deadbeat is the cheapest man in ten counties. Why, he was so cheap that on his honeymoon, thirty-five years ago at their first breakfast, he asked for separate checks.

Abraham Lincoln, commenting on the importance of preparation: "If I had eight hours to chop down a tree, I'd spend six sharpening my ax."

There are some gerontologists who recommend that men in their sixties make the best, most patient fathers and should just go ahead and have babies. One thing is sure, they never complain about having to get up at two o'clock to feed the baby because when a guy is over sixty, he has to get up anyway!

A career military man, who had retired as a corporal, was telling the younger men how he handled officers during his years of service. "It didn't matter a hoot if he was a Major General, an Admiral, or the Commander-in-Chief. I always told those guys exactly where to get off!"

"Wow, you musta been somethin," the admiring young soldiers remarked. "What was your job in the service?"

"Elevator boy at the Pentagon."

A veteran of World War II was running for Congress and, as could be expected, he played on his war record in all of his pre-election speeches.

"Friends," he said, "I fought and nearly died for my country. I risked all in my fight against the German menace to our freedom; and I also helped put down the savage Italian. I have slept beneath the stars and on the field of battle covered only by the heavens. And I have marched over European soil until every step was covered with blood. I have made every sacrifice for my country except life itself and I offer that at any time my country needs it."

One time, just after the veteran had finished one of his speeches, an old fellow walked his way forward to the speaker. "I heered ya say ya had fought aginst them Germans and Eyetalians," he said. "Did I hear ya right?"

"You did that, Sir! And I'm proud of it."

"And you've slept under the hevings without no kivver, right?"

"That is perfectly right, Sir. Be assured of it."

"And your feet got bloody and kivvered the ground with blood from all the hikin' ye did?"

"Again right, Sir! You described it perfectly."

"Well, then, Mister," the old fellow said, with a slight sob to his voice, "I'll jest have to vote fur that other feller 'cause you've done a heap more fur yore country than most and more than enough already!"

There was an old man of Devizes
Whose ears were of different sizes,
    The one that was small
    Was of no use at all,
But the other won several prizes.

"What kind of woman did you marry, Peter?" his friend asked, shaking his old friend's hand in congratulation.

"I married an angel"

"You're mighty lucky. Mine's still living."

On his hundredth birthday, the old man came downstairs to greet a reporter sent to interview him on this great occasion.

After the usual greetings, the reporter asked the old fellow the reason for his rare, centennial age.

"Well, young man, you can put down that I never smoked, drank alcohol, overate, and I always exercised every day and never fooled around with whores and dangerous women like that."

"But I had an uncle just like you, who did all those very things," the reporter exclaimed, "and he lived to be only sixty-five. How do you figure that?"

"Who knows? But if I had to make a guess, I'd say that he just didn't keep it up long enough."

The same reporter - because his article was so successful and remarked about across the nation - was sent to interview another hundred-year-old man. When he visited the house, the reporter was surprised at how young and vibrant the old man was. His color was ruddy and his eyes bright. "Sir, to what do you attribute reaching your advanced age in such good health?"

The old man smiled and said: "It was assured from the time Mary said she'd marry me. We made an agreement that whenever we had an argument, we'd break it off by Mary's going to the kitchen and working...and my going out the front door and walking around the block four times. All that fresh air and all that exercise is the main reason for my age and health."

George Pitts is a powerhouse of a guy. He heads up most every organization in town. And he's the Chief, Sovereign, All Powerful, Omniscient Grand Potentate of his fraternal lodge. Still and all, he's missed the last three meetings because his wife Edna wouldn't let him go.

A golfer, now seventy years old, announced to his friends on the links that he was engaged to a lovely 21-year-old.

His friends were surprised, mystified and asked, "However did you manage to get a young chick like that to take on a guy your age?"

"I didn't tell her my true age," he replied, "I told her I was 92!"

That same young bride, married to a man many years her senior, was asked by her husband if she would still love him if he lost all of his money. She replied: "You bet I would. And I'd miss you a lot."

The young man came home from church and announced to his father that the preacher had made a wonderful speech about the proper way to look at the world. "He said, "'Let a smile be your umbrella.' Wasn't that a lovely thought, Dad?"

"Mighty nice, son. But I can tell you this. You're gonna get mighty wet."

Wife: "When I was young I could have married a real caveman."

Husband: "When you were young...that's all there were."

Back in 1879, A North Carolina newspaper greeted the marriage of 87-year-old Samuel Eshon and 22-year old Sarah Miller with this poem,

"'Tis nice to see these gay old colts
frisking like they do.
You should not ask the old man's age,
She is only twenty, too."

The difference between gossip and news is whether you hear it or tell it.

George had been quite a rounder in his younger days. But once he got married, he never drank to excess. For forty years he remained an exemplary husband. Then, one day, he ran across a bunch of fellows he hadn't seen since those great high school days. Nothing would do but that he must join with them in an all-night celebration. Before he knew it, daylight had come upon them and all were too drunk to go home. So George staggered to the phone, called his wife and cautioned her, "Don't pay the ransom money, honey. I escaped!"

You've reached old age when your wife tells you to pull in your stomach and you already have.

"How do you like the new nursing home you're living in Grandpa?" his grandchild asked. "Fine, just fine. But there's something odd about the place...the floors are so dad-blamed low that a fat guy like me can't touch his toes."

Almost every night, old Jonas had been in the habit of drinking with his buddies, until they all retired and, with their wives, went south to spend the winters. Left alone, he declared a new name for the local travel agency: the Flee Market.

The old coots were in a drug store refilling their many prescriptions when a bandit rushed into the store, pistol, mask and all. "This is a stick-up," he yelled. "Everybody fork over their valuables. I'm gonna search every last one of ya, so ya might as well fork it over now!"

One old fellow turned his head and whispered in his buddy's ear: "Here's the twenty-five bucks I owe you, George."

"I ain't much on town," said Old Reuben, from the hill country of Texas. "But when my buddy asked me to join him in a dance over to San Antonio, I said, 'Sure!' And I went. At first I didn't see any ladies to dance with, so I reckoned I was in the wrong place. Then I started lookin' around and come to a door marked 'ladies.' I opened it and, sure 'nuff, there they was."

An old timer is said to be a person who can recall when unmentionables were also unseeables.

You aren't really all that old if your fling is not flung, your song is not sung, your bell ain't rung, your spring hasn't sprung. And as long as the foregoing persists, son, your fun ain't done!

Old Charlie wasn't much on dancin' but he was asked by an old friend to dance with her at the forty-fifth high school reunion. They had barely started traipsing around the dance floor when his partner's brassiere fell off, fell down through her dress and onto the floor. Old Charlie was a right gallant fellow so he picked up the brassiere and handed it to her with the words, "Here's your ear muffs, Ma'am." Now that's gallantry.

After forty years of farming, Ernie decided to go to Europe and see the sights. And that's just what he did. When he got to Italy and the guide announced that he was taking the group to the famous "Leaning Tower of Pisa."

"Pisa? Pisa?" The old farmer tried to recall where he'd heard that word before. He shook his head, and said, "That don't sound exactly like the name of the flim-flam crook who built my silo, but I'll be damned if it don't resemble his work."

An old cowboy still worked at a dude ranch in Arizona. On the table in the main ranch house, the old fellow kept a brick and a rose, under a glass, as a kind of table decoration. He was often asked why he kept these two items.

His reply: "One time I was out in New York City having a drink in a bar. The fellows standing alongside me began to kid me about my bow-legs and they got to laughin' and making all sorts of dirty remarks about me. 'Course, I told 'em it was caused by riding hosses for so many years and to stop laughin' at me. Well, one of them jaybirds hauls off and throws that brick at me."

"But why is the rose alongside the brick?"

"That's from the grave of the fool that throwed the brick."

A seventy-five year old retiree watched a pretty girl undulate her way past him. His wife noticed this and nudged the old fellow hard - in his ribs.

"My dear," the old boy explained, "I never weary of following with abject admiration the lovely works of God's creation!"

A Congressman from the deep south was interviewed on his eighty-second birthday. "You've been a Congressman for forty years, right, Sir?" asked the reporter.

"Yep!"

"I'll wager that over all those years, you've seen mighty big changes in Congress, haven't you?"

"Yep! And I've voted against every damn one of 'em!"

Joe Edgar told his friends, gathered to celebrate his seventy-ninth birthday, that the only things in life that seem certain were death, taxes and holes in your socks.

The chairman of the Community Fund Drive went to see the richest man in town, a man who rarely gave to the Fund and then, only minimally. "Sir," the chairman began his sales pitch, "We know you are the richest man in town. Our wealthiest millionaire many times over. And yet you haven't made a contribution for many years. Please, Sir, give something."

"You don't know the facts," the one man explained calmly. "I got two sisters, both paupers. I got one grandchild with six kids who lost her husband last year. And I got a brother who is deaf and blind. So tell me, Mr. Smart Leading Citizen...if I don't give to them, why should I give to you?"

Old men get queer notions of the fitness of events in their lives. Consider this one old guy who was really put out when he had to pay the preacher $150 to tie the knot. But he was delighted to pay a lawyer $1,000 to untie it.

119

Two fraternity brothers were attending their class reunion, the first time they'd seen one another for thirty years. One asked, "Is your wife still as pretty as she was when we were all in school together?"

"Yeah, she is...but it takes her an hour longer."

The old man walked into his community bank and approached the loan officer. "Sir," he said, "I want to borrow some money."

"Certainly, Sir, and what do you have to put up for security?"

"I got this here $10,000 matured U.S. Savings Bond."

"That's just fine, Sir, and how much did you want to borrow?"

"Five dollars."

"Sir, we don't lend small, trivial amounts like that."

"Well then you told a damned lie because you advertised that you'd loan any amount with proper security. And you just said this bond was OK."

The banker nodded. "Yes, Sir, you are right and I apologize. And we'll do just what we said we'd do. Sign this note for five dollars, leave the savings bond here and all is well."

A year later, the old boy came into the bank, walked up to the same loan officer, and plunked a five dollar bill on his desk. "There's the money I owe you. This pays off that note I signed. How much interest do I owe?"

"Fifty cents, Sir."

The old man paid the debt, took back the bond and started to leave.

"Sir, one moment, please. I'm curious. Could you tell me why you borrowed five dollars, only five dollars for just one year?"

"Sure. I came in here a year ago, went to that cage over there and the woman told me a safe deposit box costs fifty bucks a year. Damned if I was gonna pay that kind of money for a puny box. So I came to see you. That way, I got that bond kept safe for only fifty cents."

Bob Hope once said, "Today my heart beat 102,269 times, my blood traveled 168 million miles, I breathed 23,400 times, I inhaled 438 cubic feet of air, I ate 3 pounds of food, drank 2.9 pounds of liquid, I perspired 1.43 pints, I gave off 85.3 degrees of heat, I generated 450 tons of energy, I spoke 4,800 words, I moved 750 major muscles, my nails grew .00056 inches, my hair grew .01714 inches, and I exercised 7 million brain cells. Gee, but I'm tired."

A wise old man once remarked that by the time some of us can afford to lose a golf ball, we can no longer hit it that far.

He's so old he gets winded playing chess.

A venerable clergyman began to eat a plate of hash but he hadn't said grace!
"John," his wife exclaimed, "Aren't you forgetting something?"
"Don't think so, I blessed it once already!"

The bellhop at the small hotel in Southern Illinois mentioned that the desk clerk was ninety-eight years old. So, as we were going into supper, we stopped by the desk to chat with the old boy. "By golly, Sir, you sure do have a lot of energy for a man your age. How do you keep that way? What do you do?"
The guy grinned a little, then leaned forward and whispered, "I ain't exactly decided yet, folks. I'm bargainin' with a couple of cereal companies now tryin' to decide on which one of 'em gits my endorsement."

Additional virtue is gained when we are old, for it is then that we make a fool of ourselves in a much more dignified manner.

It was the divorce court. His wife of many years had finally asked for a divorce.

Is it true, Sir," the judge asked, "that the last three years of your long marriage, you did not speak to your wife?"

"Yes, Sir, it is true."

"And how do you explain this unusual conduct?"

"I didn't want to interrupt her, Your Honor."

George Pecan and his wife of forty years decided to take their first vacation in all that time. They stopped at a motel and prepared for bed. But George wanted one last cigarette before retiring and left the room to go downstairs to smoke.

When he returned to his room he felt quite romantic, carefully opened the door and said, "Honey? Honey?"

There was no response.

He tried again, "Honey? Hey, Honey!" A bit louder this time.

Still no reply.

Finally, a male voice from the blackness in front of him said, "This ain't no beehive, y'damn fool. This here's the bathroom."

A wealthy man and his wife were celebrating their fiftieth wedding anniversary. They had a huge party in celebration but were saddened an shocked because neither of their two sons came to the party. One was gallivanting about Europe and the other was on his yacht sailing off New York City.

A couple of weeks after the celebration, the sons returned and made all kinds of apologies. The folks weren't impressed and the father said, "Boys, this is as good a time as any to tell you that your mother and I have never been legally married."

"That's terrible!" wailed one son. "How could you," wailed the other. "Don't you realize that you've made us a couple of bastards?"

"Yep! I sure do. And damned cheap ones at that."

The aging Arthur Godfrey once remarked, "Now that I lost my glasses, I wonder who's kissing me now."

Old Joe Buck was the cheapest guy in town. One night he went to the town's restaurant and ordered the best meal in the house. It cost all of ten dollars. When he had finished, he left a tip of twenty-five cents. The waiter said, "Thank you, Sir. This is mighty nice of you."

The old man said, "I can see you know a good man, know human nature."

"Yes, I do. And I can tell a man's nature just by looking at him. For example, I can tell that you are a bachelor, right?"

"Right. That's amazing."

"And that isn't all," the waiter grinned, "I can tell your father was a bachelor, too."

The wisest of old men always approach problems with an open mind and, most likely, an open fly.

At the turn of the century, a gang worked at counterfeiting American money. Most of it was passed in smaller, less sophisticated communities in the south. One time the gang traveled to Alabama and, when they passed into Dixon Springs, it looked just like the community they needed. So they stopped, went into the town general store and asked the old gentleman keeping store if he could change a fifteen dollar bill for them.

"You bet I can, Mister," the old storekeeper said, smiling in a right friendly manner. He rang the cash register, then said, "How would you gentlemen like me to do this? Would you prefer one three and two sixes, or do you prefer to have it in five three dollar bills?"

Harry Fountain Ashurst, an early Arizona United States Senator, once gave this advice to a group of young people. "Youth should be prudent - along with its boldness - for youth has much to loose. Therefore, do not sow your wild oats in youth; you might live to reap the terrible harvest. Sow your wild oats in your old age and you will not live to harvest them."

Two young men and an elderly gentleman were discussing death. One of the young men said that he'd like to die in the service of his country, perhaps as a spy.

The second young fellow announced, "My fondest wish would be to die as an astronaut, lost while on a flight to Saturn."

The old gentleman was quiet for a time as the young men waited for his judgment as to the way he would like to die. He sighed once, cleared his throat, nodded slowly, then said, "I don't 'specially want to die, but if I got to, well, I'd like to be shot dead by a jealous husband!"

A Republican for fifty years, old Pete Brown made it his practice to go to all the Democratic affairs. At one of them, he was approached by a man who recognized him as a Republican of long-standing. "Tell me, Sir, are you thinking of changing parties and joining us?"

"Me change parties? Hell no!"

"Then why do you come to our meetings?"

"I want to keep my disgust fresh!"

An old bachelor, ever the practical joker, decided to see if anyone ever actually heard the best wishes offered to them at celebrations. He was standing in line, waiting to offer good wishes to the grandson of his best friend, the young man who was just married in the church.

Slowly the receiving line moved along as the guests offered best wishes. Eventually, the old man offered his hand to the groom and said, smiling widely, "My wife just passed away."

"How nice," responded the young groom. "It sure is kind of you to say so." And everyone within hearing distance nodded agreement.

To cap it all, a golden girl at the end of the line smirked, "Ain't it time you took the same step?"

Oliver Wendell Holmes put it most cheerfully when he said, "To be seventy years old is sometimes far more cheerful than to be forty years old!"

Old Al Myers jokes a lot. He says that over a life that spans seventy-five years, he has learned that humor is a sharp knife that cuts a hole to let the hot air out of stuffed shirts.

Bernard Baruch was a famous citizen and world-renowned financier who, on his ninety-fifth birthday, was asked, "Mr. Baruch, do you consider that there's as much love in the world today as there was when you were a young man?"

"I think there is," was Mr. Baruch's reply. "But there's another bunch doing it!"

That man has strange and paradoxical ways, is often illustrated by the saying: "A man spends about two thirds of his life saving for his old age and the last third saying that it hasn't arrived."

While on a cruise, a cyclonic wind blew up and a young lady, leaning against the railing, was blown overboard. At once, a man jumped over the rails and swam to the girl to hold her up in that raging sea until the rescue boat could arrive. Everyone was amazed to see that the rescuer was an old man, in his eighties, and they were thrilled that someone so old could still have the bravery, the get-up-and-go to do such a brave rescue. So they gave him a banquet, a party honoring him at which he was asked to make a speech. "Speech!" the assembled diners, hero-worshippers all, cried to him. "Speech! Speech!"

The old boy rose slowly to his feet and looked over the smiling, adoring faces of the passengers assembled to honor him. "There's just one thing I'd like you good people to do for me," he said. "Find the sonovabitch that pushed me."

Next to the police, the greatest reformer is *Father Time.*

The traveling salesmen were driving through the mountainous Ozark country. They stopped before a run-down shack to ask directions, got out of the car and approached a native in faded overalls. "How do you do?" the visitors greeted him.

"Tolerable," the mountaineer replied.

"Beautiful country you have here."

"For them as likes it."

"Does it rain much up here?"

"Smidgin."

"Lived here all your life?"

"Not yit."

George Levy wanted to make some money for his senior citizens center. Since he'd been a manufacturer of ladies clothing all of his life, he decided to turn his skills to a source of income for the center. And so he invented a new birth control mechanism....a pair of ladies slacks with the legs permanently crossed.

The old boy had reached the wonderful age of eighty years but he was uncomfortable because a younger woman, a widow, was going after him tooth and nail, and with lots more, too! He simply couldn't get rid of her. Finally he told her, "Mother and Father are both against it. It won't work."

"You aren't telling me that your mother and father are alive, are you?" she scoffed.

"I am referring to Mother Nature and Father Time," he said.

D.O. Flynn: "There's no fool like an old fool...you can't beat experience."

Oscar Wilde: "The old believe everything, the middle-aged suspect everything, the young know everything."

Also: "Young men want to be faithful and are not; old men want to be faithless and cannot."

126

Old George Myers went to the theatre where the usher found him occupying three seats, simply lying across them. "Sir, you can't have all those seats," the usher said. "We have a full house tonight and we'll need them."

George didn't budge or say anything, so the usher called the manager, who also appealed to George. But George just lay there. Then the manager sent for a cop who said: "Get up, Sir. You simply can't occupy all those seats." No reply. The policeman took out his note pad and began to query the old man..."Where did you come from?"

And old George finally answered in a weak, quavering voice, "from...the...balcony."

The truck driver had miscalculated a bit and his truck was jammed under the overpass and stuck tight. So he got out of his truck, called a welder and, together they commenced to cut the bent girders and other wreckage away to free the truck. An old man from a nearby rest home was being wheeled down the road by an attendant. As they passed the truck, he called out, "Why don't you guys let air out of your tires, just enough to lower the truck so you can drive on through under it?"

The truck driver looked at the welder, scratched his head and said, "Let's try it." He did and the truck rolled through in good shape. He stopped the truck, got out and thanked the old man, saying, "What's a bright, thoughtful guy like you doing in an old folks home like that?"

The old man responded, "I may be old, crazy, senile and more. But I ain't stupid!"

An old beggar always positioned himself outside the town's drugstore across from the county seat where he offered a tray of shoelaces for sale. The town's banker always made it a practice to drop a quarter in the old man's hat and never take a pair of shoelaces. One day the beggar, on receiving the banker's quarter, tapped his benefactor on the back, saying, "I don't like to complain, Sir, but shoelaces are now 50 cents."

There was an old man in Macoupin County, Illinois, who was a jack-of-all-trades. He farmed a bit, did odd jobs and generally made do as best he could. One day, a townsman drove out to the old man's place and asked him if he would do some painting for him. The old fellow said he'd ride in with the townsman and take a look at the job and give him an estimate of cost.

As they moved toward the visitor's car, and the old man's wife called to him: "George, here you are taking off for town and there ain't a stick of wood for the kitchen stove."

"Well," the old boy said quietly. "I ain't taking the ax along with me, am I?"

On their fortieth wedding anniversary and during the banquet celebrating it, Joe Meek was asked to give his friends a brief account of the benefits of a marriage of such long duration. "Tell us, Joe," the Master of Ceremonies requested, "just what is it you have learned from all those wonderful years with Maybelle?"

"Well, I've learned that marriage is the best teacher of all," Joe responded. "It teaches you loyalty, forbearance, meekness, self-restraint, forgiveness - and a great many other qualities you wouldn't have needed if you'd stayed single."

A fat gentleman lumbered down the aisle of the train and sat down next to a little, wizened old man. There was a NO SMOKING sign in plain view above the head of the fat fellow, yet he dragged out a large cigar and match, hesitating to light it to ask the old man, "It's okay to smoke, isn't it? My smoking won't bother you, will it?"

"No," the old guy replied, "Not if my vomiting won't bother you."

An old man gives good advice in order to console himself for no longer being in condition to set a bad example.

La Rochefoucauld

Edward Montague had spent his life in the manufacture of men's suspenders. Upon his retirement, the corporation wished to place, in the boardroom, a suitable object in tribute to his stellar service. So they had a life-size painting made of a contemporary pair of suspenders and gave it the title: "To Edward Montague and the Law of Gravity."

Bob Hope once remarked that you know you are getting old when the candles cost more than the cake.

Two old fellows, one sixty and the other sixty-five, were discussing the forthcoming marriage of the latter to a young woman in her thirties. "You sure are making a mistake," said the younger man. "I can see what December will find in the liveliness of May - freshness and beauty and youth. But tell me...just what can May find in the gloom and cold of December?"
"Christmas," the older man replied.

"He's the talk of St. Petersburg."

ONE MOMENT, SIR by Marione R. Nickles

Reprinted with permission of **Penguin Books USA, Inc.**

One day an elderly couple astounded the small town populace by walking down Main Street dressed in shoes only. The old man also wore a hat and necktie.

"Holy smokes!" a friend confronted them, "Are you two streaking?"

"You could call it that, but <u>snailing</u> would be more exact!" the old man replied.

An Indiana State University graduate returned to his alma mater for his fortieth class reunion. He had not enjoyed it. "Why all my classmates were so fat and bald and near-sighted that they failed to recognize me."

Old Ebenezer had never worked a day in his life. Be assured that his wife had - almost every day of her life!

Well, one day, old Eben came rushing in the house, yelling, "Have I found a great job, honey. Four-day week, double overtime, two months holiday every year...and the use of a company car. Isn't that great?"

"So what's the catch?" asked his skeptical wife.

"There ain't no catch," Ebenezer assured her. "You start on Monday!"

There are a couple of ways to measure how old a man is. One is to observe whether he is inspecting the food more than the waitress, and the other is to ask him if he feels his corns more than his wild oats.

While jawboning with his World War II buddies at the American Legion clubhouse, Eddie Boron said that women drivers were often skilled, but that sometimes they forget, when they back out of the garage, that they backed into the night before. One of the guys remarked that his wife always slows down when going through a red light. And a third fellow remarked that if they didn't like the way women drove, they should all just get off the sidewalk.

Here are two charming stories told from
<u>Stories Told in the Kitchen</u> by Kendall Morse
by Thorndike Press in Thorndike, ME.

Old John and a few others are gone, now, but
same old stories are still being told by old timers who
were teenagers in those days. While I was buying my
tobacco, and wondering if anything new ever happened
around there, poor old Lizzie Gardner came in all
haired up, and said to Ira, "I want to buy a mouse trap.
Last night a mouse got into my drawers and chewed all
the fringe off my center piece."

The reaction over by the stove started as a snicker,
but soon they were all roaring and slapping their knees
while Lizzie stood there working her jaws in silence
wondering what they were drinking. Rufe Collins
laughed so hard he fell off the chair and bumped his
head on the leg of the stove, which only added to the
hilarity. Poor old Lizzie left not even suspecting that she
had made their day.

The store was full of idlers, as usual, all sitting in a
circle around the big Station Agent stove, and the odor
of neatsfoot oil and over-heated wool clothes reminded
me that some things never change. It was almost the
same as when I first went there with my father many
years ago. The minute we entered the store that day,
old John Prince said to my father, "I'll give you two
cents and a rusty fish hook for that boy." It nearly
scared me to death. He was so strange-looking with his
long white beard streaked with tobacco juice, and only
one tooth in his head. I didn't know what to think when
Father answered, "Daow, I wouldn't want to cheat you.
Why, he ain't worth half that price!"

If you get tired of replying to the question, "To what
do you attribute your old age?" you might answer just
as this old man did, "The fact that I was born a very
long time ago."

"Yes," said the old man to his visitor, "I am proud of my girls and I would like to see them comfortably married. As I have made a little money they will not go penniless to their husbands. There is Mary, twenty-five years old, and a good-looking girl. I'll give her $1,000 when she marries. Then comes Elizabeth, who won't see thirty-five again. I shall give her $3,000, and the man who takes Eliza, who is forty, will have $5,000 with her."

The visitor, a young Yankee, reflected a moment and asked: "You haven't one about fifty, have you?"

Elder Jones and Thomas Falcon were golf addicts. One day, on the hole near the highway, a funeral procession passed by and Elder dropped his club, clasped his hands and bowed his head. After the procession had passed, Thomas remarked how courteous it was for Elder to show such reverence before a death.

"It was the least I could do! After all, we were married forty-five years."

In Springfield, Illinois, there is a special club to which only men of over eighty years are admitted. The President was queried about admitting two men who were only seventy-five. "Well, gentlemen," he addressed the club. "Look around you. Evaluate! Then you'll see that we need some young-blood."

A wise and clever young girl married a 75-year old man, a business tycoon who was "on his last legs." This old geezer owned six palatial homes in several different countries and as might be expected, his new wife referred to them when she was asked why she married such an old and out-of-it man. "I love him!" she exclaimed. "I love him for his elegant old world manors."

Everybody knows about those pre-sale stickers that adorn the window of all unsold cars in dealer's showrooms and sales lots. They start with the basic price, then follow with line after line of built-in items such as power steering, undercoating, bumper guards, automatic shift and many more. Thus, the total price is altered beyond its original condition!

Well, one day a car dealer, who had been a farmer and wanted his own home-raised milk, appeared at the farm of an elderly dairy farmer near town. Pooter Johnson, the diary farmer, showed him several of his cows that were for sale and suggested that he select one. The dealer made his choice known and asked the price.

"Three hundred dollars," the old farmer replied.

"Fair enough. I'll take her."

"Wait! That's the basic price," Pooter replied. "There are some extras, you know." He took out a pencil, figured a bit on a piece of paper, then handed it to the auto dealer. These were the add-ons:

Basic cow	$300.00
Black and white exterior	80.00
Three extra stomachs	90.00
Storage closet and dispensing receptacle	65.00
Four faucets	60.00
Built-in-fly-swatter	40.00
TOTAL	$635.00

An old timer, out west in early days, was known among cattlemen as a "starve out." He never did any work but was always around the mess hall at feeding time. Never a worker himself, he was forever getting in the way of the men who did the work. Soon the cowboys said of him, "Here comes old Jim! When he rides in here, it's just like two good men walking out."

Birthdays tell how long you've been on the road, not how far you've traveled.

The small Iowa town's oldest resident was a notorious drunk. Everyone knew him and his habit. One night, the county sheriff got a phone call and it was from the old man, drunk, as usual. "Shay, officer," the old man said, "I been robbed. They shtole my shteering wheel, and my-my b-b-brake pedal and clutch and the whole d-d-damned d-dashboard!"

The sheriff took down all the information, got the directions and said he'd be right over.

Not more than a minute lapsed when the phone rang again and it was the old man. "Sherif-f-f, don't bother. I dishcovrered that I was s-setting in the back sheat."

The wealthy old man had reached his eightieth birthday and was in the garden planting flowers with his gardner-helper. "Man, oh man!" the gardner said, when told it was his boss' birthday, "I never would have believed that I'd be working alongside an octogeranium."

Jed Simpkins never saved a cent in all his life. When asked why he was such a spendthrift, he said, "What the heck, you can't take it with you. Furthermore, with the present value of the dollar it would seem to be hardly worth the trouble to lug it there."

And old man sat down on a park bench next to a young fellow, sighed and said, "Gosh, this mornin' I feel like I was seventy-five years old!"

"Oh dear," responded the young man, sympathetically. "That IS too bad."

"No, it ain't," the old guy replied. "Because I'm eighty-five."

It's been said that you are approaching the "senior condition" when your knees buckle out but your belt doesn't.

Old Joe refused to follow doctor's orders and take regular exercise. He explained his position as follows: "I jump the gun, fight temptation, bend the trouble, twist the facts, hunt for girls, polish the apple, sling mud, run from facts, pass the buck and lots more. I don't need no more exercise than that!"

Birthdays are like jogging shorts...they creep up on you.

Back in 1942, Dr. Edwin F. Bowers advised every man and woman over fifty to read "Alice in Wonderland" - especially these delightful verses in which Father William explains to his son just how he "gets away" with things, quite as foolish as those by which nine out of ten aging people shorten their lives.

"You are old, Father William," the young man said,
    "And your hair has become very white;
And yet you incessantly stand on your head -
    Do you think, at your age, it is right?"

"In my youth," Father William replied to his son,
    "I feared it might injure the brain,
But now that I'm perfectly sure I have none,
    Why, I do it again and again."

"You are old," said the youth, "and your jaws are too weak
    For anything tougher than suet;
Yet you finished the goose, with the bones and the beak -
    Pray, how do you manage to do it?"

"In my youth," said his father, "I took to the law,
    And argued each case with my wife,
And the muscular strength, which it gave to my jaw
    Has lasted the rest of my life."
                The Playboy Handbook-Wm. Allan Brooks, Ed.
                Knickerbocker Publishers 1942. NY

"You sure are lucky, Fred," his friend told him, "to have been married for fifty years to Susie. My wife tells me she's the best cook in town."

"Well, everybody is entitled to their opinion. I call her a biblical cook. Her recipes follow the scriptures. Everything is either a burnt offering or a bloody sacrifice."

WIM, WIGOR AND WICTORY WERSE

"You cannot keep a good man down,"
    Remarked some noble mutt,
Malicious dornicks tossed at him
    May crenualte his nut,
Outrageous slings and arrows trun
    By fortune ill may pot 'em,
But you cannot keep the good men down,
    You can't keep cream on the bottom.

The deftly wielded double-cross
    May catch you on the hip
And toss you on your vertebrae,
    But don't desert the ship;
The anvil crew may lay for you
    But never mind, dod rot' em!
The big league man can't lose his nan,
    Cream won't stay on the bottom.

"You cannot keep a good man down,"
    As Jonah told the Whale,
Within his Webster's unabridged
    There's no such thing as fail;
Such men come smiling from the floor
    Where uppercuts have sot 'em,
As I, perhaps, remarked before
    You can't keep cream on the bottom.

Damon Runyon

6

HERE
(and HEREAFTER)

On the subject (Reversed) of Evolution:

A Golden Oldie

Three monkeys sat in a coconut tree
Discussing things as they're said to be,
Said one to the others, "Now listen, you two,
There's a certain rumor that can't be true.
That man descended from our great race;
The very idea is a blatant disgrace,
No monkey ever deserted his wife,
Starved her children and ruined her life.
And you've never known a mother monk
To leave her babies with others to bunk,
Or to pass them on from one to another,
Till they scarcely know which one is their mother.
And another thing you'll never see:
A monk build a fence 'round a coconut tree
And let the coconuts go to waste,
Forbidding all other monkeys a taste.
And here's a thing a monkey won't do,
Go out at night and get on a stew,
Or use a gun or a club or a knife,
To take another monkey's life.
Yes, man descended - the ornery cuss;
But brother, he didn't descend from us!"

Anon.

Epitaphs are a classic case of split personality...both
funny and sad. Here are a few that illustrate the funny
side that turns up (or is it down?) at the end.

Finis...Maginnis. (Irish epitaph)

I laid my wife beneath this stone
For her repose and for my own.

See how God works His wonders now and then -
Here lies a lawyer and an honest man.

Here lies the body of W.W.
Who never more will trouble you, trouble you.

My time has come! My days are spent!
I was called away - and away I went!

The Baptist minister of a church far out in the Ozark hills was discouraged at how small the contributions were from his members compared to the Methodist preacher down the road. So he asked this other preacher what he did to successfully get contributions.

"During services, I hypnotize the congregation by dangling my watch before the people and say, 'I need $10 from each of you good people.'"

It seemed such a good idea that the Baptist preacher decided to try it at Sunday morning services. He dangled his watch and said, "Watch this watch, watch this watch. I want one dollar, one dollar from each person here." By golly, it worked. The collection was full of $1 bills.

A bit later he tried it again. Out came the watch and he again said the fetching words, only this time he asked for $5. Sure enough, the box came to him filled with five dollar bills.

Just before concluding the service, he dangled the watch and asked for $10 from each person. "Watch the watch, I want from each...," but the watch slipped from his fingers and smashed on the pulpit. "Oh sh-t," the preacher shouted in exasperation and it took a week to clean up the church.

There's a story floating around Lake Nebagamon, Wisconsin, that one of their citizens, a very old man, was confronted by a traveling evangelist. "Excuse me, my good friend - have you found Jesus?" the preacher asked.

"Good God, I didn't know he was lost," the old man replied.

Poor Lot's wife turned to salt, alas!
Her fate was most unkind.
No doubt she only wished to see,
How hung her skirt behind.

No use burying your charm with your hubby. Witness this obituary!
SACRED TO THE MEMORY OF JARED BATES
His widow lives at 7 Elm Street, has every qualification of a good wife, and YEARNS to be comforted.

Lincoln, Maine

To illustrate the complicated state of the legal profession, retired attorney, Bob Myers, stated that we now have 35,000,000 laws to enforce the Ten Commandments.

If all the people who go to sleep in church were laid end to end, they would be a lot more comfortable.

Emory Elwood had spent many years working in a distillery. Just a few weeks before retirement, he fell into a vat of whiskey and drowned. The undertaker reported that it took him three days to wipe the smile off Emory's face.

The old man lay dying on his bed. His sons had gathered around him for these last moments. The old man lay as if asleep.

"We better begin to think about funeral arrangements, fellows. Y'know that if we use twenty cars, it'll cost about a thousand bucks."

"What the hell do we need so many cars for! Most people will come in their own cars. Fifteen will be enough and that'll cost a lot less."

The youngest son remarked, "Hell, guys, all we need is four or five cars...just enough for the family."

Suddenly the old man opened his eyes. "Listen boys, if one of you will just hand me my pants and shoes, I'll get right up and _walk_ to the cemetery!"

A government social worker accompanied by a new young minister, were traveling in the Ozarks, trying to be of service to the mountain folks. They pulled up before a ramshackle cabin and walked to the porch where sat an old lady, smoking a pipe and chewing tobacco. They completed their social welfare business and were about to leave when the new preacher asked the old lady, "Madam, you are up in years now, and I must ask you if you've ever thought about St. Peter's reaction when you approach him at the Pearly Gates with that rank smell of tobacco on your breath?"

"Ain't nothing to worry about, Parson. When that time comes, I aims to leave my breath here in the Ozarks."

A fellow worker at the office called on Mrs. White to express his sympathy at the loss of her husband. "I'm so sorry to hear that you've lost John, Mrs. White. And I do hope that he left you well-provided for."

Mrs. White dabbed her eyes and sniffled a bit, then said, "Oh, he did! Quite well, thank you. But nothing can replace him. He left me $100,000. And I tell you this...for sure...I'd give $50,000 just to get him here again."

An old man saw his name in the obituary columns and he was furious. "How dare they," he thought, and called his lawyer to sue the newspaper. The lawyer picked up the phone and the old man told him the story.

"Where are you calling from?" the lawyer asked cautiously.

And sometimes the sorrow is stated in such a way as to indicate just the reverse. Consider these two tombstones whose words don't exactly indicate the intended meaning.

Maria Brown, Wife of Timothy Brown
She lived with her husband 50 years, and died in the confident hope of a better life.

Source Unknown

Here lies my husband, Augustus Brauder, who
was accidentally killed in his 58th year.
This monument is erected by his grateful wife.

An eighty-year-old gentleman had come to the church with his young girl of twenty or so, and walked up to the altar with her to be married. "But, sir, the font is at the other end of the church," said the clergyman.

"What the heck do I need a font for?" asked the old man.

"Oh my goodness, Sir," responded the preacher with a grin, "I thought you brought this child to be christened."

George Peterson says that he has discovered a new fact of life after visiting the cemetery where most of his friends now rest. "It's a strange thing," said George, "that as I was going from stone to stone, I realized that every dadburned one of those guys thought the world couldn't get along without him."

Riley and Casey had lost their life long friend, O'Brien. They were so down about losing him that they felt they needed a few drinks before they went to the funeral home to pay their respects. They had a few and a few more! Then they wandered their way unsteadily to the house of burial, walked inside, saw the casket and walked over to kneel beside it. The only trouble was that, in their drunken state, they mistook the piano, with cover up and keyboard exposed, for the casket. After a prayer, they got to their feet and walked out. "Riley," said Casey, "I've known O'Brien for twenty years, but I nivir knew he had sech a foine set o' teeth."

Most older Americans remember when the corner grocery store, home-owned and where you called the boss by his first name, had its own butcher shop. You gave your order and waited while the meat was cut-to-order from the carcass, then weighed on the scale. AND, with some grocers, you had to make sure the butcher's thumb on the scale did not add weight to the meat! Here's a poem to commemorate those heavy-thumbed butchers.

Here lies the body of Hays McVale,
A butcher who died with his thumb on the scale;
A customer shot him, thus causing Hays
To regret the errors of his weighs.

Some say that _death_ is no joke. But some folks grin in spite of _it._

Senator Sam Ervin, North Carolina, told about the old preacher who preached quite acceptably but often used words the meaning of which he wasn't so sure of. For example, one time he brought to his congregation a visiting preacher and, after introducing him, warned him to speak loudly, "on account of the agnostics in this heah church ain't so good."

"The tombstone is about the only thing that can stand upright and lie on its face at the same time."

Here lies my husbands, One, Two, Three -
Dumb as men could ever be.
As for my Fourth, well praise be God,
He bides for a little above the sod.
Alex, Ben, Sandy were the first three's names,
And to make things tidy, I'll add his - James.
                    Shutesbury, Massachusetts

After much arguing, Solomon Epstein went to his lawyer and had his will made. He took it home to his wife and had her read it for corrections or suggestions. And she did have a suggestion to make: "Are you real sure, Sol, that you want to have your funeral at 3 A.M.? Think, now. Three! In the morning?"

"You bet I do. I'd like, once and for all, to find how many friends we have."

There was an old coot in the choir,
Whose voice it rose hoir and hoir;
        At last one fine noight,
        It rose out of soight,
And was found next day on the spoire.

A couple of epitaphs that bear repeating:

        Here I lie between two wives.
        But I have requested my relatives to tip me a
            little toward Tillie.

Here lies Jean Kitchin, when her life was spent,
She kicked up her heels and away she went.

Paul Barker met an old friend and they started reminiscing. "I'm 80 years old," Paul said, "and the good Lord has sure looked after me. Why, every night when I get up to go to the toilet, God turns on the light for me."

"Really?" his friend remarked, astonished. "Why that's a miracle."

"It sure is," Paul agreed.

That evening the friend called Paul's daughter. He was overcome with the wonder of Paul's revelation and needed to talk to her about it. "He looks so hearty, vigorous and all," the friend told her. "And his frame of mind is superb. He told me that God talks to him at night when he gets up to go to the bathroom. God even turns on the bathroom light for him. Imagine! God made manifest."

"He is a remarkable man. That's for sure," Paul's daughter replied. "But that bathroom episode...let me tell you...he goes to the kitchen and opens the door to the _refrigerator_, not to the bathroom!"

"Operator, give me Saint Paul — er, Minnesota, that is!"

ONE MOMENT, SIR by Marione R. Nickles

Reprinted with permission of **Penguin Books USA, Inc.**

Every Sunday the pastor would observe Sam Capbell and his wife Sara, holding hands. And they held hands all through the service. It made him happy to see two such loving old folks.

One Sunday, greeting the congregation as they filed out the door, the pastor said to Sam and Sara: "It sure does my heart good to see two such loving people as you, Mr. and Mrs. Capbell. It's quite inspiration."

Sara looked up at him and grinned, saying, "That ain't love, Pastor. It's the only way I can keep him from cracking his knuckles during the service."

The average man's life consists of twenty years of having his mother ask him where he is going; forty years of having his wife ask the same question; and at the end, the mourners wondering, too.

The preacher was talking about perfection. "There are no perfect men or women in this sad world," the preacher sermonized, "And I want to know if there's anyone in the congregation who has known a perfect man or a perfect woman. If so, would you please stand?"

Old lady Robbins stood. The preacher said, "Please, Mrs. Robbins, would you tell us about your rare experience?"

"You probably want to know who it was. Actually, I did not know her. She was my husband's first wife!"

The minister had advised Eliezer to give some thought about the "hereafter." And Eliezer told him that the hereafter was hardly ever out of his mind. At least a dozen times a day he would go to do something, like going to the bathroom cabinet for his medicine, then ask, "What the heck am I *hereafter?*"

Old Tom Robinson was in church, enjoying the service. The minister was talking about love. "Is there anyone in the congregation who has not a single enemy? If there is, I'd like to have you stand up for us all to admire."

At first, nobody stood. Then one old fellow slowly raised himself out of his seat and stood to the quiet exclamations of admiration from those around him.

The preacher congratulated the old fellow on his forgiving spirit, then asked, "How do you account for this blessing, Sir? What is your secret?"

The old man thought a moment, then said, "Well, to tell you the truth, Pastor, it's just that I outlived the SOBs."

A girl, a quarrel, a room, some gas;
A hearse, a funeral, a hole, some grass.

They had just buried the town's skinflint, a man who still had the first penny he ever earned! Of course, everyone was surprised when they learned that the old tightwad had left the town's United Fund $100,000.

"Wow! Isn't that wonderful that he left all that money to charity?" someone remarked.

"He didn't leave it," was the reply of a man who had known him all his life. "They took him from it!"

Old Jerry Hickey had just lost his wife of fifty years, when he received a telegram from an old girlfriend who for years had been trying to seduce him. "I would like to take the place of your deceased wife," she wired.

Mr. Hickey wired back: "It's OK with me if you can arrange things with the undertaker."

Reported around 1880 as having stood in a Nantucket, Massachusetts graveyard:

Under the sod and under the trees
Lies the body of Jonathan Pease.
He is not here, there's only the pod:
Pease shelled out and went to God.

———————

When old Norman Jones' lawyer learned that his client had inherited three million dollars, he went to his law partner and told him that he must break the news gently to the old man for fear that he would suffer a heart attack. They discussed the problem, but before they were finished, in came the old man. "Mr. Jones, I'm glad you are here. What would you say if I told you...and this is merely hypothetical, y'know, what would you say if I said you'd just inherited three million dollars?"

The old man thought for a bit, then said, "I'd give half of it to you."

And the lawyer dropped dead.

———————

Said an ardent bridegroom, a Basque
    I'll grant any boon that you ask,
        Said the bride, "Kiss me, Dearie
        Until I grow weary,"
That Basque died of old age at the task.

———————

There was an old fellow named Ted,
Who dined before going to bed,
        On lobster and ham
        And pickles and jam,
And when he awoke he was dead.

———————

A golfing parson, badly beaten by an elderly parishioner, returned to the clubhouse depressed.

"Cheer up," said his opponent. "Remember, you win eventually. You'll be burying me someday."

"Yes," said the parson. "But even then, it'll be your hole."

At the age of ninety, Rebecca North appeared at the University and asked to be enrolled in a Hebrew class. "I've always wanted to learn the language," she told the registrar, "but I've just now got around to it."

"And how old are you, Ma'am?" she was asked.

After she told him her age, the registrar asked her to have a seat next to him. He turned to her and said, "Mrs. North, it takes years to learn a language, and Hebrew is not an easy language to learn. Do you really think you ought to begin at your age?"

"Mister," Rebecca replied, "all my life I've wanted to learn that language. But I kept putting it off. Now, at my age, I want to learn it so as to be able to greet my Creator, my Lord and Master in His native tongue."

A MORALITY TALE

Men are born, die, are interred and become fertilizer that makes the grass grow. A horse comes along and eats the grass, then converts it into a well-known by-product.

Now, the moral of this story is...Be careful where you kick. It may be your aunt or uncle.

Many is the wife who has spent a lifetime keeping house for a husband and several kids. Such will sympathize with this tombstone poem.

Here lies a woman who was always tired;
She lived in a house where help was not hired;
Her last words were, "Dear friends, I am going
Where washing ain't done, nor sweeping nor sewing;
Don't mourn for me now, don't mourn for me never,
I'm going to do nothing, forever and ever."

Source Unknown

The town's oldest and most illustrious family had only one remaining member who was old and terribly proud of her ancestry. She gave a tea party at which she asked all the guests to relate their ancestry. And they all did, except for Mary Cohen who said, "I'm sure sorry I can't give you my genealogy. Y'see, we lost all our records in The Flood."

Some folks go to church only thrice in a lifetime. Once when they're hatched; once when they're matched; and once when they're dispatched.

There was an old gal from Guam
Who noticed the ocean was calm,
   Said, "I'll swim for a lark"
   She encountered a shark,
Oh dear! Sing the 90th Psalm.

Back in the thirties, there was an old farmer who hated Roosevelt, the New Deal and everything the Democrats tried to do to put the country on its feet. He hated change. He took a trip to visit his son in a New England town, near his home, a town that was known to be 100% New Deal. They went to church. The old man used an ear trumpet to correct his hearing deficiency and he listened to the sermon with great interest, obviously disapproving of the preacher's words. When the sermon was over, he asked his son, "Who's that new preacher ya got up there?" The son replied with the name of the man, then added, "He's the son of the bishop." And the old man shouted back, "Son, ain't they all."

Here lies a woman, no man can deny it,
Who now is at peace, though she lived most unquiet.
Her husband beseeches, if near here you're walking,
Speak soft, or she'll wake, and then she'll start talking.

Two old guys, retired and living in Florida, spent all of their time at baseball games or reading about baseball or talking about the game. "Man, I sure hope there's baseball in heaven," one guy said.

"So do I...I sure hope so."

"Let's make a deal," one old geezer said, "whichever one of us gets to heaven, let's promise to let the other know about baseball up there."

"Good idea. Let's do it."

One of the men died a few weeks thereafter. The other, while watching a baseball game in Miami, thought he heard his buddy whispering in his ear. He listened very carefully. It was he, all right. "I've got news for you," the heavenly voice said, "good news and bad. The good news is...there really, truly, honest to gawd is baseball up here."

"Great. Oh, boy, I'm sure glad to know that. But the bad news?"

"You're playing shortstop on Thursday."

Epitaph: *A monumental* lie (in some cases).

King David and King Solomon,
　　Lived many, many lives
With many, many lady friends,
　　And many, many wives;
But when old age crept onward,
　　And brought its numerous qualms,
　　King Solomon wrote the Proverbs
　　And King David wrote the Psalms.

On His Wife
Here lies my wife; here let her lie.
Now she's at rest. And so am I.
　　　　　　　　　　John Dryden

One reason you can't take it with you is that it goes before you do.

Old Abe Levy had never been to Florida. Now, on his sixty-fifth birthday, his kids gave him a trip to Miami Beach. And he had a perfectly wonderful time spending day after day on the beach in the marvelous sunlight. Well, as you might suspect, he got a splendiferous tan. Unfortunately, the day before departure for home, Abe suffered a colossal heart attack and the doctors were unable to save him.

Back home, in the funeral parlor, laid back in his lovely coffin, two old biddies, lifelong friends came up to the coffin, looked at Abe, sniffled, wiped their eyes and, finally, one of them summoned up the strength to say, "Don't Abe look just wonderful...so nice and peaceful?" And her friend, standing beside her sniffled and said, "Really peaceful. And look at that tan. It looks like the trip did him a lot of good."

An optimist is a senior citizen who can say to the salesman in a tombstone sales room: "If I wait till Monday, can I get that double senior citizen discount?"

Pooter Jones was eighty years old and in bad shape, not only physically but financially. He'd lost his teeth, his hair, his hearing, eyesight and lots more. And his illnesses had about ruined him financially when, wonder of wonders, he won the state lottery and got two million bucks.

Well, old Pooter did what we'd all have done; he got a face lift, a hair transplant, new teeth, new clothes and, let me tell you, he looked wonderful, almost like a rich, handsome young man. Then it happened.

Pooter walked out of his new mansion toward his Mercedes, stumbled and fell and broke his neck. He was dead when they found him.

Not to worry. When he got to the Pearly Gates, he knocked but was denied admission. He demanded to see St. Peter and when the old boy appeared, Pooter said, "Sir, all my life I've lived a righteous life. Never smoked, drank, carried on with women, I went to church every Sunday, gave to the poor. I lived a righteous life. Why do you refuse me entry?"

St. Peter looked at him. "What did you say your name was?"

"Pooter Jones."

"Oh, for gosh sakes. Pooter Jones. Sure you can come in. You belong here."

"But why did you refuse me before?"

"Pooter, I just didn't recognize you."

When the will was opened at the attorney's office, and old Mrs. Fisher learned that her husband of forty years had left all his money to his old college sweetheart, she rushed out of the office and drove to the cemetery. She stormed into the cemetery office and demanded that the wording on her husband's tombstone be changed at once. The manager told her that such a demand was against all rules and that the present inscription, "REST IN PEACE," would have to remain.

"All right. So be it. But underneath those words, I want you to have inscribed, 'UNTIL WE MEET AGAIN.'"

A boyhood friend of Elmer Richter's came to the cemetery where rested his remains. He noticed that Elmer's tombstone was leaning badly toward the foot of the grave. "That's not right," he said to himself. "I must fix that."

So the friend got some wire out of his car, tied it around the stone, pulled the stone upright, then unrolled the wire out to a nearby telephone pole where he tied it fast, certain, now, that the stone would remain upright.

A few days later, a member of the family came to Elmer's grave to leave some flowers. When he saw the line leading to the telephone pole, he grinned and said, "If it ain't just like Elmer. He's only been here a couple of weeks and already he's got his own phone."

Suddenly a widow, old Martha Jenkins instructed the undertaker to select for her old man, the very best casket and accoutrements. Cost was no concern. But when she got the bill for $25,000, she was furious.

"But, dear lady," the undertaker exclaimed, you asked us to give your husband the very best of burials and that is what we did.

"Look," she fumed, "for $5,000 more I could have had him buried in a Cadillac!"

Veronica had been a constant sinner all of her life. Now that she was growing old, she was penitent and thought it would do her soul good to be baptized. So they took her to the creek that ran just below the church and there, the pastor asked her to get ready, to pray to have all her sins washed away.

"Holy smokes," Veronica declaimed, "You gonna try to do that in that itty bitty 'ol trickle!"

This gravestone was raised by Sarah's lord,
Not Sarah's virtues to record,
For they're well-known to the town,
But it was raised to keep her down.

The Lord, sometimes, strikes a good bargain. Just hear this interchange between a new arrival in heaven and the Almighty.

"Dear Lord, what do ten thousand years mean to YOU?"

"Two minutes."

"And may I ask, Lord, what do ten million dollars mean to You?"

"Two pennies."

"Lord, please give me two pennies."

"In just two minutes."

A bus overturned and two people were killed. One, a preacher and the other, the aged driver. When they got to heaven, the old driver was allowed in at once but the preacher was told to remain outside for a time.

Losing patience, after a long wait, the preacher demanded to know why he was kept outside.

"Well, you see," said St. Peter, "They're looking up the records. It seems that whenever you conducted services on earth, everybody fell asleep, but when this old bus driver climbed into his bus, all the passengers started praying."

Fenster Jones was known as the biggest blowhard in all of Texas. But nobody made an issue of it because old Fenster was seven feet tall, weighed 350 pounds and was a fightin' son of a so-and-so (to hear him tell it!). Well, after a long life, Fenster passed on but they could not find a casket big enough to bury this big, tough braggart from Texas. Finally, an experienced oil extractor gave the huge man an enema, after which they buried Fenster in a shoe box!

Small Boy: "Grandpa, were you on the ark?"
Grandpa: "Of course not!"
Small Boy: "Then how come you weren't drowned?"

Last spring - May 5 was the exact date, I believe - I happened to run into old Cousin Willie at The Sir Walter Hotel.

"How are you feeling?" I inquired.

"Pretty good," he replied. "As a matter of fact, I feel especially good, now that we've left April behind us."

"What does April have to do with the way you feel?"

"Well, I'll tell you. My father was born in June. He got married in June, and he died in June. I was born in April. I got married in April, and I tell you right now, I always feel a whole lot better when the first day of May arrives."

Carl Goerch

Excerpts from "Carolina Chats. 1944", "Down Home. 1943", and "Just For The Fun Of It. 1954.", written by Carl Goerch, used with the permission of the Estate of Carl Goerch.

It was the duty of every member of the Rotary Club to make a speech once a year. And this particular night was the time Eddie Hainsfurther was due. He rushed home from the office, bathed, put on his best suit, shirt and tie, then hurried down to the meeting room. But, as he walked in the door of the hotel, he suddenly remembered that he had forgotten his false teeth, without which he could not eat and could hardly talk. What to do? He explained his predicament to a new member who was sitting next to him. "Don't worry," the new member, Scot Tausend, said: "I think I've got just the thing for you." Scot reached into his pocket and pulled out a very nice set of teeth. Eddie tried them in his mouth and, while they fit poorly, he could at least make himself understood.

Eddie got away with it. His talk was a hit and everybody congratulated him. One the way out, he turned to his benefactor, Scot Tausend, and told him how lucky it was that the new member was a dentist and that they were seated side by side.

"But I'm not a dentist," Scot replied, "I'm an undertaker."

What's the one place where they have a good word for you when you are down and out? The cemetery.

Here lies the remains of old George Sleet,
Looked one way on a two-way street.

This tombstone message is supposed to be from a cemetery in Hatfield, Massachusetts. One hopes that it truly is there, it is so cute.

Here lies as silent as clay
Miss Arabella Young
Who on the 21st day of May, 1771,
Began to hold her tongue.

Mary Flannigan was a member of the Red Cross Association and, in their monthly meetings, she loved to tell stories that put men down. So, on this particular meeting night, she said, "When man was created he was instructed that he would be a man thirty years. But when mankind heard THAT, he complained bitterly of life's insufficient duration. Then the pig was created and told he would exist for thirty years. But the pig thought that was most unfair, saying that life was just too tough for pigs and that thirty years was too long. So ten years was subtracted from pig-life and given to the man. Then the horse was created and, when told that he would live thirty years, he, too, complained that to labor so hard for thirty years was a burden. And so, here, too, ten years was taken from the horse and given to the man. Next the fish was created and given twenty years about which he yelled like crazy: 'Under all that water for twenty years? Unfair!' And the man was given ten more years. Then came the bull and he was given twenty-five years, but he bellowed so loudly about it that they reduced his life to twenty years.

"And so now you understand," Mary said, "why a man after thirty, eats like a horse, grunts like a pig, stinks like a fish and ruts like a bull."

––––––––––––

An Illinois wit once remarked that the three ages of man are: 1. School tablet; 2. Aspirin tablet; 3. Stone tablet.

––––––––––––

The old lady had been married for many years when suddenly her husband died. This is what she put on his tombstone: "THE LIGHT OF MY LIFE HAS GONE OUT." Not long afterward she met, fell in love with and married another man. After thinking at some length about it, she went to the monument maker and had him add this to the tombstone:
THE LIGHT OF MY LIFE HAS GONE OUT.
P.S. I Found A Match.

IF I SHOULD DIE TO-NIGHT

If I should die to-night
And you should come to my cold corpse and say,
Weeping and heartsick o'er my lifeless clay-
If I should die to-night,
And you should come in deepest grief and woe-
And say: "Here's that ten dollars that I owe,"
I might arise in my large white cravat
And say, "What's that?"

If I should die to-night
And you should come to my cold corpse and kneel,
Clasping my bier to show the grief you feel,
I say, if I should die to-night
And you should come to me, and there and then
Just even hint 'bout paying me that ten,
I might arise the while,
But I'd drop dead again.

Ben King

"Would you repeat those terms again?"

*Reprinted with permission of the **Saturday Evening Post***

James Thurber wrote some of the funniest humor of all times and he loved to tell this story about his grandfather who was an early frontiersman and had to fight Indians many times as the pioneers advanced into the hostile west.

When the old man was on his deathbed, his minister asked: "Have you forgiven all your enemies?" "I ain't got none," the old man responded. "Well that's simply remarkable," the minister exclaimed. "But tell me...how could a tough old fighter and frontiersman like you go through life without making enemies?" Thurber's Grandpop explained it quite plainly: "I shot the sonsabitches."

————————

Almost everyone knows of the fierce cold of Maine winters. Here is a supreme example of how cold it gets up there.

"Say, Ira," I asked, "how cold was it out to your place this morning?"

"Only three degrees below zero at 6 a.m. Must be warming up some, days are getting longer now, and yesterday, it was eight degrees below. Still cold enough to freeze two dry rags together. You know, every time I see the temperature drop below zero, I'd like to have one of them summer complaints here to see it. They are always telling us what a beautiful State we live in. God's country, they call it. Well it may be God's country to them, but He sure don't spend his winters here."

"I'm glad I didn't live back in the real old days," I added. "Heard my Great Uncle Curt say that in those days it was a common sight after a snowstorm to see a man out poking around with a pole trying to find his chimney. He always said the only way to get out of the house was through the attic window on snowshoes. That was back when I was a boy and I used to wonder, with all that snow, what was the point of leaving the house at all?

"I remember one time listening to him tell some

summer people about the time he was picking blueberries, and, all of a sudden, a great big bear stood right up in front of him and let out a helluva growl. Curt said he began to run, and the bear was hot on his heels. Well, they ran that way for quite some distance, and, finally, Curt said, the only way he could get clear of that bear was to run across Round Pond. It had just frozen over thick enough to support his weight, but the bear, being much heavier, broke through the ice and Curt got away.

"About that time, one of the summer people said, 'Now wait just a minute. You were picking blueberries when the chase started -- that had to be in August, then you ran across a frozen pond? Now, I know Maine is famous for its unpredictable weather, but that's pretty hard to swallow!'

"Uncle Curt, pleased with himself that he had snared another victim, said, 'Oh, I just forgot to tell you that the bear chased me from August to Christmas!'"

"Stories Told in the Kitchen." Kendall Morse. Thorndike Press. 1981. Thorndike, Maine.

The Winterhavens

"The doctor didn't mention a side effect of a trip over the hill to the poorhouse!"

7

GRANDMAS and GRANDPAS

GRANDMA

Grandma does things backwards,
The way she uses yarns!
Sitting in her arm-chair
She's always socking darns.

When salesmen come to Grandma's door,
To sell So-po-lio,
SHE sells THEM her currant jam,
At fifty cents a throw!

Grandma's eyes are getting bad,
Two pairs of specs she's choosing;
One she puts beneath her chin,
The other's just for losing.

And when the day is over,
She has a funny look,
Turns the pages of her bed
And hustles off to book.

Source Unknown

You can live on earth only once, but if you live right, once is enough.

Old Mary Simpkins was embarrassed, at first, to answer the question of her granddaughter as to the meaning of platonic love. She thought it over quite a while, then said, "It's kinda like a fellow holding the eggshells while another guy eats the omelette."

If you're over the hill, why not enjoy the view?

"What a world this is getting to be," Grandpa exclaimed. "Why, when Grandma was a girl, she sure as heck didn't do the things girls do today. And then again," he said after a few moments of quiet reflection, "Grandmas didn't do the things that grandmas do today, either!"

Dorothy says that she dearly loves to hug her grandkids, that a hug is a _round-a-bout_ way to show affection. Her husband, too, she says, is a real good sport because he always settles every argument by letting her have her own way.

The clergyman was annoyed at the old man, accompanied by a boy. They always sat in the front row of the church and the old fellow always fell asleep half way through the sermon...so the preacher sent word to the boy that he wanted to speak with him after services.

"Young fellow," the minister said to the boy when they were alone in his office, "Is that elderly gentleman who comes to church with you each Sunday, a relative?"

"Yes, Sir. He's my grandpa."

"Oh. In that case, if you'll keep him awake during my services, I'll give you a quarter."

"It's a deal," the lad replied. And for three weeks things went fine and the old man listened attentively to the services. But after those few weeks, the old man again fell into his old ways and slept through most of the sermon.

The pastor sent for the boy and said to him, "I gave you a quarter each week and felt that the deal was settled and you'd keep your Grandfather awake during services. But you've let me down because in recent weeks the old fellow has fallen into his old ways and slept through my sermons."

"It's true that you did give me a quarter to keep him awake," the boy replied. "And I managed to do that for a time, but you see, Grandpa gave me a dollar not to bother or disturb him."

Old age: When certain parts wear out, spread out, fall out...and even squeak!

Grandmother takes her well-dressed young grandson to the beach and watches him as he paddles about. Suddenly, a giant wave carries the boy out to sea. The grandmother starts wailing to God to please return the kid and He does as another huge wave washes the boy back on dry land. The grandmother raises a clenched fists and shouts to God.

"So where's his hat?"

165

The salesgirl in ladies lingerie noticed an old man standing shyly at the entrance to the department. She walked over to him. "Can I be of service, sir?"

"Oh please," the man replied. "I want to buy a birthday present for my wife."

"And what did you have in mind, sir?"

"I really...I really don't know. But I thought a...a brassiere might be nice."

"Certainly, sir. What bust?"

"Oh, nothing! It just wore out."

"The worst part of growing old," said Grandpa Hugh Garvey, father of thirteen, "is that I have to listen to advice from my children."

It takes a baby approximately two years to learn to talk and between sixty and seventy years to keep his mouth shut.

Grandpa went to the door to answer a hard, nervous knocking. He opened it and there stood a woman with tears in her eyes. "Sir," she asked in a quivering, sobbing voice, "do you own a white cat with a black collar?"

"Yep. Sure do."

"Well, sir I just ran over it and I'm so sorry, just terribly sorry. Will you allow me to replace it?"

"Wel-l-l maybe, but first tell me...how are you at catchin' mice?"

Grandma Mary Barton had become deeply interested in Spiritualism so that one night, while reading a recent book acquisition, _The Dead Do Return_, she looked up to see a hand rising up out of the foot of the bed. Quick as a flash, she reached over and grabbed the pistol Grandpa Barton kept under the pillow and shouted, "Go away or I'll shoot! I'll give you three counts to go. One...two...three!" She fired and shot off her little toe.

Two cons were in prison and were bragging about the qualities of their grandparents. "My grandpop was a very clever guy," one boasted, "when the coin telephone first came out, he invented a slug and made a fortune."

"You think that's so great? Listen to this story about my grandma. She got ten years in the pen for stealing a hanger in a department store."

"Why such a long stretch? Just for stealing a measly coat hanger?"

"Well, you see, it was attached to a full-length mink coat."

You've joined the older generation if you can recall when the sky was the limit.

Age is mostly a matter of mind. So - if you don't mind, it doesn't matter.

Charlie Festes and his wife Mary had been married for a long, long time and they had done reasonably well at farming their 880 acres of good Illinois soil. But they did have a problem. They seemed never to agree on anything. And they argued constantly, day and night, accusing one another of this, that and t'other.

One day, Charlie had finished breakfast and was looking out the front window. He saw his neighbor driving by atop a load of hay pulled by two horses. The horses struggled together up the hill and moved on. "Honey," Charlie said wistfully, "How come you and me can't pull together up the tree of life like them two horses?"

His wife pulls herself up big as a haystack and says, "Because one of us is a dadblamed Jackass!"

Of late it seems
I have reached that age
When folks look old
Who ain't half my age.

It was such a beautiful day that Mama convinced Grandpa to take her infant to the park. So Grandpa agreed, put the baby in the carriage and pushed toward the park. Well, the baby began to scream its little head off and Grandpa kept repeating, "Easy, now, Jimmy. Take it easy, Jimmy. Relax. Steady on, Jimmy. Everything's going to be jake, OK, just dandy, Jimmy."

A nice old lady happened by, stopped to look at the baby and said, "You do such a grand job of talking to the little one. So quiet and gentle and sweet." Then she asks, "What seems to be bothering Jimmy?"

Grandpa replies, "You got it wrong, lady. He's Georgie. I'm Jimmy!"

Grandfather clock: An old-timer.

It's tough when your son loves two girls at once. What do you do? Well you duck out of it if you can, by letting Grandpa handle the deal, like this:

"Well, my boy, your dad tells me you have a problem."

"Sure do, Grandpa. I love both Kate and Edith and can't decide which one to marry."

Grandpa considers the problem, then says, "I'll give it a lot of thought and get back to you. But this much is certain...you can't have your Kate and Edith too."

"After retirement, I thought life in the fast lane would be just right for me," Grandpa said while rocking away on the front porch. "But something went wrong! I'd barely got started when I got run over!"

Grandpa Eberhart and Nellie, his wife had only one grandson and they doted on him, devoted their lives to help bring him up. When he was about twelve years old they became consumed with curiosity as to what the boy would be when he grew to maturity. So they decided on a test. First they put a ten dollar bill on the table. "This represents a banker," Grandpa told his son and his wife. "And this represents a clergyman," he said, putting down a Bible next to the money. Then he put a bottle of whiskey next to the Bible and said, "This represents a businessman."

All four of them hid in the next room, peeking around the corner to see what the grandson would do when he came into the room, to see which one of the baits he would take.

The boy looked around to assure himself that there was nobody watching, then picked up each item and examined it, even uncorking the bottle to smell its contents. Then, in one rapid movement, he put the Bible in his right pocket, stuffed the bill in his left pocket, grabbed the bottle, then walked out of the room.

Grandpa turned to his wife and said, "Whatdya know! The kid is going into politics!"

An old timer is a man who can't understand why people who make women's clothes are so determined to drive themselves out of business.

Grandma Pierik is suing George, her husband of fifty years, for divorce because of his reckless driving. It seems that, of late, he has taken to driving by her with a blond in the car.

They say grandchildren brighten up the home. That's right - they never turn off the lights.

Grandma Levy, always a regular synagogue member, had finally talked her cousin, a woman who had lived a riotous, free life into joining the Temple. "Tell me, Rabbi," the old lady asked, "Do you feel that my cousin will have her sins forgiven after all those years?"

"Yes, I do. I'm positive of it. You must remember that the greater the number of sins, the greater the glory."

"Yeah?" the old lady replied thoughtfully. "Gosh, Rabbi, I sure do wish I'd known that fifty years ago."

Grandfather Edwards was reading a magazine, looked up from it to tell his wife, "The derndest story in here, Mary, where it says this old guy my age with a wooden leg just married a gal with a cedar chest. Can you imagine what a time they'll have with splinters!"

It was probably the same old guy, Grandpa Edwards, who said to his wife, "Mary, you look like a million dollars to me." And she smiled, blushed and said, "Really? Tell me more." And the old boy added: "Green and wrinkled."

Grandmother was walking her grandchildren down the street when a lady said to her, "My what charming children. How old are they?"

"The doctor is six," the proud grandmother said, "and the lawyer is four."

It seems certain that fewer women would conceal their age if more men acted theirs.

There is nothing wrong with the younger generation that the older generation didn't outgrow.

There was a family in New Holland that had sixteen kids, so many, in fact, that both grandmothers were kept busy helping the mother take care of them. Well, one day one of the kids sneaked away from the house and ran down to the road where a road gang was black-topping the county highway. The kid spotted a barrel, climbed up on it and fell right smack dab in a barrel of tar.

The old ladies missed the kid soon after he left the house and, knowing kids so well, they suspected he'd gone down to watch the road gang. So they ran down to the road, looked around and heard the kid crying from the barrel. They rushed over and fished him out, looked him over, and one lady said, "How on earth, Melissa, are we ever goin' to git this child cleaned up!"

And Melissa replied, "Tell you what, Sarah, I'll have a talk with my daughter and see if she won't git goin' on another 'un. It'd be a danged sight easier than cleanin' this 'un up."

Grandpa Cobell said that he was sure glad that he was done, finished with bringing up children. When asked why, he responded, "For one thing, with today's styles in ladies fashions being what they are, how in heck would you know where to have your baby daughter vaccinated!"

If you kick the very person responsible for any of your troubles, you wouldn't be able to sit down for a month.

An old woman was having her picture taken at a photographer's studio. It was her ninety-eighth birthday and she wanted to give the picture to her grandson. "I hope I'll be around to take your hundredth birthday picture, Ma'am," the photographer said.

"I don't see why not," the Grandma said. "You look mighty healthy to me."

The elderly grandfather suffered badly from insomnia. His wealthy sons and grandsons tried everything without success. Finally they brought in a hypnotist who placed the old man in a chair and softly repeated, "You are feeling sleepy..." Time and time again he repeated, "You are feeling sleepy," but the grandfather's eyes were wide open.

After an hour, the hypnotist brought out a small piece of glass on a chain and slowly waved it backwards and forwards in front of the grandfather's eyes. About thirty minutes later the old man's eyes began to close and shortly afterwards his head fell on his chest.

Delighted, his children paid the hypnotist a huge fee. After he had gone, they tip-toed to the door of the room and peeped inside. The grandfather was apparently still asleep, but as they began to quietly shut the door, Grandpa opened one eye, looked around and asked, "Has that crazy nut gone yet?"

"No, I think he had it when he went in."

ONE MOMENT, SIR by Marione R. Nickles

Reprinted with permission of **Penguin Books USA, Inc.**

Grandmas soon learn that life is not one damn thing after another...it's one damn thing over and over!

———

What was considered the *"sin"* thing in grandmother's day, is now called the *"in" thing.*

———

A group of Grandma Powers' friends had come to her home to discuss plans for celebrating her hundredth birthday. "How about an airplane ride?" suggested one of her friends. "I'd be glad to arrange for it if you'd agree. You'd love it, Grandma Powers, and you really ought to try it. You've never flown, y'know."

"Thanks! But no thanks!" responded Grandma Powers who had crossed the plains in a covered wagon. "I'll jest sit here and watch television, like the good Lord intended I should."

———

"Mrs. Brown," the doctor said, "If you hope to cure the insomnia that is so bothersome to you, you must abstain from taking your troubles to bed with you."

"I can't do that," Grandma Brown explained. "You see, my husband absolutely refuses to sleep alone."

———

Grandma Susan has determined that the severity of an itch is inversely proportional to her reach.

———

Life is like riding a bicycle. You don't fall off unless you stop pedaling.

———

Edgar Dow was traveling west and stopped at a little cafe in Lantern, Iowa. He ordered the blue plate special, paid for it, then noticed the sign above the cash register, "WE AIM TO PLEASE." Before he left, he turned to the cashier and said, "You really ought to get more target practice."

Grandma Simpkins was so upset over the noise, confusion and general bedlam that had come to her daughter's house, now that the granddaughter had returned home for Christmas vacation, that she fled the home. "I just had to get away," she explained to her friend over a cup of coffee. "Melody came home from college and all her friends came over and they yakked and giggled and argued and discussed. Then they got into a hot argument over the difference between heredity and environment. On and on they argued until I just had to get out of the house. In our day, we didn't need to talk and talk over the difference. Everybody knew that if a baby looked like his father, it was heredity. And if he looked like the neighbor, it was environment. "

Matilda was frantically trying to get the housework done before going to work but her grandfather's raucous voice, singing in the bathroom, was driving her nuts. "Grandpa," she yelled to him. "Please. Why must you sing in the shower?"
"Because there ain't no lock on the door!"

"I have noticed," said Grandpa Jim, "that the members of the younger generation are alike in many disrespects."

Grandpa Brown remarked to his son that raising the retirement age is a good deal like moving the finish line when the horses are coming down the homestretch.

Grandpa Hatmaker says that kids today are sure different, much more biased than when he was a kid. For example, when he takes them to the store, they say, "Bias this" and "Bias that."

It's a real shocker to realize how many of your high school buddies have become highbrows (when they emove their hats!).

Old Jonas was a crotchety fellow who always took breakfast with his wife. He would read the morning newspaper while she fumed at his neglect. This being their fortieth wedding anniversary, she yelled: "Henry! Henry! Please put that paper down and let's talk about how we are going to celebrate our wedding anniversary today. What do you suggest?"

Jonas put his paper down, removed and polished his glasses, stared for a moment into the distance, then said, "How about two minutes of silence?"

"I NEVER NAG WALTER, BUT BUYING THAT CAR BACK IN 1958 WAS STUPID..."

Fun is like life insurance...the older you are the more it costs. My grandson bought a retirement policy. All he has to do is keep up the payments for 20 years and the salesman can retire.

An example of the endearing horse sense that comes with age, is illustrated with the story about the matron who asked if she'd gone to Florida to visit her son who had recently married. "No," she replied. "I don't think it's time yet. I thought I'd wait till after they have the first baby. I've got an idea that they'd welcome a grandmother more cheerfully than a mother-in-law."

"Grandma, what's a girdle?" the grandson asked.
"It's an article of clothing that keeps a broad misfortune from spreading," she replied.

An old man was asked if his wife of fifty years was economical. He replied: "Yep! Sometimes. This last year she used only fifty candles on her sixtieth birthday cake."

Patricia was really confused. Her sweetheart's birthday was near and she was at a loss as to what he'd appreciate having her give him. So she went to her grandmother for advice. "Grandma, my boyfriend Tony, is very rich, has everything he needs, drives a Cadillac to work, a Rolls Royce from his city home to his country estate, and uses a yacht to go fishing. He's got oodles of socks and shirts and he must have a hundred ties. He owns a box full of diamond rings, another box of watches, and he belongs to six athletic clubs. What can a girl like me give him for his birthday?"
"Encouragement," replied Grandma.

Could anyone deny that a screen door is an article that grandchildren get a bang out of?

"Grandma, I don't want my face washed. Please don't."

"Every little girl needs to have her face washed when she gets up of a morning, dear. Then she should wash three times a day in addition. I've always done that."

"Yeah! Sure! And just see how your face shrunk!"

As we get older, we understand the saying: "Take good care of yourself. You'll find it hard to get a replacement."

It's the optimist who sees the donut, the pessimist who sees the hole, and the realist who sees all those calories.

He's so danged old that he doesn't read stories that end, "to be continued."

There is a central and overwhelming advantage that old folks find in thinking and reminiscing about the past...it's a helluva lot cheaper!

"I tried life in the fast lane," said Grandpa from his rocking chair. "But I got run over."

When you stop to think of it, we haven't progressed all that far. After all, Grandfather didn't need one-tenth the stuff to conquer the entire wilderness that we need for a cookout.

Birthdays tell how long you've been on the road, not how far you've traveled.

You look like a million...every year of it.

An old man, a grandpa, took snuff,
He said he was happy enough.
    For he sneezed when he pleased,
    And was pleased when he sneezed,
And that's more than enough about snuff.

Grandchildren of any age can always make their grandparents happy just by saying, "I'm hungry!"

Among the things that are quite easy, even simple for a child to operate, are the grandparents.

An old-timer is one who remembers when a woman looked the same after washing her face.

When your grandson is ready for college it is a grand idea to advise him to be sure his brain is engaged before he puts his mouth in gear and takes off.

Old age has been defined as that time in life when you know all the answers but nobody asks you the questions.

Elmer Weiskopf says that if living conditions don't begin to stop improving so dang much in this country, we're going to run short of humble beginnings for our great men.

The little grandson rattled his grandaddy's newspaper for attention. When Grandpa put the paper down, the kid asked: "Is it true that God gives us our daily bread?"

"Yep! Precisely."

"And Santa Claus brought me all those toys at Christmas time?"

"Of course he did."

"And our new baby, Susie, came from Heaven above?"

"She sure did."

"And Mom takes care of us, the house, the food and all?"

"Never misses a day at it."

"Then tell me Grandpa, what does Dad do around here?"

Grandpa Myers said that over his eighty years he had learned that life was kinda like licking honey off the thorns of a rose bush.

"If spinach is so good for you," Johnny complained to his mother, "Then why don't you make grandpa eat it?"

Grandfather: A fellow whose daughter married a guy very much her inferior but who later produced grandchildren of absolute genius.

Why did Grandma put wheels on her rocking chair?

Because she always had wanted to learn how to do rock and roll.

A sourpuss
        Was dour Grandma May
    Her welcome mat
        Said "Stay Away!"

There's a club for men and women who are seventy years or more and it meets weekly (not weakly!) in Burlington, Iowa. One elderly chap arrived early at the meeting hall and thought to wait at an adjoining park, resting on a park bench. A lady passed and sat on an adjoining bench.

"Do you belong to our Over-Seventies Club?" the senior citizen asked her.

"I should say not!" was the reply. "I ain't anywhere never seventy and mind your own business!" she snapped.

"Sorry," the old man apologized. "All us old coots in the club like to brag about our age. Mind tellin' me how old you are?"

"A woman's age is her own business and nobody else's," she told him.

"True," the old man replied. "And it appears that you've been in business a helluva long time."

"Grandma, how long have you and Grandfather been married?" asked the granddaughter.

"Fifty years," Grandma replied.

"Isn't that wonderful," exclaimed the granddaughter. "And I'll bet that in all that time, you never once thought about a divorce...right?"

"Right. Divorce, never...Murder, sometimes."

A young boy, some six years old, was studying his grandmother. Soon he asked, "Grandma, are you a lot older than my Ma?"

"I sure am, honey, lots older," she replied.

The boy nodded. "I figured that," he said, "But I got to tell you that her skin fits a whole lot better than yours."

Grandma Peters defines pregnancy as a woman so swelled up over her husband's work that she puts up a big front.

180

Grandma Fentserwald has this to say about aging. "You can prevent wrinkles by cream and massage; and you can dye grey hair, but there's no graceful way you can prevent a small boy from offering to help you across the street."

Grandma Brown took her two grandchildren to the zoo. Walking about the generous grounds, they stopped before a huge cage of storks. Grandma told the two youngsters that these were the birds that brought both of them to their dad and mom.

The two children looked at one another, then the oldest leaned over and whispered in his sibling's ear, "Don't you think we ought to tell Grandma the truth?"

"Roger is going through a phase."

Reprinted with permission of the **Saturday Evening Post**

Down in South Carolina, they were engaged in burying a war hero revered by all the inhabitants of the small mountain community. It was a military burial with color guard, bugler and all.

Amid much weeping, the bugler blew taps and the guard of honor fired a salvo for the last salute. The crash of the weapons was just too much for the hero's little grandmother, who fell over in a dead faint.

There was a moment of silence broken by a small boy's yell, "Gawdam! They shot Grandma!"

The old lady was in the hospital bed, busy chatting with her visiting grandson. She talked...and talked...and talked on and on while her poor grandson busied himself finishing off a bowl of peanuts sitting on her bedside table. At last she shut up and the lad apologized, saying: "Granny, I'm so sorry. I didn't realize that I was eating all your peanuts. I'll replace them, ok?"

"Don't worry. Doesn't matter now. Y'see, I ate all the chocolate off them yesterday."

Do they fight? Well I guess. Been fighting for forty years. A Justice of the Peace didn't marry those two, it was the Secretary of War.

Grandmother Robinson was so delighted to learn that her grandchildren were coming to visit her that she gave ten dollars to the church. After they left she gave twenty dollars!

A grandmother of sixty years (more or less!) said to her friend, "I'm mighty uncomfortable! I've got on my sitting-down shoes and my standin'-up girdle!"

A newly married man noticed that every time his bride put a roast in the roasting pan, she cut off both ends of the beef. He asked why she did this. She replied, "Because my mother always fixed a roast just that way."

One evening at his mother-in-law's home, he noticed her doing the very same thing. "Why do you do that," he asked, "cut both ends of the beef?"

"Well, that's the way my mother always did it," she explained."

Inevitably, the young man finds himself at his wife's grandmother's home, watching her prepare the roast for dinner. So he asks her why she cuts off both ends of the roast beef before putting it in the pan.

"Because," replied the grandmother, "this durned pan is too short for the beef."

8

NOSTALGIA

If you are over sixty, you have been witness to more changes - good and bad, heavenly and hellish, than any other generation from Adam and Eve on. Wow! What a time to have lived. Consider the following:

Consider the changes! We were born before television, before penicillin, before polio shots, frozen foods, Xerox, plastics, contact lenses, Frisbees, and the Pill.

We were before radar, credit cards, split atoms, laser beams, and ball point pens, before pantyhose, dishwashers, clothes dryers, electric blankets, air conditioners, drip-dry clothes...and before man walked on the moon.

We got married first, and then lived together. How quaint can you be?

In our time, closets were for clothes, not for "coming out of." Jeans were scheming girls named Jean and Jeanne, and having a meaningful relationship meant getting along with your cousins.

We thought fast food was what you ate during Lent, and Outer Space was the back of the Strand Theatre.

We were before house-husbands, gay rights, computer dating, dual-careers, and commuter marriages. We were before day-care centers, group therapy and nursing homes. We never heard of FM radio, tape decks, electric typewriters, artificial hearts, word processors, yogurt, and guys wearing earrings. For us, time-sharing meant togetherness...not computers or condominiums; a "chip" meant a piece of wood; hardware meant hardware and software wasn't even a word.

In 1940, "Made in Japan" meant junk and the term "making out" referred to how you did on your exams. Pizzas, "Mac Donalds," and instant coffee were unheard of.

We hit the scene when there were 5 and 10 cent stores, where you bought things for five and ten cents. Sanders or Williams sold ice cream cones for a nickel or a dime. For one nickel you could ride a street car, make a phone call, buy a Pepsi or enough stamps to mail one letter and two postcards. You could buy a new Chevy coupe for $6,000.00, but who could afford one - a pity too, because gas was 11 cents a gallon.

In our day, cigarette smoking was fashionable, grass was mowed, coke was a cold drink, and pot was something you cooked in. Rock music was Grandma in a rocking chair, humming a lullaby, aids were helpers in the Principal's office, and mother was one word...not two!

We were certainly not before the difference between the sexes were discovered, but we were surely before the sex change - we made do with what we had. And we were the last generation that was so dumb as to think you needed a husband to have a baby!

No wonder we are so confused and there is such a generation gap today!

But we survived. What better reason to celebrate?
Author Unknown

Remember back then when "enter" was a sign on a door and not a button on a computer?

And if you think that concern for air pollution, automobile fatalities, high divorce rates, poison gas and germ warfare are now concerns, take a peek at these worries of fifty-four years ago (1926)!

GOOD NEWS

If ever I saw happy faces around me it was in the early weeks of August, before the presidential campaign had got into full swing. Every other day brought its budget of good news.

First came a report from the Weather Bureau stating that the air over New York was more heavily polluted than at any time in the last five years. People repeated the news with beaming faces and congratulated each other. It meant that more smoke was coming from the factory chimneys. Prosperity was headed back. Everybody was happy. Needless to say the book reviewers went out and danced in the streets.

Next I recall what a mighty cheer went up when it was announced that automobile fatalities were climbing rapidly. It meant that more cars and gasoline were being bought, and more liquor was being consumed, all tending to more employment.

Next there were jubilant editorials in the newspapers calling attention to the fact that divorce was on the upgrade, after a tragic slump extending over several years. It meant that times were getting better. People were beginning to step out again and had the price of a ticket to Reno.

The best news of all was the report that all the nations were making preparations to bombard the enemy's crops with poison gas and germs in the next war. This meant that civilization was saved, for the end of the wheat surplus was in sight.

Ah, it was good to be alive in such times.

Oscar M. Ridge
As I Look Back
Doubleday Doran & Co.
Garden City, NY 1937

The bathtub was invented in 1850 and the telephone in 1875. It is interesting to consider that if you had been living back then, you could have luxuriated in the bathtub for twenty-five years without hearing the telephone ring.

George Petefish has maintained for several years now that the fact that George Washington could throw a dollar across the Potomac is not so strange, not strange at all. "It's just that a buck went a helluva lot farther in them days," he says.

There was no distinctive lipstick flavors when Grandpa was a young man. He says that when you kissed a girl all you could taste was girl.
Democrat, California, MO.

A wise man once remarked, "In the old days, when you wanted a horse to stand still, you tied him to a hitching post. Today, you bet on him."

You know you are a senior citizen when the money needed to send your grandson to college for one semester is only a bit more than was needed to put you through four years at the university.

It is hard to adopt a philosophy of life in this world when, if a man runs after money he's money-mad, and if he keeps it he's a miser, and if he spends it, he's a wastrel, and if he fails to get money, he's a ne'er-do-well, and if he simply won't try to get it, he lacks ambition. Further, if he gets money without working for it, he's a parasite, and if he gets and keeps a fortune after working hard all his life, people say he's a damn fool who never got a thing out of life. Kinda makes a person wonder how to go about things...doesn't it?

A penny saved is...not worth much today.

An old timer is a guy who recalls when people could hold onto a ten dollar bill long enough to fold it.

There are still plenty of old-fashioned mothers around who can recall their husband's first kiss...But they have daughters who have a hard time remembering their first husbands.

Another way to tell that you are part of those "old folks" is to listen to modern popular music. If it in no way resembles the music you love, well, you're gettin' up there, brother, if not there already! And if you can't arrange your arithmetic to fit that category, try this one...Do you remember when the word GAY meant that you were having a wonderful, rollicking good time?

One of the hazards of biding your time is revealed in this two-liner.

> All things come to those who waits:
> But then they sure are out of date.

An old timer is one who can recall that a kid who called himself part of the "beat generation" was a youngster coming out of the woodshed."

You know you are up there among the hoary oldies when your grandkid's motorbike costs more than your first car - that lovely old Studebaker - cost you, back in 1939!

For my first twenty years, I thought the world was flat. And for my next thirty years, I thought it was round. But now, at seventy-five, I'm positive it's crooked.

A group of city hunters were chatting in the home of their old guide out in West Virginia. They admired a huge gun hanging on the wall above the fireplace. The guide said it was his favorite weapon. "I killed plenty ba'r, deer, wild turkey, quail, and pheasant with that ol' gun. And that same old gun got me two son-in-laws, too."

There is an insightful, wise Yiddish proverb that goes: "Old age to the foolish is winter; to the wise, it is harvest-time."

Old George says that the girls of his generation learned to cook to find the way to a man's heart, but these derned modern girls _thaw_ an easier way.

You're getting old when the gleam in your eye is from the sun hitting your bifocals.

190

Jim Edgar went back to his college for his fiftieth reunion. And he had a wonderful time. When he got back he told his friends that the most remarkable change of all was that they put both men and women up in the same dormitory.

Don't worry about your wrinkles, they merely indicate where many smiles have been.

The old lady remarked, during a bridge game, "I used to be a mighty popular gal, way back when, but now all that's chasing me is Father Time."

Martha Edwards says her memory is just awful except for one thing...she can always remember what things used to cost.

In this day of women's lib and short skirts, old man Jones figures that it's the woman - not her wrongs - that ought to be redressed.

The old man was taken to the high school graduation of his granddaughter. After the ceremonies were over, he was asked what he thought of the way young people dressed today. He replied, "Those mini-skirts are somethin' I'll tell ya. Why, when we was high school kids the only way you could tell iff'n a girl was knock-kneed was to listen."

Those good old moral days date back to the time when, if you looked in backyards you saw the product of marriage, triangles on the clothesline and not in the courtroom.

Nowadays it takes darned near as much brains to fill out your income tax as it does to make the money.

Then there was a young professor lecturing to teachers on modern methods of education. He informed them that if a child disobeyed, or became noisy, the teacher should switch the child's attention. An old man, a visitor, sitting in the back of the room, arose and announced that when he was a boy, attention wasn't what got switched!

Today you can't judge a woman by her clothes. Why? Insufficient evidence.

An old timer is a man or woman who can remember when a child had more sisters and brothers than he had fathers.

Age is sure deceiving. It is astonishing how much faster 60 comes after 50 than 50 after 40!

A famous actor was celebrating his seventieth birthday. A reporter came up to him and asked if he was having as much fun now as he had as a younger man.

"Young fellow," said the actor, "I am now seventy years old. I must tell you that nothing...nothing at all is as much fun as it used to be."

An old person is one who remembers when the hero only kissed the heroine at the end of the movie.

You are truly old when you lived back in those days when a girl married a man for his money instead of divorcing him for it.

Remember when there was a time when we would talk out problems over coffee and a cigarette? Now they are the problems.

The young fellows in the lodge took me to town with them one night last week...to a disco. Well, let me tell you, I ain't never seen nothin' like that before. The squirmin' and the wigglin' of those young ladies made me tired just to look at 'em. Why everything moved but their bowels. If my dog acted that way, I'd have given him worm medicine.

———————

An old timer is one who can recall those long-dead times when a baby was prized as a new wonder in the family and not a tax deduction.

———————

An old timer is a person who can remember when charity was a virtue and not an industry.

———————

One proof of having reached senior citizen status is if you can remember when the cafe _and_ the beggar on the street asked only a nickel for a cup of coffee.

———————

Bill Crook says that young men today will stand for anything...for anything except a woman on the bus.

———————

Some judges can be wonderfully understanding of the elderly. As an example, in Boston, when an old lady was called to the stand, the judge instructed, "Permit this witness to state her age. After that she may be sworn."

———————

There is a sign in the country village of Greenview, Illinois, that reads, "Do you remember those grand old days when sex was dirty and the air was clean?"

———————

A senior citizen is one who remembers when to give a woman more rope meant she would string up another length of clothesline.

A young lady was describing to her grandfather, her experience at the theatre the preceding evening. "Why, I was really shocked," the young girl said. "Everybody in the place was 'snuzzling.'"

"Snuzzling? Just what is snuzzling?" grandpa asked.

"It's the same thing you called 'necking,' Grandpa."

"Maybe so," Grandpa replied. "But now I call it 'reminiscing.'"

An old timer is one who can remember when the height of indiscretion was to _type_ a love letter.

It seems a very long time ago that, when you had a serious automobile accident, the first thing you asked for was a doctor...not a lawyer.

Old Pete Jones said that money may not bring happiness but he sure does wish that he'd had a chance to find it out for himself.

Old days: The time before the dime store had a lay-away plan.

An old timer is a fellow who remembers when he bought $6 worth of groceries and had to hold the bag from the bottom!

An old timer is someone who remembers when a girl walked backwards in a high wind, and a time when...the sky was the limit! And he recalls that a girl used to stay home when she had nothing to wear.

The old man was about to marry a girl much younger than he. And this worried the old fellow's son who suggested that before he went through with the marriage, he consult a physician. The old boy thought this was a first-rate idea and went to see his doctor.

When the father returned to his home, he sat his son down and reported, "The doctor said something I thought I understood but now I'm not so sure. You've been through college and all so that perhaps you can explain what the doctor meant when he used a word I didn't understand. Tell me, son, just how many times a week is semi-annual?"

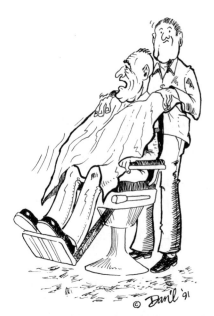

THE USUAL WAY, MAX.... EASY ON THE SIDES
AND NOT TOO MUCH OFF THE TOP!

Seventy years ago, the magazine *"Farm Family"* published this touching and funny poem. It seems that some things never change whether they be part of the 1920s or the 1990s.

"DIAMOND"

You say you're getting 'long in years,
    And short in cash, and old?
Just drive them horrid thots away!
    Don't let your love git cold!

You was a good old waggin once,
    An' if yer busted now,
I sure can't see as it's your fault,
    I blame myself somehow.

Don't think I'm gonna give you up,
    Because you're losin' speed,
I'm slacking up a lot myself,
    You're jest the one I need!

I love you jest the way you is!
    I love you now, - because
It issent what you is today!
    It's what you used to was!

Remember that your pal's no kid,
    I'm follerin' right along.
We need our lovin' more today
    When everything seems wrong.

The road is gittin' little rough,
    The evenin' air is chill,
But when we reach the jump-off place,
    Let's be together still!

Let's don't git careless 'bout our love
    Whatever else we do!
Imagine that your hair is black,
    And that my eyes are blue!

196

Now put your arms around my waist,
     And hold me on your knees,
Our honeymoon will last as long
     As we have young ideas!

And ev'ry quarrel that we've had
     I've plum forgot, I vow,
And all the love and joy of life,
     Comes rushin' on me now!

It makes my heart go "thumpy-thump"
     With gratitude, old boy!
See? Ain' I blushin'? Tears? Ha-ha!
     Why them is tears of joy!

Kiss me again! There! Atta boy!
     My sweetheart ain't so slow.
Why darn you! You hain't changed a bit
     Since fifty years ago!

                    Chas. Valley

The Winterhavens

9

THAT WONDERFUL HUMOR

OF THE PAST

Here are some hilarious stories about life in North Carolina by Carl Goerch, early newspaper columnist and radio broadcaster from Raleigh, North Carolina. These tales of the 1940s offer wonderful examples of typical, classic American humor.

Down in Washington, N.C., there used to be a crabbed, crusty old carpenter by the name of Walker. He didn't have much to do with anybody and was generally regarded as an old grouch; something of which I wasn't aware of at the time.

I'd meet Mr. Walker on the street and say: "Good morning."

The old man paid no attention.

Next morning the same thing would happen. And it also happened three or four mornings afterwards.

Once more I met him with the customary greeting: "Good morning."

Mr. Walker stopped in his tracks, glared at me and then shouted: "Good morning, good morning, good morning, good morning, good morning! THERE - let that do you for a week or so and quit bothering me with your damned 'good mornings'."

Excerpts from *"Carolina Chats. 1944", "Down Home. 1943", and "Just For The Fun Of It. 1954"*, written by Carl Goerch, used with the permission of the Estate of Carl Goerch.

Norm Jones says that worrying about what's in outer space seems rather silly in view of the fact that few of us know what's in the glove compartment of our own automobile.

REAL ESTATE NOTE

A newly married couple was looking for a house in the country and, after finding what they decided was a suitable one, were making their way home. The young wife, after reaching home, happened to think that they had not noticed a water closet on the place, and she decided to write the owner about it.

Being very modest, she hesitated to spell out the words "Water Closet" in her letter, so she decided to refer to it as "W.C." The owner did not readily understand just what she meant, so after pondering a long while, he decided that she must have reference to Westminster Church, a well-known church in that section. He answered her letter as follows:

Dear Madam: I regret very much the delay in answering the letter you wrote me and now take great pleasure in informing you that "W.C." is located only seven miles from the house and is capable of seating 700 people.

This is very fortunate indeed, if you are in the habit of going regularly; but no doubt you will be interested in knowing that a great many people take their lunch with them and make a day of it, while others cannot spare the time generally and are in too big a hurry to wait if the place is crowded.

The last time my wife and I went was about six years ago, and we had to stand up all the time.

It may interest you to know that it is planned to hold a bazaar to raise funds for plush seats for the "W.C.," as it is a long-felt want.

Raymond Pollock of New Bern was in Raleigh while the legislature was in session and told me of a little experience that he and Mrs. Pollock had with a maid whom they had hired a couple of weeks before.

She was a girl from the country and hadn't worked out before. She found it mighty hard to get the hang of things and made a lot of mistakes. However, Mrs. Pollock was very patient and did her best to teach the girl how her work should be done.

One day Mrs. Pollock had to go to some kind of a

meeting down town. Before she left, she made out a list of things she wanted the maid to get from the store while she was gone. She wrote out the various items very plainly and distinctly. Like this:

1. Chicken.
2. Tomatoes.
3. Potatoes.
4. Biscuits.
5. Lemon Pie.

The maid was determined that this was going to be one job that should be done right. She took the list and went to the store. She bought the various items. When Mrs. Pollock got home, she found one chicken, two tomatoes, three potatoes, four biscuits and five lemon pies.

A man is as young as he feels--after trying to prove it.

Undoubtedly there have been many times when you've been on a train and have looked forward to sitting down and enjoying a couple of hours of quiet reading. Sometimes you get by with it: other times some talkative individual will take the seat next to yours and will start a conversation in which you have absolutely no interest.

It's hard for the average person to get rid of somebody of this type without being deliberately rude, which is something that most of us don't want to be. So we just sit there and abandon all our plans for reading. We answer his questions and try to be as polite as possible. Under these circumstances, we'd give almost anything in the world if we just knew how to escape. Here's how Pete handled it.

Pete had to go up to New York recently on a little business trip. He spent the night and started on his return journey the following morning. He had with him a book which he had been wanting to read for some time. So just as soon as he got settled down in his seat, he opened his suitcase, took out the book, stretched himself out comfortable and started to read.

He read for about ten minutes. The book was interesting and he was enjoying himself thoroughly.

And then it happened.

A tall, gangling individual came strolling through the car. The seat next to Pete was vacant. The stranger paused. Then he smiled what was supposed to be an ingratiating smile and said: "Brother, do you mind if I sit here?"

"Not at all," said Murphy untruthfully.

The stranger seated himself. He looked around for a minute or two. He glanced at Pete several times, but that gentleman gave him no encouragement. Unfortunately the man was of that type which needs no encouragement. And so the conversation started.

"Nice day, isn't it?"

Pete said that it was a very nice day indeed.

"You going far?"

"Salisbury."

"Where's that?"

"North Carolina."

"What might be your name?"

"Walter Murphy."

"I used to know a Murphy in Toledo, Ohio. Samuel Murphy was his name. Any kin of yours?"

"I don't think so."

"He's in the hardware business. What business you in?"

"I'm an aviator."

The guy looked Pete over very carefully. "Aren't you a trifle old to be an aviator?" he inquired.

"My age doesn't have anything to do with it, but I'm afraid that my general physical condition is going to keep me from doing any more flying."

"You look to be in pretty good health."

Pete shook his head sadly.

"You mean you don't feel well?"

Pete leaned over and put his hand on the other chap's knee. "My friend," he said, "you are gazing upon an individual who soon will leave behind him all the cares and worries of this terrestrial sphere. I have just returned from the South Pacific, where I was stationed for fourteen months. I lived a goodly portion of that times in the jungles of Satu Baku. Of course, you've heard of Satu Baku?"

"Seems to me I have."

"Certainly you have. You impress me as being a very intellectual gentleman. As I have just said, I spent many weary months in the jungle. One day I was making my way through the dense undergrowth when I was stung by a tiva-duva fly. I contracted the dread disease of muspatosis. The terrible poison has gradually spread through my system. The doctors in New York have informed me that when it reaches my heart, I shall die. It still has three inches to go."

"Gosh! That's terrible!"

"Yes, it is. But that isn't the worst of it."

"What do you mean?"

"The doctors in New York told me something about muspatosis that I never knew before."

"What is that?"

"They said that it was highly contagious: that it could be picked up by anybody who came in contact with me. They urged me to go back to my home in Salisbury and remain as closely confined as possible. When I think that I may be the means of bringing this disease to other people, it fairly makes my heart bleed, and under existing conditions my heart has no business bleeding. Why even now, with you sitting close beside me, the virus may be... Hey! Wait a moment: I want to tell you the rest of it."

The stranger had risen to his feet. "I've got somebody waiting for me in the other car," he said hurriedly. "Sorry, but I must be going."

"Good day," said Pete. "I enjoyed talking to you."

The man mumbled something in reply and then disappeared. Pete picked up his book again with a sigh of content. He resumed his reading where he had left off and thoroughly enjoyed the rest of his trip back home.

An old-timer is a person who can remember when you could carry money around in your pocket long enough to wear a hole in it.

Mike Myers holds that the declining years are those in which a man declines dang near everything.

All of us old-timers remember when it was taken for granted by everyone that "Laughter is the best medicine." It was as certain a cure as was Lydia Pinkham's Vegetable Compound that worked wonders for the ladies of the family. And now the matter of laughing, of laughter, has become a subject for university study and academic concern. There are humor sessions, classes, conferences and so on. Well, Old Josh Billings (1818-1885), in the 1870s knew all about laughter and the good it does. And he didn't need to go to college to learn it! Take a peek at his analysis of "*Laffing*" as he and his fellow Americans considered the subject over 100 years ago.

Josh liked to use phonetic spelling, a humorous form (back then) of comic literature, and it takes a few moments of reading to get used to it. But do stay with it because Old Josh is a jewel and worth the effort.

LAFFING.

Anatomikally konsidered, laffing iz the sensashun ov pheeling good all over, and showing it principally in one spot.

Morally konsidered, it iz the next best thing tew the 10 commandments.

Theoretikally konsidered, it kan out-argy all the logik in existence.

Analitikally konsidered, enny part ov it iz equal tew the whole.

Konstitushionally konsidered, it iz vittles and sumthing tew drink.

Multifariously konsidered, it iz just az different from ennything else az it is from itself.

Pyroteknikally konsidered, it is the fire-works of the

soul.

Spontaneously konsidered, it iz az natral and refreshing az a spring bi the road-side.

Phosphorescently konsidered, it lights up like a globe lantern.

But this iz too big talk for me; theze flatulent words waz put into the dikshionary for those giants in knolledge tew use who have tew load a kannon klean up tew the muzzell with powder and ball when they go out tew hunt pissmires.

Laffing iz just az natural tew cum tew the surface as a rat iz tew cum out ov hiz hole when he wants tew.

Yu kant keep it back by swallowing enny more than you kan the heekups.

If a man *kan't* laff there is sum mistake made in putting him together, and if he *won't* laff he wants az mutch keeping away from az a bear-trap when it iz sot.

Sum pholks hav got what iz kalled a hoss-laff, about halfway between a growl and a bellow, just az a hoss duz when he feels hiz oats, and don't exackly kno what ails him.

Theze pholks don't enjoy a laff enny more than the man duz hiz vettles who swallows hiz pertatoze whole.

A laff tew be nourishsome wants tew be well chewed.

There iz another kind ov a laff which I never did enjoy, one loud busst, and then everything iz az still az a lager beer barrell after it haz blowed up and slung 2 or 3 gallons ov beer around loose.

There iz another laff whitch I hav annalized; it cums out ov the mouth with a noise like a pig makes when he iz in a tite spot, one sharp squeal and two snikkers, and then dies in a simper.

This kind ov a laff iz larnt at femail boarding-skools, and dont mean ennything; it iz nothing more than the skin ov a laff.

Genuine laffing iz the vent ov the soul, the nostrils ov the heart, and iz jist az necessary for helth and happiness as spring water iz for a trout.

Thare iz one kind ov a laff that I always did reckommend; it looks out ov the eye fust with a merry twinkle, then it kreeps down on its hands and kneze and plays around the mouth like a pretty moth around the blaze ov a kandle, then it steals over into the dimples ov the cheeks and rides around in thoze little whirlpools for a while, then it lites up the whole face like the mello bloom on a damask roze, then it swims oph on the air, with a peal az klear and az happy az a dinner-bell, then it goes bak agin on golden tiptoze like an angle out for an airing, and laze down on its little ed ov violets in the heart whare it cum from.

Thare iz another laff that noboddy kan withstand; it iz just az honest and noizy az a distrikt skool let out tew play, it shakes a man up from hiz toze tew hiz temples, it dubbles and twists him like a whiskee phit, it lifts him up oph from hiz cheer, like feathers, and lets him bak agin like melted led, it goes all thru him like a pikpocket, and finally leaves him az weak and az krazy as tho he had bin soaking all dy in a Rushing bath and forgot tew to be took out.

This kind ov a laff belongs tew jolly good phellows who are az helthy az quakers, and who are az eazy tew pleaze az a gall who iz going tew be married to-morrow.

In konclushion I say laff every good chance yu kan git, but don't laff unless yu feal like it, for there ain't nothing in this world more harty than a good honest laff, nor nothing more hollow than a hartless one.

When asked how old he was, an old Chinese replied, "Me full-bloom."

Many of us have wondered why retired folks give up their lifelong homes and move to desert places like Arizona, New Mexico and the like. Perhaps these observations by Dick Wick Hall, back in 1926, could help us understand it. Dick Wick Hall established his own town in the desert and called it Salome. He claimed that the population was 19 people and one frog named (what else?) The Frog. Born and raised in Salome where water was scarcer than hen's teeth, The Frog never learned to swim. The town worried that he'd fall into a bucket of water (when the town got one) and drown! At any rate, there is something "Salubrigous" and "Invigatory" in the Salome water and desert air.

Folks live a very long time in Salome. In fact, they started a cemetery many years ago but have never had anyone to put in it. They are figuring on shooting a visitor one day in order to get the cemetery going!

Dick Wick Hall was the editor and publisher of the town newspaper, "The Salome Sun," from which the following observations were taken. His philosophy of bygone days was wise, witty and just a touch nostalgic. Most senior citizens today can recall this type of writing as offerings of the balance and direction that kept Americans sane, wise and decent.

Back in 1968, Frances Dorothy Nutt assembled the best of Dick Wick Hall's writings and put them in a book titled, "DICK WICK HALL: Stories from The SALOME SUN" published by Northlands Press, Flagstaff, Arizona.

Golden Age: Thin on the top and not on the bottom.

Our new Private Grave Yard is now Open for Business and not only fills a Long Felt Want but it is a Public Improvement that the Town can be Proud of. We are Proud of it ourselves, as a Business Asset to the Paper. Two Delinquent Subscribers have already come in and Paid Up, after seeing and inquiring about What it was For. The first hole was dug by mistake, the time the Reptyle Kid laid out Wiggle Ear Watson and folks thought he was dead at first until he come to again' but it don't matter much because Our Cemetery is located as a Placer Mining Claim and the work will count for the Assessment required by law, and we can use the Hole for anybody that it Fits. The other Vacancy is waiting for Gila Monster Jake, who is about Ripe for Picking and Planting. No extra charge for services. It will be a Pleasure in some cases.

When I said that a Bump was just a Chuck Hole bottom side Up, I was talking about the County Roads and didn't mean the Bump some folks have on top of their Necks - even though Some of them don't Use it for anything but a Hole to Throw Chuck into three times a day.

Good Clothes and Good Neighbors both Wear Longest when they ain't Used Too Often.

A Placer Miner was in from Pinto Creek this week for Grub and Excitement and among other things bought a new pair of Shoes, which Squeaked so bad that Chloride Kate wouldn't let him stop at the Blue Rock Inne. She said he was a Stranger to her and from the Noise he made when he walked, she thought he was some Tourist with a Bad Case of the Asthma and she didn't want him dying on her hands.

The town has its own golf course too, and it is twenty-three miles of fairway. As you can imagine, it takes days to play around the course. But that's Salome for you! Here's one rancher's observation about the course.

Old Tutt Tuttle was in from his ranch the other day and Archie Bald Doveface took him out to show him the Greasewood Golf Course and try and talk him into subscribing for the paper, which he didn't do. I asked him what he thought of Golf and he said the World was sure going to the Devil and Folks must be Crazy, paying 75¢ for a little white ball and then spending Four Dollars for a Club* to try to knock it off into the Brush and Lose it and then have to hunt for half a day to find it, and then when you did find it, the dog goned fool knocked it off into the Brush again and Lost it.

*Remember...the time is 1920s.

Six Shooter Sims is our Conversationalist Two Gun Man and is Supposed to be Bad, according to his Talk and Reputation, which is Self Made. He ain't ever killed nobody since we come here, Twenty Five Years ago, but since so many Tourists commenced to go through here on their way to California, he has Scared a Good Many of them Almost to Death.

What For Folks come here for don't seem to Worrty Strangers near so much as Wondering Why they stay here when there is a Good Road leading Both Ways out of town. They don't stop to think that Most Folks don't stay here on account of the Climate or to Make Money but most generally because it is so Easy to Live here.

Out here in the Desert you Don't Need Much--and You Don't Get Much either--and after awhile you get so as you Don't Want much--and when you get that way there ain't Much Use in going somewhere else to starve to Death, and it is a Lot easier here than going to the trouble of moving, so we stay here.

Most of the time is spent going after the Mail in the morning and meeting the 9 o'clock Train at night, to be sure it gets through town all right. The rest of the time, if you are not too tired, you set around and Wait for Something that has Never Happened yet. A man can put in a good deal of time setting and looking out across the Desert, past miles and miles of Greasewood and through the wiggly heat waves at the sun burned Mountains in the distance, setting there just the same as you are, waiting for something to Happen.

After awhile you get so as you are just about the same as the Mountains, only they have set there a little longer than Most of us and are a little more Sun Burned - and they don't have to meet the 9 o'clock Train like we do. Whoever it was that said a Thousand Years is like a Day and a Day like a Thousand Years, he Knew his Cactus and said about all there is to say about the Desert.

An old geezer is one who can remember when the richest man in town owned a two-car garage.

Carl Goerch worked with radio and newspapers in North Carolina. He published a superb collection of his articles in a 1943 book titled, *"Down Home."* In one article, he listed many words that were and are in common use in other parts of the nation. Consider this explanation of "hush puppies," an article of food we all enjoy. And there are many other slang words, innovative and descriptive to a point bordering on poetic genius. See how many of these old-fashioned American words you know.

ODD WORDS AND EXPRESSIONS

During the thirty years that I have been a resident of North Carolina, I have constantly been running across words and expressions that I never have heard before. Some of these are used solely in this state: others are also heard in Virginia, South Carolina and Georgia.

Take the world "hush-puppy" for example. It's a kind of cornbread, fried in grease, and is mighty fine to eat, especially with fish. I believe the expression originated down in the lower part of Georgia, or the upper part of Florida. Negro fieldhands used to have fish fries. They'd sit around a fire, telling stores. Their dogs, hovering around, would smell the fish cooking and would start whining. One of the men would reach for a small piece of cornbread and throw it in the direction of the dogs with the admonition: "Hush, puppy!" and that's how the name is said to have started.

All-overs: To be nervous, as "I have the all-overs."
Antigodling: Criss-cross, or out of plumb.
Barning: To harvest tobacco.
Bless: To cuss. As "I'm going to bless him out."
Branch: A small stream of water.
Buss: A kiss.
Caved: To be delirious. As "He caved all night."
Check: A light lunch. As "A little check to eat."
Cooter: A turtle.
Cribber: A wind-sucking horse.

210

Fault: (As a verb). To blame. As "I didn't fault him for doing that."

Fernent: Beyond or opposite.

Gallery: A porch; particularly an up-stairs porch.

Goobers: Peanuts.

Go-poke: A traveling bag. Most frequently heard in Macon County, although used elsewhere as well.

Gross: To find fault or complain. As "What are you grossing about?"

Ground Peas: Peanuts.

Gumshot: A slingshot.

Hanker: To want; to desire.

Hassle: To pant. The lungs and heart are among the organs which form the haslet of animals; hence the usage.

Heading: Pillows. As "Have you enough heading?"

Heft: To feel the weight of an article.

Imitate: To look like. As "He imitates his father."

Latch pin: Safety pin.

Laying-by time: The off-season in farming operations.

Laying-off: Planning or intending. As "I've been laying off to do that."

Leather britches: Beans dried in the hull.

Mincy: Fastidious.

Mind: Heed, or attention. As "He paid me no mind."

Nannypod: Banana.

Nard: (Also Narr'd). Referring to a variety of homespun.

Nellify: To balk; to refuse to go forward.

Passle: Quite a number. As "A passle of young 'uns."

Peart: Lively, or in good health.

Pocosin: Swampy or marshy tract of land,t he rim of which is higher than the interior, thereby keeping the water from draining off.

Penders: Peanuts.

Plumb: Entirely. As "I plumb forgot."

Poke: A paper bag.

Pus: (Pronounced "bus"). A small bag, or a small "poke."

Ramps: Wild onions.

Red: To clean out or sort. As "I'm going to red out

this trunk."

Right much: Considerably; frequently. As "I see him right much."

Ruthers: Choice. As "I gave him his ruthers."

Sass: Garden vegetables.

Savannah: An open and uncultivated tract of land.

Scimption: A small quantity.

Stob: A stake.

Swivvet: Hurry. As "I'm in a terrible swivvet."

Take out: to unhitch horses and mules. Usually expressed as "taken out."

Tote: To carry.

Excerpts from *"Carolina Chats. 1944", "Down Home. 1943", and "Just For The Fun Of It. 1954."*, written by Carl Goerch, used with the permission of the Estate of Carl Goerch.

Worry is interest paid on trouble before it is due.

Carl Goerch published this story titled, *"The Zipper Story"* in 1937. It was a big hit, appearing in many newspapers across the land and, in translation, in France. Mr. Goerch achieved fame, if not fortune, from the article. He never revealed whether it was true. But, from the thrust of it, one would have to assume that the event really happened. Here it is, set at a time when the zipper was a recent invention.

It may sound funny to you and to me, but it was almost tragic to the people who were involved in the incident.

It happened in the State Theatre in Raleigh.

There's a certain gentleman in Raleigh (we'll call him Mr. Brown for the sake of convenience) who weighs well over 200 pounds. One night last week he went home to supper and found that his wife had prepared backbone and dumplings-a dish of which he is particularly fond.

So he sat down at the table and gorged himself until he could hold no more.

Then he suggested that they go to the State Theatre and see a picture. Mrs. Brown was agreeable, so down town they went.

They found seats at about the center of the theatre,

and after they had settled themselves comfortably, proceeded to enjoy the picture. Mr. Brown began to feel that his belt was too tight. Inasmuch as the theatre was dark, he didn't hesitate to unloosen it. But even then he didn't feel exactly right: there was still too much pressure around his middle.

He had on a pair of trousers with zippers down the front, so he reached down and ran the zipper-jigger down a few inches.

After that he felt fine and gave a huge sigh of relief as he prepared to enjoy the picture.

Everything went along fine, for ten or fifteen minutes, and then a lady, sitting on the same aisle, about three or four seats away, decided that she had seen all she wanted of the show and got ready to leave. The people sitting next to her obligingly rose in order to make way for her. When she approached Mr. Brown, he too rose to his feet. And then he suddenly remembered that his zipper was unfastened, so he reached down hurriedly to pull up the jigger.

When he did, he caught the lady's dress in the zipper and couldn't work the thing up or down to save his life.

She felt a tug at her dress and turned around to give him a hard look. She felt another tug, whereupon she leaned forward and hissed: "What are you trying to do?"

That attracted Mrs. Brown's attention. She turned to her husband and whispered hoarsely: "John, what are you trying to do to the lady?"

"Not a thing," whispered back John.

"He is, too," said the lady. "He's tugging at my dress."

Mrs. Brown half-way rose from her seat. "Turn her loose this instant!" she commanded. "Whatever in the world has come over you?"

"I can't turn her loose!" protested Mr. Brown.

"Why not?"

"Her dress is caught in my pants."

Mrs. Brown gasped, and so did the other lady. People sitting behind them were beginning to get impatient and there were cries of "Sit down!" and

"Down in front!"

Mr. Brown began to perspire freely. He tugged at the zipper for all he was worth, but the more he tugged, the more firmly the lady's dress became entangled in its meshes.

"What are you-all trying to do?" asked a gentleman sitting directly behind Mr. Brown.

"Her dress is caught in my pants!" hissed Brown.

"Good Lord," said the man behind, and after that he didn't say another word.

"Do something!" insisted the lady.

"I'm doing all I can." growled Mr. Brown, "but it's getting worse and worse all the time."

By that time everybody in the neighborhood was taking a keen and unholy interest in the proceedings.

"We'll have to go out in the lobby," finally said Mr. Brown.

"Together?" she asked.

"You're darned right-together," he told her. "Think I'm going to take off my pants and let you walk off with them?"

She agreed that there was nothing else to do but act upon his suggestion. Moving slowly toward the end of the aisle, she led Mr. Brown along with her.

Then they started toward the lobby. It was the side of her dress that had been caught in the zipper and so, while she was able to walk along all right by taking rather short steps, Mr. Brown had to go sideways, somewhat like a crab on the beach.

Folks sitting on the aisle almost fell out of their seats as they saw what was taking place. their eyes followed Mr. Brown and the lady as they waltzed in the direction of the lobby.

By the time they got there, both of them were so mad that they couldn't see straight. One of the ushers-after the situation had been explained to him-took them into a little sideroom, where Mr. Brown took out his knife and proceeded to do some effective work with it.

At last the lady was free. She shook down her dress, shook herself all over, gave Mr. Brown a final dirty look and sailed majestically out of the theatre.

Mr. Brown returned to his seat, where he had to

listen to Mrs. Brown's whisperings and also to the chuckles emanating from all the seats in his immediate neighborhood.

He sat through the rest of the show with his belt tightly fastened and with the zipper pulled all the way up, but the damage had already been done and he really didn't get much pleasure or enjoyment out of the picture.

If anybody wants a pair of pants with zipper attachments, I can tell him where he can get them at a very reasonable price.

He'll have to be a rather fat man, however.

Excerpts from *"Carolina Chats. 1944."*, *"Down Home. 1943."* and *"Just For The Fun Of It. 1954."*, written by Carl Goerch, used with the permission of the Estate of Carl Goerch.

Memo to the early American: Life is like riding a bicycle. You don't fall off unless you stop pedaling.

Can you remember when Ada Jones and Billy Murray sang, *"In the Shade of the Old Apple Tree?"* Did you see movies of Fatty Arbuckle? Ben Turpin? Keystone Cops? Do you remember the Hupmobile and the Stutz Bearcat? Well, even if you don't recall all of these treasurers of the past, you'll enjoy reminiscing with Carl Goerch, as if you did. It's a lovely reminiscence of days in North Carolina.

MEMORIES OF THE PAST

I've often heard it said that the first sure sign of getting old is when you begin to find more pleasure in thinking about the past than you do in considering present-day events. I couldn't help but think of this when I went to a picture show not long ago and saw a film that depicted scenes of the Gay Nineties era.

There's a lot of enjoyment in bringing back to mind some of the things we experienced many years ago and which have largely faded out of the picture. For instance:

I like to recall the days when we got up on a cold morning, grabbed our clothes and ran down to the kitchen to dress; when there was a wash-stand in the bed-room, with a huge bowl and pitcher on which flowers were painted, and when the thundermug was considered a most necessary article of furniture.

I enjoy envisioning the parlor as it was in boyhood days, with its hair-stuff furniture, its rubber plant and the picture of Granpa and Grandma hanging on the wall. She sat with her hands on her knees, and he stood behind her with one hand resting on her shoulder.

I'd like to see again the old plush album on the center table, the collection of shells on the what-not in the corner, and the stereoptican views of Niagra Falls, Fujiyama and Yellowstone Park. Also the phonograph with the beflowered horn, which you cranked by hand. The records were cylindrical in form, and a special brush was kept on hand so that they might be dusted off each time before playing. When you turned on the machine there was a lot of scratching, and then a voice would say "In the Shade of the Old Apple Tree, as sung by Ada Jones and Billy Murray. This is an Edison Re-cord."

Yes sir, when you begin to think about "the good old days," you sort of wish you could go back again to some of those things which now are only fond memories.

I'd like to go to church on Sunday and hear again a real honest-to-goodness, hell-fire-and-brimstone sermon, with the preacher paying his respects to those sinners who participated in dancing, card-playing, going to theatres and indulging in other worldly amusements.

I'd like again to be a member of Jackson Engine Fire Company No. 1, and join the other fellows in pulling the big hose cart to fires. There was one fat member, name of Lefty Powers, who stumbled one night, fell flat on his stomach, and sixteen men and the cart ran over him. He didn't like it, so he resigned the following day.

I'd like to have another watch-fob-made of shoe-laces...peg-top trousers that were so narrow at the bottoms you could barely get your feet through them, and so wide at the top that they billowed in the wind like a balloon getting ready to rise...also the long coat that came almost to your knees...and patent-leather shoes you fastened with a button-hook. What a thrill it would be to go to the beach and see some women wearing stockings, and skirts that came to their knees! And on rainy days I'd like to stand in front of McCutcheon's Hardware Store and watch the ladies go by, raising their long skirts and displaying two or three inches of ankle.

I'd like to walk down the street and hear someone holler: "Oh, you kid!" and "Twenty-three, skidoo!" And hear folks whistling "Everybody's Doing It," "Wait 'Til the Sun Shines, Nellie," and "A Bicycle Built for Two."

I'd like to go to the movies one time more and look at the silent pictures. And wouldn't it be great to see on the screen again such actors as John Bunny, Lillian Walker, Fatty Arbuckle, Ben Turpin and the Keystone Cops!

I get quite a thrill, too, when I think of Old Man Weeks. We used to have street lights that burned when two pieces of carbon were in contact with each other. Arc lights, I believe they were called. Old Man Weeks would drive all over town in a horse and dilapidated shay, pulling down the lamps, throwing away the worn-out carbon and putting in new sticks.

And then, too, there was Old Man Foley, who drove a street-sprinkling cart to help lay the dust, because we had very few paved streets in those days. What a delight it was to walk along behind the cart and let the water spray all over you!

Another well-known character was Uncle Rufe Thomas, who drove the ice wagon down our street. It had a little step behind. Sometimes there would be as many as five or six kids on that step, snitching small pieces of ice out of the wagon. Uncle Rufe didn't care- so long as we didn't take big pieces.

I like to think back on Fulcher's blacksmith shop and watch Henry Fulcher shoe horses...Lord, I can almost smell the place right now; and almost hear the clink, clink, clink as he pounded a red-hot shoe with his big hammer. One day, while I was watching him, a big gray mare hauled off and kicked him in the stomach. Just as soon as he could get his breath back, Henry swore for five minutes without stopping or repeating himself.

The old livery stable, and the harness shop with the big wooden horse out in front also are vivid memories, to say nothing of the cigar-store with its wooden Indians.

When I left school and started work, I got my dinner at noon in a down-town restaurant. I usually got soup, some kind of meat or fish, two vegetables, bread and butter, coffee and dessert, and it cost me 25 cents per meal.

I'd like again to have the experience of having Mr. John Crenshaw stop and invite me to ride in his new automobile. It was an Oldsmobile, with a curved dashboard in front, and you steered it by using a long handle. The motor was underneath the seat and was cranked from the side. I remember the early speed law in our town was eight miles an hour, and there was quite a fight when it was proposed to raise it to ten miles an hour.

I'd like to see again the old Maxwell-Grisco automobile, or a Hupmobile, Haynes-Apperson, Winton, Locomobile or Stutz Bearcat. And if I had an opportunity of riding just once in them, I'd like to put on a long duster, big gauntlets and a cap with goggles appended thereto.

Yes, when you stop to think about it, there are a lot of things which we took as a matter of course in our younger days, but they seem remarkably beautiful, interesting, exciting and worthwhile now.

Excerpts from "Carolina Chats. 1944", "Down Home. 1943", and "Just For The Fun Of It. 1954.", written by Carl Goerch, used with the permission of the Estate of Carl Goerch.

The stories that comprise *"Tall Tales of the Devil's Apron,"* by Herbert Maynor Sutherland, are set in the extreme southwest part of Virginia, an isolated area - even today it remains that way - that has given rise to some of the most delicious folktales in all America. Here are two stories that deal with older folks in a way the reader may find surprising.

UNCLE IRY'S TRANSMIGRATION

It remained for Brandy Bill to tell the tale to end all tall tales of the Devil's Apron. As best I can recall it went something like this:

"Oncle Iry an' A'nt Nicey Dutton had done spent most of their lives on their leetle twenty-acre farm up thar ferninst the Kaintucky line. They had brung up a whole passel of young'uns, but in the due cou'se of time they all got married an' moved a-way whar they could find jobs.

"So them two ol' people was left thar all a-lone, but that didn't seem to trubble 'em much. All they ever knowed was hard work, an' they managed to git a-long jest a-bout like they allus had. Some of the young'uns tried to git 'em to come an' live with 'em, but Oncle Iry an' A'nt Nicey jest wouldn't leave the ol' homeplace.

"As time passed Oncle Iry got to thinkin' a leetle a-bout hisself an' whut might be a-head of him. He knowed that he was a-gitten' a-long in years, an' mebbe didn't have much more time left. He never had been much of a feller to go to meetin's, an' he hadn't never give much thought to re-ligion, er whut might happen to him in the worl' to come.

"So he got down his ol' Bible, an' started to readin' it at night. He read it from kivver to kivver, an' atter that he hunted a-roun' amongst his neighbors an' sich, an' he read 'em all. Then he got aholt of a book that told a-bout some heathen country whar they be-lieved that the soul of a man would come back to this worl' atter he died an' it'd be in the body of some animal er t'other. I fergit now whut they called this hyer be-lief."

"Transmigtation of Souls," I interrupted. "The theory of the Hindoos in India."

"That's it," agreed Brandy Bill. "Anyhow Oncle Iry he read that book plum through an' one night whilst him an' A'nt Nicey was a-settin' afore the fire he finished it, an' then he turned to A'nt Nicey and says:

"'Nicey, I've been a-radin' this hyer book an' it tells as how the soul of a man atter he dies come back ag'in in the form of some livin' critter. Now, I be-lieve this book, an' when I die I want ye should bury me up thar on that hill whar we put our two babies, an' then I want ye to watch all the lettle critters that come to this farm. I'm astin' ye to keep a eye on all the lettle pigs an' calves, an' chickens, an' pups, an' ever'thing, an' ef'n I can, I'll come back to ye, Nicey.'

"She promised him she'd do that, an' not long atter that Oncle Iry got sick an' died. She had him buried in their lettle graveyard up thar on the hill, an' then fer a year she kept a close watch on the lettle pigs an' chickens, an' kittens an' sich, but she didn't see nary a sign of Oncle Iry.

"She got to worryin' a-bout that, an' she had done give up jest a-bout all hopes of ever seein' him ag'in in any form er animal. Then one day somebody told her a-bout a woman-name of Smith-that could talk with the sperrits of the de-parted. This woman lived down thar in Ohio acrost the river frum Catlettsburg, Kaintucky, so A'nt Nicey got on a train an' went down thar.

"She found somebody to show her whar at this sperrit woman lived, an' she went up an' knocked at the door. A voice told her to come in, an' she said that when she got inside the house, it was a skeery-like place, all hung with black curtains a-roun' the walls, an' thar wasn't no place to set down. By that time A'nt Nicey said she was a-gittin' purty shakey in the knees.

"A-bout this time the sperrit woman come through them curtains, an' A'nt Nicey told her as how she wanted to speak with the sperrit of her de-parted husban'. The Smith woman she p'inted towarge a table that stood in the middle of the room, an' on it was a horn a-bout six inches wide acrost the mouth an' mebbe two foot long."

"'Go over thar an' pick up that horn,' says the sperrit woman, 'an' ef'n it gits heavy in you're han's, it means that the sperrit of the de-parted is ready to talk to ye.'

"A'nt Nicey sorty sidled over thar, an' picked up that horn. It looked like it was empty, but purty soon it started to git heavy like somebody was a-pourin' melted lead in it. A'nt Nicey she gripped that horn plum tight to keep frum drappin' it an' helt it up ag'inst her bosom.

"Then sudden-like thar come a voice outta that horn,

an' it was the voice of Oncle Iry.

"'Howdy, Nicey!'

"'Howdy, Iry! How air ye?' gasped A'nt Nicey.

"'Jest as fine as frawg-h'ar, Nicey. I wisht ye could be hyer with me. It's the purtiest place ye ever seed-jest wide, rollin' medders as fur as ye can see, an' the grass knee-high ever'whar. The leetle flowers air a-noddin' of their leetle' heads, an' the leetle birds air a-singing' of their leetle songs, an' all of my com-pan-yuns air fe-male, an' they're jest a-standin' a-roun a-lookin' me with their big soulful eyes-.'

"'But Iry,' gasps A'nt Nicey, plum flabbergasted, 'I didn't figger as how they let sich goin's-on be done up thar in Heaven.'

"'Heaven!' snorted Oncle Iry. 'Who said anything a-bout heaven? I'm a penny-ryal bull on a blue grass farm in Kaintucky. Moo-o-o-o!'"

SOPHYGENE and HER HALF-BROTHERS

I had started fishing down on Pound River the other afternoon when I happened to run into the boys from the Devil's Apron gathered at Dutton's store. They were engaged in an animated discussion on some subject, and I walked over and joined them to hear the news.

"Well, what brought all of you fellows out today?" I queried, when they halted their conversation.

"Ye got hyer jest a leetle late," declared Little "Bijie with a grin. "We was all at the weddin' at the Hard-Rock meetin'-house a leetle while ago, an' we jest drapped by hyer to git a leetle eatin' terbacker an' a few things like that."

"A wedding!" I ejaculated. "Who got married?"

"That youngest gal of Dooless Dave Farmer's-the one they call Sofygene," explained Brandy Bill. "She got married up with ol' Hop Hill's son, Oval."

"A church wedding?"

"Shore, an' they done it up in style," Brandy Bill assured me. "Good 'Lige he married 'em, an' they're a-havin' a big in-fare dinner at Dooless Dave's this evenin'. They didn't in-vite none of us fellers."

"Some of the boys was a tellin' of a tale up thar at

the meetin'-house that kinda tickled me," continued Brandy Bill with a twinkle in his eyes. "Ye know, ol' Dooless Dave he has allus been a-doin' ever'thing he could to keep that gal frum gittin' married. Him an' his ol' woman had done raised a passel of young'uns, but all of 'em had got married an' left home but Sofygene.

"Now, I don't have to tell ye fellers hyer on the Apern that Sofygene was mighty purty-just a-bout the purtiest that was ever seed in all these parts. She wasn't more'n fifteen when she had all the boys a-buzzin' a-roun' like flies a-roun' the mo-lasses jug. Fer a year mebbe it looked like she couldn't make up her mind an' then she slowed down an' started to goin' steddy with Oval.

"But Dooless Dave's ol' woman was ailin' most of the time an' wasn't able to do much of the work a-bout the place. An' Dooless Dave was too lazy to work so he figgered he'd be in a bad shape ef'n he lost Sofygene. He'd either have to go to work hisself am' mebbe do all the cookin' an all, er hire somebody to do it.

"Frum whut I'd allus heerd, Sofygene was a mighty good cook, an' Dooless Dave he aimed to keep her home re-gyardless. When he seed that she was a-gittin' plum thick with Oval, he de-cided that it was time that he was a-doin' somethin' a-bout it. So he tuck Sofygene to one side an' says to her:

"'Honey, air ye an' Oval a-fixin' to git married?'

"'I reckon we air,' she says with a giggle.

"'Ye can't do that, Honey,' he tells her in a whisper. 'It's ag'inst the teachin's of the Bible. Ye see, Oval's yore half-brother.'

"Wall, that put the skids under Oval right plum quick, an' a leetle later she started courtin' up a storm with Cal Collige, one of Bizz'ness Bill's boys. Dooless Dave he seed how that was progress', an' he was plum pleased with hisself on how he got rid of Oval so he figgered on tryin' the same trick ag'in. An' it shore e-nough worked a secon' time when he told her that Cal Coolige was her half-brother, too.

"Sofygene she looked a-roun' an' purty soon her an' a boy frum over thar a-bout town was a-sparkin' to beat the band. An' Dooless Dave he kept a clost watch on her an' this boy by the name of Higgins, an' when it looked like they was a-goin' to git hitched, he tells her that this Higgins boy was a-nuter of her half-brothers.

"Right thar was whar Sofygene blowed up. She told Dooless Dave that ef'n he was the pappy of all of the boys in the state, she was a-goin' over in Kaintucky, an' git her a man. Dooless Dave he didn't say nothin', but he shore wasn't aimin' to let her git a-way ef'n he could help it. He still figgered he'd pulled a mighty smart trick.

"But Sofygene she went straight to her mammy an' told her a-bout her pappy a-claimin' to be the daddy of all of the boys she went with. Dooless Dave's wife she set thair in her rockin' chair an' lissened to the story without sayin' a word. Then she sorty smiled an' patted Sofygene's hand.

"'Sofygene,' she says soft-like, 'Ye go a-head an' git married to the boy ye like the best. It wouldn't be no sin even ef'n he was the pappy of all them boys bekaze, Honey, ye ain't no kin to yore pappy.'"

Life was not easy at Devil's Apron, for men, children and certainly not for the women folks. The very first time that Herbert Sutherland came to the place, he was eyed with suspicion by a group of men sitting on the porch of the house he approached. They all made moonshine, of course, and didn't know whether or not he was a federal agent. Finally, to break the ice, he told them he was hungry and would appreciate a bit to eat. One of the men called to his wife plowing the field behind a mule, "Old woman, come feed this man." She came, prepared a wonderful meal and Mr. Sutherland tried to talk to her while he ate, describing the countryside in glowing tones. "Must be a wonderful place to live," he said.

"Wonnerful, huh!" she snorted, "It's shore fine fer men and dawgs but it's pyore hell on mules and wimmin."

Wife to her elderly husband at dance, "Waltz a little faster, dear, this is a rumba."

Josh Billings had wonderful observations about most aspects of American life. Here are a few more of his sayings about us old folks. You will understand why his contemporaries called him the American Ecclesiastices.

When i see an old man marry a yung wife, i consider him starting out on a bust, for I am reminded uv the parable in the Bible, about new wine, and old bottles.

Old age iz covetous, bekauze it haz larnt bi experience, that the best friend a man haz in this wurld, iz hiz pocket book.

Three skore year an ten iz the time allotted to man, and it iz enuff. If a man kant suffer awl the misery he wants in that time, he must be numb.

The devil iz the father ov lies, but he failed tew git out a patent for hiz invenshun, and hiz bizzness iz now suffering from competishun.

A cheerful old man, or old woman, is like the sunny side ov a wood-shed, in the last of winter.

Cheerful old girls are the bridesmaids ov society.

Some folks az they gro older, gro wizer; but most folks simply grow stubborner.

The man who wrote, "I would not liv always, I ask not tew sta," probably never had been urged sufficiently.

"On A Slow Train Through Arkansas," by Thomas W. Jackson, was one of the biggest selling books in America at the turn of the century. Published in 1904, in cheap paperback, it was sold by "train butchers" on all passenger railroad cars. These "butchers" or salesmen roamed the cars with baskets of these hilarious joke books that helped the passengers pass the time on the prolonged trips across country.

Here we present a selection from Jackson's first book and his best-seller. Corny? Sure. Funny? It's still funny. Great literature? As Thos Jackson would be the first to admit: That it ain't. And yet it sold hundreds of thousands of copies!

ON A SLOW TRAIN THROUGH ARKANSAS

You are not the only pebble on the beach for there is a little rock in Arkansaw. It was down in the state of Arkansaw I rode on the slowest train I ever saw. It stopped at every house. When it came to a double house it stopped twice. They made so many stops I said, "Conductor, what have we stopped for now?" He said, "There are some cattle on the track." We ran a little ways further and stopped again. I said, "What is the matter now?" He said, "We have caught up with those cattle again." We made pretty good time for about two miles. One old cow got her tail caught in the cow-catcher and she ran off down the track with the train. The cattle bothered us so much they had to take the cow-catcher off the engine and put it on the hind end of the train to keep the cattle from jumping up into the sleeper. A lady said, "Conductor, can't this train make any better time than this?" He said, "If you ain't satisfied with this train, you can get off and walk." She said she would, only her folks didn't expect her till the train got there. A lady handed the conductor two tickets, one whole ticket and a half ticket. He said, "He's a man. Under twelve, half fare, over twelve, full fare." She said, "He was under twelve when we started."

The news agent came through. He was an old man with long gray whiskers. I said, "Old man, I thought they always had boys on the train to sell the pop corn, chewing gum and candy." He said he was a boy when he started. They stopped so often one of the passengers tried to commit suicide. He ran ahead for half a mile, laid down on the track, but he starved to death before the train got there.

We had a narrow escape of being killed. Just as we got on the middle of a high bridge the engineer discovered it was on fire, but we went right across. Just as the last car got over, the bridge fell. I said, "Conductor, how did we ever get across without going down?" He said, "Some train robbers held us up."

The conductor collected half fare from a lady for her little girl. It made her so mad she asked the conductor what that said on his cap. He said, "Train conductor." She said it ought to be "Train robber." He said he only took what was fare.

There was a lady on the train with a baby. When the conductor asked her for her ticket, she said she didn't have any, the baby had swallowed it. The conductor punched the baby.

There were three kinds of passengers who rode on that train. First class, Second class and Third class. I said, "Conductor, what is the difference between the First class and Third class passengers, they are all riding in the same car?" He said, "Just wait a while and I will show you." We ran a little ways and stopped again. The conductor came in and said, "First class passengers, keep your seats; Second class passengers, get off and walk; Third class passengers, get off and push."

The conductor was the tallest man I ever saw. I said, "Conductor, what makes you so tall?" He said it was because he had had his leg pulled so often. He said he was born in the top of a ten story building. He came

226

high, but they had to have him.

He said he had been running on that road for thirty years and had only taken in one fare, that was the World's Fair.

An old lady said to the porter, "Are you the colored porter?" He said, no, he wasn't colored he was born that way. She said, "I gave you a dollar, where is my change?" He said, "This car goes through; there is no change."

There was a Dutchman on the train, he was trying to ride on a meal ticket. The conductor told him he would have to pay his fare. He said, "How much does it cost to ride to the next station?" The conductor said, "Thirty cents." The Dutchman said, "I will give you twenty-five." The conductor told him it would cost him thirty. The Dutchman said, "Before I will give more than twenty-five I will walk." The conductor stopped the train and put him off. The Dutchman ran ahead of the engine and started to walk. The engineer began to blow the whistle. The Dutchman said, "You can vissel all you vant, I wont come back."

There was an old man and woman on the train by the name of Jessup. There happened to be a place where the train stopped by the name of Jessup's Cut. The old man went to the car ahead. When the brakeman came in and hollered, "Jessup's Cut!" the old woman jumped up and hollered, "My God! who cut Jessup?"

They ran a little ways further and stopped again. Somebody said, "Conductor, what have we stopped for now?" He said, "We have reached the top of the hill. It is now downgrade; we will make a little better time and have an entire change of scenery." And so we did.

The stations were so close together when they stopped at one they had to back up to whistle for the next.

The conductor told a fellow that the next place was where he got off. He said, "Which end of the car shall I get off of?" The conductor said, "Either one, both ends stop."

There was a young fellow on the train. He couldn't get a seat. He was walking up and down the aisle and swearing. There was a preacher in the car. He said, "Young man, do you know where you are going, sir? You are going straight to Hell." He said, "I don't give a darn; I've got a round trip ticket."

The brakeman came in and hollered, "Twenty minutes for dinner!" When the train stopped we all rushed for the dining-room. I ordered two soft boiled eggs. When the waiter brought them in, she opened one and said, "Shall I open the other?"

I said, "No, open the window."

She said, "Ain't the eggs all right?"

I said, "Yes, they are all right, but I think they have been mislaid."

One fellow in the excitement drank a cup of yeast thinking it was buttermilk, He rose immediately.

The waiter was handing me my coffee just as the conductor was hollering, "All aboard." She slipped and fell and spilled the coffee down my back. When she got up she said, "Excuse me, will you have some more?"

I said, "No, you can bring me an umbrella."

Pretty soon they hollered out, "Skeetersville!" That was my town where I got off. I saw a sign that read "Hotel." I went over and registered.

Skeetersville was a very appropriate name for the place, for the musquitors was all there. They would come around and look on the register to see what room you had. The landlord told me he had just adopted a new set of rules. He handed me a list of them. They read something like this:

If you want the bellboy, wring a towel.

If you get hungry during the night; take a roll in bed.

Base-ball players wanting exercise will find a pitcher on the table.

If you want to write take a sheet off the bed.

If you find the bed to be a little buggy and you have a nightmare, just hitch the mare to the buggy and ride off.

Guests will not be allowed to tip the waiters, as it is liable to cause them to break the dishes. (I promise you there was no dishes broken while I was there.)

Married men without baggage will leave their wives in the office.

Old and feeble gentlemen will not be allowed to play in the halls.

They gave me a room on the first floor, that is from the roof. It was one of those rooms when you rent it the roof uses it. When I went to bed I had a creeping sensation come over me. I got up and told the landlord that there were bugs in the bed. He said there wasn't a single bedbug in the house! I told him that he was right about it, they were all married and had large families.

The following story is from the delightful, revealing collection of Virginia folktales told by Herbert Maynor Sutherland in his superb book, "*Tall Tales of the Devil's Apron,*" published in 1970 by Commonwealth Press of Radford VA.

KING SOLOMON'S DIET

"That shorely was a powerful sermon ye preached up at the meetin'-house last Sunday," complimented Brady Bill to Good 'Lige as the latter joined our circle around the stove at the grist-mill last Saturday afternoon. There was a chorus of affirmative grunts from the others, but Good 'Lige merely nodded his thanks.

"Ye know," continued Brandy Bill after a brief silence, "ol' King Solomon must a-been much of a man - a-doin'all of them things that the Good Book says he done."

"An' that's the gos-pel truth!" ejaculated Little 'Bijie with enthusiasm. "He shore must a-been a plum on-usual sort of a feller that could build him a temple, an' run his army, an' hold cou't to try folks fer evil-doin', and still make ever'body happy. It's no wonder they called him the wisest man that ever lived."

"Wall now, I don't know a-bout that," spoke up Business Bill, shaking his head. "Him a-marryin' up with a thousan' wimmin thataway don't look to me like he had much sense. He'd ort to a-knowed that one was a Gawd's plenty."

"Say, Good 'Lige!" called Little 'Bijie. "Do ye think

he reely had a thousan' wives at the same time er was he jest braggin' a leetle or somethin'?"

"It's writ down thar in the Book in black an' white," replied the old preacher emphatically. "All of ye heerd me read it last Sunday word fer word an' line fer line."

There was a silence for a full minute, and then Business Bill cleared his throat.

"King Solomon must a-been a rich man, too, er he couldn't a-kept that many wimmin. I'd shore hate to turn a thousan' wimmin' loose in one of these big dee-part-ment stores an' then have to foot the bill. Come wintertime, it'd bu'st a millun-air jest to buy a pair of shoes for each one of 'em."

"Whar at did he git all his money nohow?" demanded Little 'Bijie a bit suspiciously.

"He had a few gold mines in Africa," I explained, proud of Biblical knowledge. "They were located in Ethiopia, I believe."

"Wall he shore did need 'em," growled Bad 'Lige. "I bet he had to work 'em double shif'."

"Like I was a-sayin'," persisted Little 'Bijie, "he shore must a-been a-bu'stin' out with wisdom ef'n he knowed how to keep the peace betwixt a thousan' wimmin. Ol' Tucker Floyd he had him jest two wives, an' they fit an' pulled ha'r all over the place."

"I've jest been a-wonderin'," said Business Bill, again pushing his views into the conversation, "how he managed to feed 'em. Take a thousan' people thataway an' they can eat a powerful lot of vittels ef'n he fed 'em three squar' meals a day. Must a-had him a whale of a big cookstove in that thar palace."

"Whut did they eat mostly back in King Solomon's time?" queried Little 'Bijie. "I mean did they raise corn an' 'taters an' beans an' sich? I know they had sheep, but a feller can't eat mutton all the time."

"I think I've read somewhere that they ate locusts and wild honey," I ventured uncertainly.

"Ye mean them seventeen-year locusts like we've got?" Little 'Bijie's brows were deeply creased. "Must a-ben a hell of a long time betwixt meals."

"Ye've got yore Bible mixed up a leetle," Good 'Lige corrected me softly. "It was John the Babtis' that et the locusts an' wild honey. That's in the New Testy-ment, an' not in King Solomon's time."

Undaunted, I continued to diseminate my store of information.

"I have heard that one of the favorite foods that the old Sheiks of Arabia were accustomed to serving in their harems was a baby camel boiled in milk. It was said that this diet kept the complexions of the women as pink and beautiful as the clouds at the first blush of dawn."

"Ye don't say!" murmured Little 'Bijie wonderingly. "Wall, I'm afeard that'd be jest a leetle too rich fer Snowdy Jane's blood."

"Comin' back to them locusts," interrupted Business Bill, "how do ye reckon they cooked 'em? Fried or b'iled er roasted?"

"I imagine they fried them," I explained. "They consider fried bees quite a delicacy in those countries over there."

"Fried bees an' baby camels b'iled in milk!" exploded Business Bill with a shrug. "King Solomon must a-been bad in need of them thousan' wimmin ef'n he'd put up with sich as that."

"All that don't make me no never-mind," said Little 'Bijie. "I don't keer whut them thousan' wimmin had fer breafas'. Whut I want to know is whut they fed to King Solomon."

Here's a few more sayings and aphorisms of Josh Billings.

One ov the privileges ov old age seems tew giv advise that nobody will phollow and relating experiences that everybody distrusts.

I luv tew see an old person joyful, but not kickuptheheelsful.

When we are yung, we change our opinions tew often. When we are old, tew seldum.

Let him go, mi son, an ancient father said tew hiz boy, who had caught a yung rabbit, and when he gits bigger, ketch him again. The boy did az he waz told, and haz been looking fer that rabbit ever since.

Thare iz but very phew men whoze wisdum lasts them their lives out.

Well, it's time to shut down this chapter of fun, and we can think of no better, more fitting and pleasant way to do it than to include another wonderful "essay" by that national treasure, the comedian that Abraham Lincoln thought the best judge of human nature since Shakespeare - the one and only Josh Billings. Here he is to tell us about the Joy of The Kiss - back in the 1860s!

KISSING.

I hav written essays on kissing before this one, and they didn't satisfy me, nor dew I think this one will, for the more a man undertakes tew tell about a kiss, the more he will reduce his ignorance tew a science.

Yu kant analize a kiss enny more than yu kan the breath ov a flower. Yu kant tell what makes a kiss taste so good enny more than yu kan a peach.

Enny man who kan set down, whare it is cool, and tell how a kiss tastes, haint got enny more real flavor tew his mouth than a knot hole haz. Such a phellow wouldn't hesitate tew deskribe Paridise as a fust rate place for gardin sass.*

The only way tew diskribe a kiss is tew take one, and then set down, awl alone, out ov the draft, and smack yure lips.

If yu kant satisfy yureself how a kiss tastes without taking another one, how on arth kan you define it tew the next man.

I hav heard writers talk about the egstatick bliss thare waz in a kiss, and they really seemed tew think they knew all about it, but these are the same kind ov folks who perspire and kry when they read poetry, and they fall to writing sum ov their own, and think they hav found out how.

I want it understood that I am talking about pure emotional kissing, that is born in the heart, and flies tew the lips, like a humming bird tew her roost.

I am not talking about your lazy, milk and molasses kissing, that daubs the face ov enny body, nor yure savage bite, that goes around, like a roaring lion, in search ov sumthing to eat.

Kissing an unwilling pair ov lips, iz az mean a viktory, as robbin a bird's nest, and kissing too willing ones iz about az unfragant a recreation, az making boquets out ov dandelions.

The kind ov kissing that I am talking about iz the kind that must do it, or spile.

If yu sarch the rekords ever so lively, yu kant find the author ov the first kiss; kissing, like mutch other good things, iz anonymous.

But thare is such natur in it, sitch a world ov language without words, sitch a heap ov pathos without fuss, so much honey, and so little water, so cheap, so sudden, and so neat a mode of striking up an acquaintance, that i consider it a good purchase, that Adam giv, and got, the fust kiss.

Who kan imagin' a grater lump ov earthly bliss, reduced tew a finer thing, than kissing the only woman on earth, in the garden of Eden.

Adam wan't the man, i don't beleave, tew pass sich a hand. I may be wrong in mi konklusions, but if enny boddy kan date kissing further back, i would like tew see them dew it.

I don't know whether the old stoick philosophers ever kist enny boddy or not, if they did, they probably did it, like drawing a theorem on a black board, more for the purpose of proving sumthing else.

I do hate to see this delightful and invigorating beverage adulturated, it iz nektar for the gods. I am often obliged tew stand still, and see kissing did, and not say a word, that haint got enny more novelty, nor meaning in it, than throwing stones tew a mark.

I saw two maiden ladys kiss yesterday on the north side ov Union square, 5 times in less than 10 minnitts; they kist every time they bid each other farewell, and then immediately thought ov sumthing else they hadn't sed. I couldn't tell for the life ov me whether the kissing waz the effekt ov what they sed, or what they sed waz the effekt ov the kissing. It waz a which, and tother, scene.

Cross-matched kissing iz undoubtedly the strength ov the game. It iz trew thare iz no stattu regulashun aginst two females kissing each other; but i don't think thare iz much pardon for it, unless it iz done to keep tools in order; and two men kissing each other iz prima face evidence ov dead-beatery.

Kissing that passes from parent to child and back agin seems to be az necessary az shinplasters, to do bizzness with; and kissing that hussbands give and take iz simply gathering ripe fruit from ones own plumb tree, that would otherwise drop oph, or be stolen.

Tharefore i am driv tew konklude, tew git out ov the corner that mi remarks hav chased me into, that the ile ov a kiss iz only tew be had once in a phellow's life, in the original package, and that is when...

Not tew waste the time ov the reader, i hav thought best not tew finish the abuv sentence, hoping that their aint no person ov a good edukashun, and decent memory, but what kan reckolekt the time which i refer to, without enny ov mi help.

*vegetables.

234

10

BOOZE

and other

STUPIDITIES

Jones had spent forty years as a con man and he was a good one! It so happened that while he was casing a new town, he wandered into a bar. The bartender asked, "What'll you have?" and Jones ordered a whiskey and soda. He got it, drank it and turned to walk out.

"That'll be three bucks, Sir," the bartender said.

Jones turned a quizzical look on him. "Are you crazy," he said. "I came in here to rest my feet and you invited me to have a drink. Now I should pay for it?"

"What are you talking about," the angry bartender shouted. "We have a business here and we sell drinks, don't give 'em away."

"But you asked me to have a drink," Jones repeated.

A man at the end of the bar stood and said, "That's right, bartender. I was sitting here and distinctly heard you invite the man to have a drink. I'm a lawyer and I witnessed this entire matter."

The bartender swallowed hard, turned red-faced, and gritted out: "You win. Now both of you get the hell out of here and don't come back."

They left. But the next day Jones came back, looked around and soon the bartender saw him and yelled, "Hey mister, I told you never to come back here. Ever."

Jones said, "What are you saying? I've never in my life been in here before."

"The hell you say," the bartender yelled. "You came in here yesterday and cheated me out of a drink."

Jones stood tall, cleared his throat and with great

dignity said, "Bartender, I've never been in this place before...ever."

The bartender is confused now and realizes for a moment, then says, "Well, all I can say is you must have a double."

"That's kind of you," Jones said, "But go easy on the soda."

———

The elderly geezer from South Carolina liked his whiskey straight and old. He used to hold a glass of whiskey, then say, "I want you guys to blindfold me so's I won't see or smell the whiskey. Because if I see it or smell it, my mouth will water and dilute this good whiskey and I just purely do hate water in my booze."

———

An old codger who had had far too much to drink, got on the crosstown bus and started toward a seat, bumping passengers, stumbling and staggering to a seat where he sat down next to a dignified matriarch who sized him up, shook her head in disdain and said, "Sir, you are intoxicated and going straight...to...hell!"

The drunk staggered to his feet exclaiming, "Holy schmokes! I'm on the wrong bus-s-s!"

———

"Did you have any trouble meetin' the ladies at the dance, Zeke?"

"Nawp. I just opened the door marked 'ladies' and, by gosh, the room was full of 'em."

———

The government has just released the results of a multi-million dollar study. They report that older people would live a lot longer if they didn't die sooner.

———

His teeth are like the Ten Commandments - all broken.

Two old geezers decided to have a last fling in Chicago. They boarded the train, rode up there, got a nice room, and proceeded to get liquored up. They kept the door open and all evening people came in and out to drink with them.

Next morning when they awakened, one of them had a broken arm, a bandaged leg and head. One eye was black and there were numerous bruises all over his body. He asked his buddy, "How did I get in this fix?"

"Well," his friend replied, "You took bets that you could jump out of our window at this hotel, fly like a bird and come back to land safely on the window sill."

"You didn't let me do it, did you?" the damaged old boy asked.

"Let you do it? Hell, man, I lost thirty bucks betting that you could!"

"On the third day of the cruise it got so rough they had to lash Fred to the bar."

*Reprinted with permission of the **Saturday Evening Post***

The town drunk had pursued that distinction for fifty years until one day he passed a sign that read, "Ring bell for undertaker."

So he rang the bell and the caretaker opened the door. "What do you want, old man?" And the old buy replied, "I want to know why in the hell ya can't ring that bell y'self."

For many years a certain old codger had played piano at the most popular bar in town. Not much of a drinker, on this particular night he took a yearning for liquor. It was his 25th anniversary at the tavern. He had several drinks and, eventually, had to stagger to the bathroom where he relieved himself and walked back toward the piano in highly unsteady steps. But he made it. As he pulled the piano stool in position, an old lady came up to him and asked, "Old fellow, do you know your zipper is open and that your dingus is hanging out?"

"Not right...off...offhand," the old man replied unsteadily. "But if you'll jush hum a phoo bars...I'm shoor I'll 'member it."

An artist was painting a lovely landscape in the beautiful hills of southern Missouri, when an aged hill country farmer happened by and stopped to see the painting. "Hello," said the artist. "I see you, too, are a nature lover, enjoying he splendor of great skies, the lovely old colors of sunset, the bright golden orbs of sunrise, the utter loveliness of hills and valleys and trees and nutritious grass. You sense all this, don't you old timer?"

The old farmer shook his head and said, "Mister, I ain't had a drink in a dang near five years!"

And, to improve your memory, lend people money.

There was an old bum in a bar room,
	He sat there all day and got loaded,
The bartender threw him out in the street,
	Whereupon the old bum - exploded.

A reporter was interviewing the town's oldest man, who was 100 years old. "Why have you managed to live so much longer than others?" the reporter asked. "Have you done anything special that might have contributed to your longevity?"

"I figure I've lived this long because of my sober, steady, moderate life...no liquor, red meat or tobacco. And I'm in bed every night at 10 PM."

"Astonishing" the reporter remarked. "But what's all that noise I hear in the next room? I can hardly hear myself think!"

"Oh, don't worry about that. That's my daddy who always comes home drunk. He's been out all night."

Ben Franklin: "There are more old drunkards than old doctors."

There's an old barber in Carlinville who has shaved everybody, cut hair and trimmed beards for fifty years. He was quite a drinker. Well, one day a Methodist minister came into his barbershop for a shave. Of course, he smelled the whiskey breath and noticed with alarm the trembling hands. And the old barber did cut the minister's chin.

"I don't mind the cut, old fellow, but now you can see that from that cut what evil comes from drinkin' whiskey."

"Yes, Sir!" agreed the old barber. "And beyond that, drinkin' has sure made your skin tender."

The delivery man left the box at Uncle John's front door, where Uncle John, sitting on his porch, motion to him to put it. Huffing and puffing, the delivery man sat down to rest himself and said, "My, Sir, this sure is a nice place you got out here away from the hustle and bustle of town."

"Yep! It does me right good," the old fellow replied. "But I got to walk a mighty long ways to git me a shot of whiskey."

"Well, why don't you get yourself a jug of whiskey and keep it out here, near you?"

"Bad idea," the old man responded. "Whiskey don't keep worth a damn out here."

If you let a smile be your umbrella, you're gonna get awful wet.

The smart aleck asked a golden girl about the marks on her nose. "What caused 'em, Ma'am?"

"They were made by glasses," she replied haughtily.

"Well, fer gosh sakes, Ma'am, you oughta tilt your head back further; besides, booze pours easier thataway."

She was such a hot kisser that she melted all my gold teeth.

A man and wife are sitting at the bar, having a few quiet drinks before returning home. Near them sits an old drunk now deep in his cups. Suddenly the drunk cuts loose with a phenomenal belch. The sedate man near him, sitting with his wife, says, "How dare you belch like that before my wife?"

"I sure am sorry, mis-shter. I shimply dind't know shwas her turn."

Norman Seigel, in his late seventies went out on the town and didn't return home for dinner that night. This upset his wife, especially when he didn't come home until the next morning, drunker than a hog on sour mash. She finally got him undressed and put to bed after worming from him where he'd been the night before. Norman had been, he told her, "to the Nirvana Grill and Bar where the restrooms were all gold. The urinals and ever'thing, were sholid, just sholid gold. Ain't seen nothin' like it in all my born daysh!" Then he fell asleep.

That evening, overcome with curiosity, Norm's wife called the Nirvana Grill and Bar. "My husband was down at your place last night and he tells me that you have a restroom with gold appointments, gold urinals and all. Is that true or was he lyin' to me?"

There was a brief pause, then she heard the voice on the other end of the line call out, "Hey, Joe, I think I've got a line on that feller who pissed in your saxophone last night."

———————

Old Elijah Chase was known as a hard drinker but a steady and responsible one. And so when the boys were gathered at the town tavern and old 'Lije took a big glass of whiskey, then asked the bartender for an eye-dropper, everyone was curious. They were even more curious when 'Lije took the eye-dropper and put three, exactly three drops of water in the whiskey glass.

"Tell me, 'Lije," one of his buddies asked, "Why are you doing that?"

"Boys, I'll tell ya somethin'. I can still drink more whiskey than any of you fellers and hold it better, too. I've always been mighty proud of my ability to drink and hold my whiskey! But to tell ya the truth, fellers, I can't hold my water like I used to could!"

———————

No woman ever makes a fool out of a man...she merely directs the performance.

Two old guys were sitting in the lounge of the Chicago University Club. Each had a drink and they were content. "It sure is fine here," said one old fellow. "It's almost as good as sittin' in the grandstand at the Illinois State Fair and watchin' the automobile races."

"That's what you say," another oldster remarked. "But I figure it's like being in Yankee Stadium and watching the world series."

An old black man served their drinks, then said, "Has either of you two gents ever tried watermelon?"

My grandfather lived to be 95 and never needed glasses. But then lots of people drink from the bottle.

Two elderly widows, naive as could be, decided to take a trip to New York. There they went to the Waldorf Astoria Hotel, walked into the elegant dining hall and seated themselves. When the waiter appeared, one woman said, "My nephew told us about an elegant bit of appetizer he had here a few months ago. It came in a tiny glass with a tiny green olive that was covered, he said, with a delicious, crystal-clear sauce. We'll have two of those."

At the senior citizens' center, one old fellow, normally quiet and subdued, took a pint of whiskey out of his pocket and drank it. A short time later, he took another pint out and downed it, too. Well, as you might expect, he became frisky as a young kid. "Be your age, old man," a worker admonished him. "Settle down."

But the old guy continued his friskiness and took off after a young secretary. The worker grabbed him and said, "How can two pints of simple whiskey make you act so foolish?"

"Don't forget," the old man told him, "that two pints sure do make one c...cavort."

A really nice guy, passing an apartment house in the small hours of the morning, noticed an old man leaning limply against the doorway.

"What's the matter?" he asked. "Drunk?"

"Yep."

"Do you live in this house?"

"Yep."

"Do you want me to help you upstairs?"

"Yep."

With some difficulty he half dragged, half carried the drooping, grey figure up the stairway to the second floor.

"What floor do you live on?" he asked. "Is this it?"

"Yep."

Rather than face an angry wife who could take him for an accomplice, he opened the first door he came to and pushed the limp figure in.

The good guy then went downstairs. As he was passing through the vestibule he was able to make out the dim outlines of still another oldster - apparently in worse condition than the first one.

"What's the matter?" he asked. "Are you drunk, too?"

"Yep," was the feeble reply.

"Do you live in this house, too?"

"Yep."

"Shall I help you upstairs?"

"Yep."

The good Samaritan hauled the drunk to the second fellow, where this man said he lived. He opened the same door and pushed him in.

As he again reached the front door, he discerned the shadow of a third man, obviously worse off than the other two. He was about to approach him when the drunk stumbled out into the street and threw himself in the arms of a passing policeman.

"For Heaven's sake, off'cer," he gasped, "protect an old man from thish evil fellow. He's done nothin' al night long but carry me upstairsh and' throw me down th' elevator shaf'."

YOU'RE DRUNK

When your knees hit hard
And your head feels queer
And your thoughts rise up,
Like the foam on beer,
And the street moves around
As you stumble along,
And you start in singing
Some darn fool song-

When you see two glasses,
And there's only one,
And you're spending your "roll"
Just to get up a bun,
And you're "settin' 'em up"
To every rummy you meet,
And throwing your nickels
To the kids in the street-

When you start on a run
And you really can't stop,
And you get in a fight
With a big Irish cop,
When you get talking war
And you start in to brag,
And feel just as tough
As though you could wave a big flag-

When you get to your house,
And your head starts to swim,
And you wait for the milkman
To come let you in,
And you get inside
And you can't really think
Put your umbrella to bed
And sleep in the sink-
You're drunk, old man, you're drunk!

What's new...besides your teeth and hair?

244

The horse and mule live 30 years
And nothing know of wines and beers.
The goat and sheep at 20 die
And never taste of Scotch or Rye.
The cow drinks water by the ton
And at 18 is mostly done.
The dog at 15 cashes in
Without the aid of rum and gin.
The cat in milk and water soaks
And then in 12 short years it croaks.
The modest, sober, bone-dry hen
Lay eggs for nogs, then dies at 10.
All animals are strictly dry;
They sinless live and swiftly die;
But sinful, ginful, rum-soaked men
Survive for three score years and ten.
And some of them, a very few,
Stay pickled till they're 92.

                                          Anonymous

That soprano has a large repertoire. And that dress
doesn't help it any.

Be tolerant of those who disagree with you - after all,
they have a right to their stupid ridiculous opinions.

Mrs. Custer, elderly and unworldly, visited Chicago
for the first time. Before leaving home, a friend asked
him to visit a relative's grave. So, the first thing that
Mrs. Custer did was to visit the cemetery where the
friend's beloved was interred. There, she asked for the
whereabouts of the grave of a "Mister Edward Jones."

The caretaker consulted his records and said,
"Madam, we have at least fifteen Edward Jones' buried
here."

"I thought you'd tell me that, so I came prepared.
Here's his picture."

Year after year, the members of the Irish Grove Methodist Church had considered replacing the inadequate lighting in the sanctuary. This year they were determined to change the lights.

A self-appointed board had considered several alternatives and now proposed to the assembled congregation that a new chandelier be purchased at a cost of one thousand dollars.

Old Percy Boyer stood up, so excited he could hardly stand still. "Feller members!" he began, "I been acomin' to thiseyer church for nigh onto sixty years an' I ain't never had no cause to complain about things. Now you folks want to spend a p...p...pot full of money o n a c h a n d e . . . c h a n d e . . . l e e r. One...thousand...semolains! An' I know dadblamed well, same as you folks know it, that there ain't one single person, man or boy or woman or girl among us that ever played one or even knows how to play on o' them blamed things, so why waste the money?"

He's been drinking so much for so long, he looks like the first husband of a widow.

Norman was the laziest man in town. In all of his seventy-five years, he had never done a lick of work. One day his wife announced, "I'm so ashamed of us, of how we live. Your brother pays the rent. Your cousin buys our clothes. Your sister sends us food and my brother pays for our vacations..."

Norman replied, "You certainly ought to feel ashamed. You've got three brothers, too, and they never sent us one...single...penny."

Old Jeb McTavis was the town's single, most notorious miser. For example, he never rode the bus to work but always ran behind it thus saving himself one dollar a day. One day, when he felt like splurging, really letting go, he ran behind a taxi and saved ten bucks for himself.

I went on a vacation to forget things and when I opened my suitcase, I found out I'd succeeded!

The old Senator from North Carolina, Senator Sam Ervin, told some wonderful stories. There's the one about the North Carolinian who was about three ounces short of a quart. He was asked if he knew what country he lived in. "Nawsir," he replied. Then he was asked if he knew the name of his state. "Nawsir," he said. Finally, someone asked if he had ever heard of Jesus Christ. "Naw," he answered. "Well, then, have you ever heard of God?" another person asked. "Yawsir, I do believe ah have," he said, "Is his last name Damn?"

Pete is the town's laziest guy, and yet, he's a model husband...but not a working model!

Sam Jones had worked hard for thirty years and never taken a vacation. Finally, at age fifty, he took his first vacation to India! It was a wonderful experience and when it was time to return to the United States, he felt that he ought to send something, some memento, home to his father who was in his eighties. So he shopped around and finally bought a beautiful live peacock, a male with brilliant plumage. Assured that it would get to the United States in good shape, he mailed it home.

When he arrived home and asked his father how he liked the bird, the father said, "Delicious! Tasted just great!"

If you think time heals everything, try curing yourself waiting in your doctor's office.

Here's to those wonderful days of my life,
Spent in the arms of another guy's wife
...My Mother!

A DRUNKARD'S ODE

How well do I remember, 'twas in the late November,

I was walking down the street quite full of pride,

My heart was all a-flutter as I slipped down in the gutter,

And a pig came there and laid down by my side;

And as I lay there in the gutter, all too soused to even mutter,

A lady passing by was heard to say:

"One may tell a brute that boozes by the company he chooses,"

Hearing this the pig got up and walked away.

"The Playboy's Handbook" 1942

"He had a nap this afternoon."

ONE MOMENT, SIR, by Marione R. Nickles.
Reprinted with permission of **Penguin Books USA, Inc.**

R-E-M-O-R-S-E

The cocktail is a pleasant drink,
It's mild and harmless, I don't think.
When you've had one, you call for two,
And then you don't care what you do.

Last night I hoisted twenty-three
Of these arrangements into me;
My wealth increased, I swelled with pride;
I was pickled, primed and ossified.
     R-E-M-O-R-S-E!
Those dry martinis did the work for me.

Last night at twelve I felt immense;
Today I feel like thirty cents.
At four I sought my whirling bed,
At eight I woke with such a head!
It is no time for mirth or laughter-
The cold, grey dawn of the morning after.

If ever I want to sign the pledge,
It's the morning after I've had an edge;
When I've been full of the oil of joy
And fancied I was a sporty boy.
This world was one kaleidoscope
Of purple bliss, transcendent hope.
But now I'm feeling mighty blue-
Three cheers for the W.C.T.U.!
     R-E-M-O-R-S-E!
The water wagon is the place for me.

I think that somewhere in the game,
I wept and told my maiden name.
My eyes are bleared, my copper's hot;
I try to eat, but I can not;
It is no time for mirth or laughter -
The cold, grey dawn of the morning after.

George Ade

Talk about a nutty conversation! Take a look at this one.

It was midnight and the phone rang. The old man hopped out of bed, picked up the phone and said, "Yes-s-s?"

"Sir, is this one one one one?"

"Nope. Sure ain't. This here is eleven eleven."

"Are you dead sure this isn't one one one one?"

"Hell yes, Man. I've lived here thirty years. I oughta know. It's eleven eleven."

"Hey man, I'm sorry."

"That's OK. I had to get up anyway 'cause the damn phone was ringing."

Time waits for no man, but it sure does stand still for a woman of 60.

W. C. Fields was once asked, "What do you suppose your daddy would have said if he had known that you drink two quarts of booze a day?"

"He'd have tagged me a sissy," Fields replied.

A drunk and his equally inebriated buddy were seated at a bar.

"Whasha time?" asked the one drunk.

"Thash exactly right," said his buddy.

"Thanksh," replied the drunk.

He has pullman car teeth...one upper and one lower.

The drunk was arrested for driving down the wrong side of the one-way street. The cop asked him where in the devil he thought he was going.

The drunken guy admitted that he wasn't at all sure, "But wherever it is, I musht be d-d-damned late, 'cause everbody sheems to be comin' back already."

A fervid evangelist stomped into the frontier saloon and demanded quiet. Holding up his arms to get attention...and he got it...he yelled, "Don't you men know that drinkin' that vile and obnoxious stuff will send you straight to hell? So come along with me and all you sinners who hope to go to heaven come stand alongside me."

All came but one drunk. The evangelist yelled at him, "Hey, you, don't you want to go to heaven?"

"Nope. Sure don't," he yelled back.

"Honest injun, ya dern fool! Ya don't want to go to heaven when you die?"

"Oh, so that's it," the drunk yelled back. "When I *die*! I figgered you was makin' up a load now."

They tell the story in a State Street tavern, in Chicago, about the guy at the bar who was drinking martinis. The odd thing was that after each drink, he'd carefully eat all the glass and then set the stems in a neat row in front of him. After watching him down half a dozen drinks, and eat the glass, the bartender remarked to another customer, "That guy is plumb nuts, crazy, out'n his mind!"

"I sure do agree with that," the customer said. "He's leavin' the best part, them stems."

If you don't know what's up, you haven't been buying liquor lately!

A hillbilly's old wife sent him to town to get something to rid the place of moths that had troubled them. The druggist sold him a box of mothballs.

Months later, the hill man came into the drugstore, complaining that "them mothballs wouldn't work nohow, noway. Marthy and me we aimed carefully, too. But we ain't hit a single moth! Maybe you got a bigger size, like one of them pool table balls."

251

If such a hillbilly seems too stupid to be true, consider his son whose stinky feet really irritated the lady school teacher. She told the boy that he simply must put on a fresh pair of socks every day. This the boy did. But real soon, after only six days, he couldn't get his shoes on over the six pairs of sox.

An old man was really high and was riding home on the bus. As the bus moved, the old fellow tore pieces from his newspaper and threw them out the bus window.

"Hey old fellow, what are you doing, throwing those pieces of paper out the window?" another passenger asked.

"Don't you know. It scares tigers away."

Thinking to humor the old guy, the passenger said, "Hell, old man, there ain't any tigers out there!"

"Effective, ain't it!" said the old guy.

Doctor: "Which would you rather give up...wine or women?"
Patient: "It depends on the vintage."

"I notice that you use snuff," I said to the patient.

"Yes, it's excellent for skin rashes and dandruff."

"But you don't *have* skin rashes or dandruff."

"I know. Really works, doesn't it?"

Walter S. Feldman, M.D.

The most expensive vehicle to operate, mile for mile, is a shopping cart. And my wife took hers for a 1000-mile check up.

Old age: A condition that in no way limits a man in his learning new ways to be stupid. J.C. Salak.

252

The senior class at medical school was listening to a visiting physician's lecture on the local incidence of lead poisoning from paint. He pointed to a patient under observation-a small wrinkled man, well into his sixties. "Notice the lead line on the patient's gums," said the physician. "Now, if each one of you will step up and examine him..."

"Oh, that ain't necessary," munched the old man, as he removed a full set of dentures. "Here, just hand 'em around."

Charles Miller, M.D.

Mary Swanson helped herself to a couple of drinks before supper and her friend Maria asked, "I thought you'd quit drinking, Mary?"

"I did quit, but I'm having a bad time with insomnia."

"Oh, yes, I see. A couple of drinks help you sleep, right?"

"Not really, but when I have to stay up it doesn't bother me nearly as much!"

By the time a guy is rich enough to sleep late, he's too old to enjoy it.

Old Pete Brown and his buddy were staggering down the street and stopped before a liquor store. They saw a sign that stated, "DRINK CANADA DRY!"

"Hey! Look at that invitation," Pete said.

"Let's give it a try," said his buddy.

That same Pete Brown was having a wonderful time at his nephew's wedding reception, enjoying toast after toast after toast. His wife turned to him and said, "Pete, don't you think you'd better ease off on the whiskey, now?"

"Why?" Pete asked.

"Because it does seem to me that your face is beginning to blur."

Why does a woman say she's shopping when she hasn't bought anything?

Same reason a man says he's been fishin' when he hasn't caught anything!

Percy Smith should have retired from tending bar years ago but he loved his job and wouldn't quit. Well, one day a man as old as he came in, sat at the bar and said nothing. "Care for something? How about a drink?" Percy asked.

"Don't believe so," the man replied. "Tried whiskey once and didn't like it."

Twenty minutes later, Percy walked up to the man and said, "Mister, I'd sure like to give you something. How about a cigar?"

"No, sir! Thank you, but no. Tried it once and didn't like it."

Finally, after half an hour passed, Percy walked once again to the man at the bar and said, "Mister, we got a card game going in the back room and if you'd like to join the fellers, I'd be glad to take you back there."

"Thanks a lot," the man replied. "I tried cards once but didn't like it. I'll just sit here and wait for my son."

"An only child, I presume," said old Percy.

One day an old duffer walked into Percy Smith's bar and he seemed mightily confused. Percy asked him if anything was wrong and did he need help.

"I don't know...I don't know," the old geezer muttered. "Gosh! I never had nothing like that happen before...."

"What happened!" Percy asked.

"Well I put a quarter in the scale outside and the derned thing said I weighed one hour!"

"I understand you used to earn a salary that went into five figures?"

"That's right. My wife and four sons."

254

George suggested to his wife that they go into a bar and have a drink. She replied that it was only ten o'clock in the morning and that it was very bad for them to drink before noon. George said, "Heck fire, Susie, it's already two in the afternoon in India."

———————

Grandpa Peters walked to the bar and ordered his usual scotch and soda. "Do you remember me?" he asked the bartender.

"Don't think I do," said the bartender. "Should I?"

"I'd have thought so," Grandpa said. "I was in here a few months ago, couldn't pay for my drink and you threw me out. You broke my leg."

"Oh, I'm sure sorry about that," said the bartender.

"Don't bother to apologize," Granpa said, downing his drink, "because I'm afraid I'm going to have to trouble you again."

———————

You're a senior citizen when...you begin to feel on Saturday night the way you used to feel on Monday morning.

"Changing Times"

———————

You're well-seasoned if you can remember when both panhandlers and restaurant owners asked only a dime for a cup of coffee.

———————

For sure you're a golden ager if you can remember when it was easy to distinguish between a bathing beach and a nudist colony.

Al Spong

———————

Cliff Hathaway would get tough when he drank. But he never got down to fighting. He'd get out of it by saying something to get his drinking buddies laughing, like: "I'd like to kick him in the teeth, but why should I improve his looks?"

255

Grandpa Friedberg was from the small town of Jacksonville, Illinois. He took a long-delayed trip to New York and had a wonderful time. On his last night in the big city, he went into a bar, sat down and was soon joined by a young lady who sat next to him. Suddenly the girl stood up, shouting, "You scum! What do you mean propositioning me to go to your hotel room!"

Grandpa was really disturbed at this unprovoked outburst. He stood and walked to a table to avoid the angry comments and grim looks of the other people at the bar.

Soon the young lady walked up to him and said, "Gee, Mister, I hated to do that to you, but I'm doing a master's degree thesis in psychology and I needed to get your reaction to my putdown."

Grandpa Friedberg decided to teach her a lesson. He got to his feet, pointed his finger at the girl and shouted, "One buck for half an hour? You nuts? You ain't worth that kind of money in or out of bed."

You're a golden-ager if you can remember when charity was a virtue instead of an industry.

"Changing Times"

The early western frontier bars were not only tough, spartan, but they filled a desperate need to dispel cowboy loneliness. These tough, sometimes lethal bars, not only dispensed booze but with almost every glass came a humor chaser. Consider these old signs, hung over the bar for the edification of our late nineteenth century grandparents.

This house is strictly intemperate.
None but the brave deserve the fare.
No shooting, unless in self-defense.
Persons owing bills for board will be bored for bills.
No more than five to a bed.
Sheets will be changed nightly - once a month.
When bedding down remove your spurs, it's hard
    on the sheets.

All monies to be left with the clerk as he is not
    responsible.

or this one:
    A word to the wise: All confidence sharks,
    Thimble-riggers, bunco-steerers, sure-thing-men
    and all other objectionable characters:
    STAY AWAY! (or face drastic action).

The nature of the action is not specified. Or this price
list:

    Snacks - two bits.
    Square meal - four bits.
    Belly ache - one dollar.

    Oh, bury me with my knife and six-shooter,
    My spurs at my heels, my rifle at my side;
    And place on my coffin a bottle of brandy,
    For my ghost to swallow, when he goes for a ride.

    "I drink," said Jackie Gleason, "to remove warts and
pimples from the people I'm looking at."

    A man is old for sure, when he waits in line to take
the escalator to the basement floor!

    Now that he had retired, Johnny Gingold spent most
afternoons in Norbandy's, the neighborhood bar. One
day, about four o'clock, he staggered out of that bar
and flagged down a cab, slid into the seat and ordered
the driver to: "Take me to Norbandy's bar."
    "Whatd'ya know," said the cabby, "We're there
already!"
    "Thanks a million," Johnny said, "But, really, you
shouldn't drive that fast."

When Phil Robinson got drunk he embarrassed us. One time he drank soup and six couples got up and danced.

A set of twins, the McGuire sisters, walked into a bar and ordered martinis.

Soon after their entrance, a drunk walked in the bar, saw the twins, did a double take, then walked to the bar. He ordered a drink, then took it over to where the identical twins were sitting, rubbed his eyes twice and stared at the girls.

"Don't be disturbed, old man," one of the twins said. "We really are identical twins."

The old drunk shook his head as if to clear it, squinted at them again and said, "All four of you?"

Edgar James got bored watching the grandkids and, as soon as he could, he turned them over to grandma and hurried to the tavern nearby. There he met a stranger and they talked, drank, told stories and soon were fast friends. At the end of the evening, Edgar suggested to his new friend that, when he returned to visit the grandchildren one year hence, that they meet in this very same tavern and resume their friendship. "Agreed," said his new friend. "See you a year from today."

Exactly one year later, Edgar returned to his grandkids' city and, as soon as he could, hied himself to the remembered tavern to look for his friend. To his surprise, the fellow was sitting in the very same place, on the same stool as the year before.

"My goodness, I never thought you'd be here when I came back," Edgar told him.

"Back?" said the other fellow. "Who left?"

An old timer is a person who believes that the best thing about the good old days was the taxes.

Two guys left the Senior Citizens' Center and walked to a nearby bar. When they got inside the bar, one asked where the check room for coats was located. "You go down the hall to your left, and enter the third door on your right. They'll take care of your coats."

The fellow made a mistake and opened the _second_ door that lead to the elevator shaft. Down he went, falling ten feet. A few steps behind him came his buddy who asked, "What the heck are you doing?"

"Hanging up my coat. You better do the same. But watch out for that first step, man! It's a sonovagun!"

It is amazing the odd, stupid things that drunks do. Consider Elmer Winters who had been drinking all evening, then left the bar to get in a cab and tell the driver to take him around the block fifty times. About the fortieth time around, Elmer pounded on the glass and yelled, "Hey, driver! Please speed it up, can't ya! I'm in a hurry!"

A bit later, Elmer was arrested for drunkenness. At his trial, his attorney quizzed the police officer who had made the arrest. "Just because Elmer was on his hands and knees in the middle of the road doesn't prove that he was intoxicated," the lawyer said.

"I understand that," the officer said. "But your client was trying to roll up the white line in the middle of the road!"

A man, up in years, staggered out of Oxtoby's bar and stopped a passerby. "Sir, could you pleash tell us or me or whoever ish taklkin' to ya', where I yam?"

"Certainly. You're at the corner of Second and Jefferson."

"No, No! Not the details, jush tell me what city thish ish."

A guy walks into a bar and he is obviously disturbed, shaking all over and his eyes are wild. "Gimme a double vodka martini, he whispered to the bartender."

When the drink was in his hands, he gulped it down, turned to the bartender and asked how tall penguins were.

The bartender thought a bit, then turned to the back wall and measured a height of about two feet. The man nodded, thanked him and ordered another double, drank it down and asked the bartender to be sure of that measurement and would he do it on the wall, once again. The bartender obliged him, whereupon the shaken guy ordered another double. Now worried, the bartender asked the man what his problem was. The man downed his third double martini and said, "If penguins are only that tall, man, well...I guess I just ran over two nuns!"

A veteran of World War II walked out of a bar and asked the gentleman in uniform, standing outside, to call a cab.

"I am not a doorman, Sir," replied the uniformed gentleman. "I am an officer in the U. S. Navy!"

"Oh, escuse me. Then would you pleash call me a boat!"

A Priest and a Rabbi wandered into a bar and were escorted to a table by a cocktail hostess. "Please be seated gentlemen," she said, "And what will you have?"

"A Manhattan, if you please," said the Rabbi.

"And you, Father?"

"Please!" expostulated the Priest. "I do...not...drink! Period! Rather than drink I would sooner commit fornication."

"Oh, young lady," said the Rabbi, "If there's such a choice, I'll have the same as Father John."

He is not drunk who, from the floor,
Can rise again and drink some more;
But he is drunk who prostrate lies,
And cannot drink, and cannot rise.

Eugene Field

You might not believe it but there is an old guy in Bloomington who is so dumb that, when he finally got married, he stayed up all night on his wedding night! You see, he'd heard that you have relations on your honeymoon, so he did the logical thing and waited up to greet them when they arrived.

Reprinted with permission of the Saturday Evening Post

Some old guys are mean, man. One is so mean he reminds me of a toothache I once had.

When a man has a birthday he takes a day off. When a woman has a birthday, she takes a year off.

You can be sure that you've reached senior citizen status when you've arrived at that "Please repeat that" stage.

There is a rule to drink,
I think,
A rule of three
That you'll agree
Cannot be beaten,
And tends our lives to sweeten:
  Drink ere you eat,
  And while you eat,
  And after you have eaten.
         Wallace Rice, 1885

Work is the curse of the drinking class.
        (Old Saying)

It is difficult to gainsay the words of religious teachers. Consider this poem by Dr. Henry Aldreich, Dean of Christ Church, 1647 - 1710:
 If it be true that I do think,
 There are five reasons we should drink:
 Good wine -- a friend -- or being dry --
 Or lest we should be by-and-by --
 Or any other reason why!

Jed Stith had been a drinking man all his life. But, as he grew old, the habit began to tell on him so that he went to see his doctor, who gave him a thorough examination.

"Jed," the doctor observed, "Now that I've been though all your tests, been over you thoroughly, I think I can safely say that drinking has caused all your problems. My advice to you is . . . quit drinking and you'll feel thirty years younger. I promise it!"

"Thanks a million, Doc," Jed replied, "But when I'm drinkin' I already feel like a man thirty years younger."

Old man:	"Yer darned tootin' I was in the service! The Navy. Served four years too."
Young ensign:	"That's most interesting, Sir. What was your capacity?"
Old man:	"Derned near three quarts a day!"

A few days before he was due to retire from the brewery where he had worked all his life, Pete Endicott fell into a huge beer vat and drowned. A fellow worker remarked, "The poor man never had a chance."

"That's not quite true," one of his co-workers remarked. "I saw him climb out twice before he died, and go to the bathroom."

Jimmy Peters and Paul Coutrakon had been high school buddies but hadn't seen one another since graduation, forty years ago. Nothing to do but go to the tavern, have a few drinks and recall old times. Well, the old friends had more than a few. Suddenly Jimmy turned to Paul and said, "Y'know, Paul, I think I'll go to the airport, hop a plane, fly to Africa, and buy all the diamond mines."

"Oh yeah," sneered Paul. "And just suppose I won't sell 'em to ya?"

Back in the days of Prohibition and the Volstead Act, Berton Braley wrote this poem that celebrates the "morning after." Yes, dear reader, there once as an Austin automobile. (See the fourth verse.)

WHY?

Why did I take that other drink?
  That little more, how much it is!
I was respectable, I think,
  Until I got that extra fizz.
Thereafter -- well, it would appear
  My story's writ in purple ink,
(I do not know, but so I hear)
  WHY did I take that other drink?

It seems that, as a merry lark
  I scaled a wall, a fence or two,
Rode buffaloes in Central Park,
  And tried to wrestle with the Gnu;
How I got out I do not know,
  Nor how I dodged a night in clink
To tap-dance in a burlesk show;
  Why DID I take that other drink?

Where did I get the hansom cab
  In which I drove to Hackensack?
And from what boathouse did I nab
  The birch canoe I paddled back?
Whence came the baby crocodile
  That's basking in the kitchen sink
Wearing a Mona Lisa smile?
  Why did I TAKE that other drink?

Whose Austin is that in the hall?
  Where did I find that coat of mail?
That hydrant over by the wall,
  That statue and that butcher's scale?
Whose roulette wheel is that? And what
  Explains this Chinese suit of pink?
Where did I get this wife I've got?
  Why did I take that OTHER drink?
        Berton Braley

Known as the town's confirmed drinking man, Old Chauncey Follet stumbled out of his favorite bar and smashed into the corner lamppost. He staggered back, rubbing his nose to be sure it wasn't broken, turned, and tripped over a fire hydrant. He stumbled back from that encounter and ran up against an iron railing guarding the steps down to the basement. Inching his way along the railing, he came to the steps, took a step backward and fell downstairs, landing in a dazed heap at the bottom before the basement door. "To hell with all this ruckus," Chauncey mumbled to himself, "I'll just curl up here and get a good sleep until this damned parade passes."

There is an ancient *midrash* about the biblical story of Noah. According to the story, Noah planted a vineyard and had Satan for his partner. To fertilize the soil, Noah and Satan killed a lamb and let all the blood sink into the vineyard soil. Then they did the same with a lion, a monkey, and a pig. After that the vines started to grow big and strong.

How do we know this? Easy! When you drink a little wine you feel gentle and sleepy as a lamb. Drink a little more and you feel fearless as a lion. You can whip anybody anytime! Drink still more and you start hopping and skipping and jumping about like a monkey. But if you drink more, you wallow in your own filth like a hog!

James Truslow Adams used to tell the story of two sailors thinking and talking about old days. They were in a bar talking about the old-time barrooms with brass rail and sawdust on the floor and other nostalgic recollections.

"Well I guess there's gotta be change, Jerry, I can understand that. But I sure do miss those bright and shiny brass spittoons."

"I know, buddy, but then you always did."

265

Back in the 1940s, an old man went to see his physician. "I'm not feeling well, Doc. I got so many aches and pains I've forgotten what it's like to feel good."

The doctor examined the old boy and then said, "What you need is a bit of stimulant. Take four or five shots of whiskey every day and you'll feel fine again. I'll send a jug of good whiskey."

"But, Doctor," the old man groaned, "I'm a firm Baptist and neither I nor my family can have liquor in the house. My family simply wouldn't allow it."

"I'll send the whiskey and then you take it in hot water, five or six times a day. Your family needn't know a thing about it."

"But when I send down for hot water they are sure to suspect me."

"You just send your shaving mug downstairs and request they fill it with hot water. They'll think you need it to shave and you'll be fine."

The patient left and then days later the doctor called the house to find out how the old man was feeling.

"He's doing all right, physically, Doctor," the old fellow's daughter replied. "But he's gone bonkers, completely out of his mind. He's been shaving every ten minutes and we're about to go nuts sending up hot water every time he calls for it. Can you help us?"

———————

Let us endeavor so to live that when we come to die even the undertaker will be sorry.

Mark Twain

———————

Shortly after the repeal of Prohibition, a Chicago bar put up this sign:

PLEASE DON'T STAND UP WHILE THE ROOM IS IN MOTION.

———————

Herb Cantill advised his son-in-law to quit drinking for the wife and kid. . .neys.

You can determine the very essence of a person by noting three things: His cup (what happens when he drinks). His pocket (how he spends money). His anger (what he says when provoked).

Two old ladies, lifelong friends, met on the street and began to talk. After a while, they moved to a restaurant to have coffee and continue their reminiscences.

Seated, one old girl asked, "And how is hubby Gerald?"

"Oh, I lost him a year ago."

"Oh my! I didn't know. But he seemed so young...not over sixty, was he?"

"Sixty-three. But the poor man got to drinking, drank too much and that caused it all."

"Cirrhosis of the liver?" murmured her friend.

"Nope. Dog food. When he drank he craved dog food. Used to eat it every morning 'stead of cereal. Then again at night for a bedtime snack."

"Oh, my goodness. How strange!"

"Yep! That's what killed him. Got to chasing cars and one of 'em ran over him."

Life would be infinitely happier if we could only be born at the age of eighty and gradually approach eighteen.

Mark Twain

Two old geezers had been on an all-night spree. As they staggered home, they got diverted down a railroad track and, after a time of walking, one old guy says, "Wow! I'm s-sure tired. Ain't we never goin' t'git t'the bottom of these here stairs?"

The other old geek replies: "It ain't these stairs that b-bother me. It's these here l-low bannisters that're gittin' me down."

267

An old drunk gets on the bus, staggers down the aisle and sits down next to a prim old lady. She looks him over, makes a face and says, "Old man, I can tell you one thing for sure, you are on your way to hell!"

The old geezer stumbles to his feet, turns to the old lady, and says, "Holy smokes, Ma'am, I'm on t-t-the wrong t-train!"

The old boy walks into a candy shop and is met by a clerk. "Can I help you, Sir?" she asks.

"You bet," the old guy replies. "You got any candies with liquor in the middle?"

"Sure do. How many did you want?"

"Oh...gimme two quarts of middles."

Four guys were attending their fiftieth fraternity reunion held at the Waldorf Astoria in New York. Well, they got pie-eyed as old friends are wont to do. They stumbled out of the hotel and the doorman put them in a taxi and told the driver: "This guy goes to the Drake. This fellow goes to the New Yorker, this fellow goes to the Claridge and this last one here, he goes to the St. Regis." The taxi pulled away.

Very soon the same taxi is back at the Waldorf, and the driver leans out and says, "Sort these old fellers out for me once again, will you? I hit a bump!"

An old guy always spent his evenings in the same bar. Night after night he would walk there, order his same drink, repeat the order time after time, finally pay his bill and go home.

But one night after he had paid his bill, he stood up, walked to face the wall, walked up the wall, across the ceiling, down the opposite wall to the door, and then outside.

"Now that is mighty strange," the bartender mused. "Every other night he always said 'Good Night' before he went home."

During a revivalist's tent meeting, the preacher was sermonizing on the evils of liquor, all liquors of every kind and description. And he was boiling mad at saloon keepers. "Who has the most expensive automobiles? The saloon keeper. Who has the finest home, eats the most expensive food? The saloon keeper. And who pays for all these luxuries, these properties of the very rich saloon keepers? You do, my friends. You do!"

Some days later the preacher met an old man whom the preacher had known for many years, had known him to be a confirmed drunkard. The old drunk congratulated the preacher on his wonderful sermon.

"I'm glad to see you sober, my friend," said the preacher, "and to have had a part in getting you to give up your excessive boozing."

The old man replied, "Well, Reverend, I ain't exactly given it up, y'know. What I've done is. . . .I've bought a saloon!"

A professor of English Literature had a few too many drinks at the party and on his way home, was arrested for speeding and hauled to the small town court, charged with being drunk and disorderly. "Have you got anything to say for yourself before I sentence you?" the judge asked.

The professor stood up and said, "Man's inhumanity to man makes countless hundreds mourn." The professor then strode back and forth shouting, "I'm not so degraded as Poe, nor so unkind as Keats, nor so intemperate as Tennyson or so vulgar as Shakespeare."

About that time the judge shouted, "Shut your mouth. That'll be thirty days!" Then he turned to the bailiff and said, "Take down that list of names and round those guys up. Why they're as bad as he is."

There's no trick to being a humorist when you have the whole government working for you.

Will Rogers

269

The bell captain at the Hotel Pierre got a call from a guest at 3 A.M. "What time does the hotel bar open?" an old, quavering voice asked.

"Ten o'clock," the bell captain replied.

At 4 A.M., the old guy calls again: "What time does the hotel bar open?" And the bell captain answers as before, "Ten A.M., Sir."

A couple of hours later the bell captains gets a third call from the same guy, who asks the same question. This angers the bell captain who yells into the phone, "Dammit, Sir, Don't bother me again with that silly question. Nobody can open that bar before ten! It's the law! Got it?"

The old guy then replies, "Who wants to get in? Hell, man, I want to get out!"

At the Senior Citizen's Center, a physician was giving a lecture on the physical effects of alcohol. He put a worm in water and another worm in whiskey. Then he held up both glasses, saying, "You see what happened? The work in water is alive and swimming. The worm in whiskey is dead. Now, tell me, what does that say to you?"

An old man held up his hand. "Yes?" the doctor recognized him. "What does the experiment tell you, Sir?"

"Seems plain enough," the old man replied. "If you drink whiskey you don't get worms."

George Peters is spending his last few days on this earth in hospital. But he hasn't lost his sense of humor. When anyone knocks on his hospital room door, he replies, "Friend or enema?"

They say that W. C. Fields yearned all of his life to compose drinking songs. But he had this hang-up, this fixation. He simply could not get past the first two bars.

Percy Teleth was a meek kind of a man and let his wife make all the decisions for the family. And she did a good job of it, too. One time she had to go to the dentist with Percy. When she got there, she told the dentist, "I got to have a tooth pulled and I want it done now, at once, and get it over as soon as possible because I've got a million things to do."

The dentist was a good guy, smiled and said, "I admire your courage, Mrs. Teleth. Just tell me which tooth is causing you trouble."

She turned to Percy, saying, "Get in the chair there, Percy, and show the dentist which tooth is bothering you."

The nightclub had a piano bar and the pianist was chatting with one of the customers, telling him that he had learned to read music as a young man with his first instrument, a violin. After that he took up the piano.

"Why did you give up such a lovely instrument as the violin? " the customer asked.

"Because the wine glasses wouldn't stay on," the pianist replied. "They kept sliding off!"

They say down in Ozark County, during Prohibition and when moonshine liquor was a good source of income to the hillbilly Ozarkers, they estimated their corn crop in gallons. . . not in bushels. And so it happened that one day an Ozarker fell head first into a huge vat of moonshine liquor. Unable to get out, he drowned and it took the undertaker two days to wipe the smile off his face.

Ben Barnees spent four years in the service in World War II. Ever since, says Ben, "I've suffered from 'bottle fatigue.'"

Mary Jo Simpson was a bit liquored up when the old girl decided to walk home. Confused, she headed through the cemetery only to fall in an open grave. Not to worry. . .along came another drunk, a man, and he, too, fell into the grave. After a bit, Mary Jo said, "Gosh all fishhooks but it's cold in here." Whereupon the other drunk replied, "Well, for gosh sakes, what'd ya expect, ya kicked all that warm dirt off'n ya."

Very, very, very few
People die at ninety-two.
I suppose that I shall be
Safer still at ninety-three.
                    Willard R. Espy, "Actuarial Reflection."

In his introduction to *"Tall Tales of the Devil's Apron,"* Herbert Maynor Sutherland tells of a lawyer who had been reduced to a vegetable because of his excessive drinking. This lawyer, Willie B. Fuller, took exception to an article that Mr. Sutherland, a newspaper reporter, had written concerning life in Devil's Apron, Virginia. The area gained its name because the devil, with a load of bad tidings in his apron, had once been bound for Kentucky where he planned to dump it all, and instead stumbled and dumped it on this area of Virginia!

In fact, of all the men I grew to know on the Devil's Apron only the alcoholic Kentucky lawyer remained a comparative stranger year after year, until one day after I had acquired the local county paper I received a letter from him addressed to my office. It said:

"Dear Editor;
"I notice from time to time that you seem to take a special delight in publishing articles in regard to the drinking habits and propensities of the inhabitants of this section, known to many as the 'Devil's Apron.' Judging by the tone of your writings, I gather that it is your considered opinion that the men over here spend

practically all of their time imbibing the 'mountain dew' for which these hills are justly famous.

"It is quite true that some of us, when we feel so inclined, do partake of a medicinal toddy made from the finest old apple brandy that ever soothed a man's palate, or from pure malted corn, backed and doubled in the manner our forefathers made and loved. We consider that modern 'sugar-top' concoction that goes by the name of moonshine to be an abomination in our sight and we will not tolerate it.

"But to be perfectly honest with you, I have on my desk before me as I sit at my typewriter, a bottle of the finest applejack that was ever distilled in the purpled shadows of the age-old Cumberlands. I can close my eyes and smell the sweet odor of the apple-blossoms, and even hear the songs of the little birds whose music went into the soul of this applejack. I can detect the smell of ripening mellow apples as they are carefully gathered and stored away for Thanksgiving pies and Christmas toddies and eggnog.

"In a moment, I shall take a moderate drink of this ambrosia, and if it meets with my palpitant anticipations, I shall probably take another. It is my sincere and confirmed belief that for anyone to attempt to stop me would be an invasion of my personal liberties which I will deeply resent. I have tasted a few drops of this brandy, and I am convinced that by so doing I have not in any manner invaded the rights of any other person on earth.

"Just to show you that I don't give a hang how much you talk about us fellows over here in the Devil's Apron, I have taken another drink of this aforesaid highly medicinal brandy, and I will say to you that it is just about the smoothest concoction that ever trickled down a man's gullet. This second drink, or maybe it's the third, makes me feel that I don't give a whoop what you say or who you say it to.

"Now, Mr. Editor, I, and my buddies over hear, ain't bumn, and you can&t make us bums. I like a little drinl now and thwn as I said before, and as I will repeat if I want to anf when I want to. I have tajen a third drink, and maybe a fourth, and I am more than ever convimced that I have done nothing to whivh any man can take exception to whatever.

"If Me and the boys wan't to get togeser on satirday night to have us a little fun, and if we take a few drinis and don&t harm nobpdy but ourselfs then what I say is that it ain't noboy's bizness, no matter if he thinls it is his. That&s the way I feel abouy it.

"I want&t to sa to yyiu that this likker is all rught. A lot of it wouldnT do on np harm. When we need stimulay we need it. My granfyer wus broughr up on moobshine an' had it in the house al the time. He drunk it freelu, and even the Ministew dranj it when he coom to our housee. It&s a prettu kind of a cointry when a grabson is bettre than his gunfaher. I can drink this kind of brandu all day and nit be no worse a cicozen than I was befote. I could drink this hole quaet aud negger bat a etelashe.

"Bue whay I weant of yiou is to remund yio thqt you arw wronb ober againain and agnian thqt you arw wronb ib comfsing evert bony whu drinkd as a bougm. We ain&t crimilas.

"Rexcevtfilly Yiotdx, O8Bd.srff. wILLIE b. fULLER."

"I'm afraid that's a little higher than I care to get."

*Reprinted with permission of the **Saturday Evening Post***

11

AMERICAN TALL TALES

A unique American phenomenon is the BURLINGTON LIAR'S CLUB. This marvelous organization of people who love to tell whoppers or windies or, to be more literate, righteous LIES, has been functioning since 1929 and has elicited some of the most delicious lies ("twisted reality") that defy description and exist simply because they are great and innocent fun. Every year they run a contest for the best lie of that year and entries are received from all over America and beyond. Since these fantastic tales are so much fun and part of American folklore, here are a few of the early championship lies beginning 62 years ago, as awarded by the royal jury of the Burlington Liar's Club, Burlington, Wisconsin.

Orrin Butts (honest, folks, that is his true name), back in 1921 wrote to notify the Burlington Liar's Club that he had saved the life of the man he worked for. His boss was a farmer and, one day, a bull gored the farmer so dreadfully that "immediate and heroic action was indicated." So Mr. Butts, the savvy hired hand, proved equal to the occasion. He killed a sheep, transferred the entire innards of the animal to the gored-out farmer's innards, sewed up the farmer, and the good farmer recovered, thanks to Butts. But a peculiar thing happened. Orrin Butts reported that his boss refused to sleep in his own home, ate nothing but hay, grew a set of magnificent horns, and the second year, "he yielded a clip of 40 pounds of wool." Since Mr. Butts is from Bay City, Michigan, we have to assume that his story is immaculately true.

Old timers will recall those distant days when corn was shucked from the stalk and thrown against a high board on the opposite side of the wagon, called "the bangboard." The ear of corn would hit the "bangboard" and drop from it into the wagon. After about fifty bushels were shucked, they would take it to the farm elevator and hand-shovel/scoop the entire load into the corn crib. Well, Mr. Frank Norton told the Burlington Liar's Club, back in 1939, that he and his father got so good at shucking earcorn and hitting the "bangboard" with it that they could play easy tunes on that "bangboard," tunes like "Asleep in the Deep" and "Onward Christian Soldiers." Easy stuff.

But as the season progressed, they got better at making corny music, They got so good at it, in fact, that they could play "Darktown Strutters Ball" and even bugle calls.

Then, one year on a fall day, they took the place of the town band in the annual band contest and won first prize (and we quote) "with a masterpiece of 'bangboard' music," their own arrangement of "Chopsticks."

Although Bruno Ceresa swears it is true, we kind of figure the following story may be somewhat tall - just a teenie weenie bit!

It seems that Mr. Ceresa's grandfather had a clock that was so old that the shadow of its pendulum, swinging back and forth over the generations, had "worn a hole in the back of the case!"

Prize Winning Lie, 1934

Mr. Osborne wrote us regarding the exceptional training of his mule, which he rode when hunting jackrabbits. While hunting one day he took out after a "jack" which fled across a mesa, and close pressed, plunged headlong over a 10,000 foot cliff. The mule, trained to follow rabbits, never hesitated, but plunged off after it.

"I thought my hour had come," wrote Osborne, "but

276

then I remembered how well trained that mule was, so I sat quietly in the saddle until we were about 10 feet from the ground and then hollered, 'WHOA!' The mule stopped in his tracks, and I stepped off, unhurt."

Verne Osborne
Centralia, Washington

Prize Winning Lie, 1947

"Me and my friend Charley Skorpea were playing that night for the championship of the Boggy Creek Bottoms, and it was his shot. Just as he started to shoot for the 8-ball a fly lit exactly on top of the ball. 'I am going to kill that fly with this shot,' he said.

"Time stood still while two boys booked bets on whether he would or not. Believe it or not, the fly also stood pat. Everybody in the house was expecting Charley to loft the cue ball so it would light on top of the insect and exterminate him.

"When they finally got all their bets made, Charley chalked his cue and knocked the 8-ball out from under that fly so quick that it fell on the table and broke its back!"

John C. Hopley
San Antonio, Texas

Prize Winning Lie, 1943

"When I first came into the army they sent me to the state of Maryland. Now if you've never been in Maryland you don't know how bad mosquitoes can be. Those in Maryland were of the P-38 type, and when they landed on you they always filled both fusilages. The first day they completely drained me of blood. The second day I was giving I.O.U.'s. In fact, months later, when I was stationed in Alabama, to my surprise the Maryland mosquitoes sent me a card on Father's Day because they had so much of my blood in them."

S. Sgt. Baron S. Fonnesbeck
Dugway Prov. Grd.
Tooele, Utah

They tell this story about the oldest man in Carlinville, Illinois. He was given to telling lies. He called them tall tales and others called them whoppers. Still others called them windies. But they were all...all lies and the preacher was worried. "He's going to pass on, one of these days, and it's a shame that he can't present a better record to St. Peter than the one he's got. I think we ought to talk to him about his lying and endangering his future security with all those big lies he's been telling."

The congregation agreed and delegated four men to accompany the preacher to the old man's farm. They met to discuss the project and the preacher said, "I think we ought to make him see how awful his habit is. I think we ought to tell him the biggest lie, a real blanket-stretcher...the most high fallutin' story we can think of and show him the error of his ways by example. You all agree?"

The delegation all nodded and they started off for Limpton Joneygan's farmhouse. Limpton met them at the door, invited them in and the preacher began his talk-story.

"Limpton, all five of us came out to tell you a story and to see if you get the point. Is that all right with you?"

"Sure, 'nuff. Go right ahead, Parson. Only don't tell me no lies."

"Limpton, we had the most awful thing happen last Sunday. I was goin' about the business of preachin' when in through the window come ajumpin' a huge mountain lion. And who do you think was chasin' him? A fice, a little spotted dog lookin' like a minature coon hound. Well, that little dog jumped that big mountain lion and they fought and fought till the fur was aflyin' everywhere. Women screamed. Men yelled. It was the awfulest commotion we ever had but, you know what, that little fice completely whipped that big mountain lion and drove him clean out of the church! Now, Limpton, what do you think of that? You believe me all the way, don't you?"

"Well, sure I do, Parson. Of course. And why not? Heck fire, Parson, that little fice that whupped the lion? Why, he was my dog!"

278

It may seem strange to outsiders who don't know much about small towns, but there is a town in Iowa so small that it doesn't have any pay restrooms...only pay bushes!

Old-age diabetes is quite common among us older folk. And it is a good thing that those of us so affected do not live in Okinawa. As Gunnery Sergeant Joe Sage tells it, in Okinawa, they have a unique bird known as the Saccharin Swallow whose song is so sweet that diabetics are forced to wear earmuffs to shut out its voice.

Mr. John P. Zelenak, Jr. of Tacoma, Washington, claims that he has about the laziest wife in the nation. He writes, "My wife is so lazy that she feeds the chickens popcorn, so that the eggs will turn themselves when she fries them."

It is said that a very lazy man read that story when it was printed as the best tall tale of 1937, went on a diet of popcorn so that he would not have to turn himself over in bed...the popcorn would do it. Now, THAT is lazy.

Back in 1941, R. C. Cross of Wausau, Wisconsin, wrote: "You should have gone fishing with me in the old days in the Unadilla. One of the natives accidentally spilled a bottle of hair tonic in the river, one day, and all the fish started to grow long beards. All we had to do to catch them was to stick up a red-and-white-striped barber pole, hang out a copy of the *Police Gazette,* and holler, 'NEXT'!"

Lou Powers of Ortonville, Minnesota reminds us just how cold it can get in Minnesota. 1958 saw him reporting this winner lie to the Liar's Club:

"One morning last winter it was so cold that when I set out a tea kettle full of boiling water, it froze so fast the ice was warm."

A curious thing happened in the service, during WW II. Captain Hope Harrin was mess officer and so knew a lot about dehydration. So he wrote this girl to go to the dehydration plant, get herself dehydrated, then have her mother mail her overseas to him. This was done and when the Captain received the letter with his dehydrated girlfriend in it, he "poured water over her dehydrated body, and quickly restored her to her natural self. In half an hour, she was as good as before - and here with me!" Now that's about the closest thing to Resurrection that we've heard of!

A kind of inactivity (some call it laziness) does afflict the older folks and nothing describes their take-it-easy attitude so much as the sneezers in the town of Jacksonville. There it takes two to sneeze, one guy to throw his head back, and the other has to go "Achoo!" Now that IS kinda lazy.

But they aren't much worse than the two old fellers in Fancy Prairie. When they need firewood, it takes two of them to get it. One swings the axe and the other guy grunts. And if they need a lot of wood, they call in a third old man to do the sweating.

Then there was the senior citizen who had grown so absent-minded that he put his shirt to bed and sent himself to the laundry for a washing! And that's not all. This old geek didn't realize the dumb thing he'd done until they tried to iron him. But he wasn't half as "gone" as another old guy from a nearby town. This oldie put his cat to bed one night and then put himself outside. And he didn't figure he'd done a stupid thing until a vicious dog chased him and he discovered that he could not...climb a tree.

Charlie Levy had been a submarine sailor in World War II and he had a battleship tattooed on his chest. But, as he grew old, he got so thin that that blamed battleship shrunk to the size of a rowboat. Honest!

Old George Edwards returned from the first decent vacation he'd had in thirty years. He vacationed in Nebraska and when he returned and reported to the office, he was asked how he liked his vacation. "Folks," old George began, shaking his head, "I had the best time I ever had...except for those windy days. I stayed on a ranch of my cousin's and the dadblamed wind never did stop blowing. Didn't bother my cousin 'cause he hinged his house so that when the wind blows it over, all he has to do is pull her straight again. Why, that wind blew so hard it blew all the barbs on his fence down to one side. My cousin told me that at this time of year, he has to feed all his hens buckshot to keep from having them blow away! And I, myself, saw something happen to one of his hens that you won't believe. That hen layed an egg into the wind and it had to lay that same egg six times before she could get it to stay down - not blow back inside her. Further, do you know the wind blew so strong from the west that it took the sun an extra three hours to set? And that was the good season in Nebraska. Think I'll stay home from now on."

Here are some more wonderful tall tales from that superb organization, THE BURLINGTON LIAR'S CLUB of Burlington, Wisconsin, the Winning Lie for 1952.

Now comes a story of an American GI in Japan. He seems to have come upon mosquitoes the likes of which had never before been seen. Witness this as it emerged from the truthful lips of (then) A/3c Harry Cummings:

"One night in July, I had just turned in for the night when I heard the door open. At first I thought it was one of the other guys who slept in the room with me. When I got a better look, I saw it was two mosquitoes. They stood nearly six feet tall and believe me, I was too terrified to move, so I just laid where I was and kept still when they approached my bed.

"Suddenly I heard one of them say, 'Do you think we should eat him here, or should we carry him home?'

"After a moment's consideration, the other replied,

'Let's eat him here. You know very well if we take him home our big brothers will take him away from us!'"

In 1978, things were really tough in Mayville, Wisconsin, says Winfred Herberg. Inflation was wild. "Why," he writes, "my wife and I built a house we could afford. But we couldn't live in it. It was so small my wife didn't have room to change her mind." Winning Lie for 1978.

And, a year later, C. A. Laurie of Eckland, Missouri, told of his revelation on a cold, cold winter day. He was walking down the street when, "I saw a politician standing on a street corner with his hands in his _own_ pockets." Winning Lie for 1979.

Here are some more wonderful whoppers (tall tales) from the championship liars of the Burlington Liar's Club, Burlington, Wisconsin.

Small-town folks are reputed to be mighty tight with a dollar. That may or may not be true, but when Old Mary Jane Hustlebuck passed on and arrived at the Pearly Gates, she claimed overtime. Why? Well, she had always been late for everything she ever did in her entire life. But, you see, she was on time (first time) for her funeral. Hence, she claimed overtime. Makes sense once you think about it, right? If any reader doubts this phenomenon, he can write to the teller of this tale, Philip Strandvold of Pilot Rock, Oregon. (Of course, one can be pardoned for suspecting that Philip was a mite like the man who was such a liar that he had to get his neighbors to call his dogs for him, as reported by Lester Connally, of McGregor, Texas.)

Carl Fisher married his third wife who was mighty lazy. "She's so lazy," Carl told his buddy, "that she uses only drip-dry dishes."

Zeke Martin and his wife are both 72 years old, and both are known to be soft-hearted. But Zeke has the softest heart of the two. Why, when his wife has hard, heavy work to do around the house, old Zeke just can't stand it...he simply has to put on his hat and go to the tavern!

Zeke is one strong fellow. He's so strong he can pull himself two feet off the ground by his coat collar. Not many men his age can do that. Of course, he's a show-off and does it often to impress people.

He's tall too, so tall that people get a stiff neck from looking up at him. Not everybody believes her when his wife says that he is so tall that, of a morning, he has to put on his pants by pulling them on over his head.

Zeke says he still chases after the girls, "now and then." "But," he adds, "they got to be going downhill."

An old man, retired, decided to take up painting. Well, they discovered that he had real talent, especially for realistic painting. As a matter of fact, he painted a dog so real that the derned beast bit him.

Of course, he should have known better because he once painted a sunny July scene so perfect, so real that the people who saw it suffered heat stroke. After that the authorities would not let him paint winter scenes for fear that viewers would catch cold. Now that is true artistry.

Another time he painted a hunting scene with six duck decoys and a hunter in the blind on a lovely winter day. A live cat wandered by that painting, saw the ducks and thought they were real, ate the heads of four of them before the painter got around to shooing him off! Talk about artistry!

Before we approach more such tall tales, let's take a look at those American heroes who are simply the world's greatest! And we don't expect the Baron Munchausens of the world. No, Sir!

It's a fact that no nation can match our mythic, larger-than-life heroes like Paul Bunyan, Pecos Bill,

Davy Crockett, Mike Fink, John Henry and lots more. These guys and *their ladies* reflect the attitude of Davy Crockett: "BE SURE YOU ARE RIGHT...THEN GO AHEAD!" That attitude built and still builds this nation. For such as Davy Crockett and all those other heroic types, nothing was impossible. And that attitude holds as true today as it ever has. Americans are a "can do" people and their mythic heroes reflect that "can do" attitude.

Here are some prototypes, just a bit larger than life, typical of the "Go Ahead" American. Tall heroes? Yes. Tall Tales? Sure! Or are they...?

Consider Pecos Bill. That old boy confronted a tornado, lassoed it and, as it pulled him off the ground, Bill twirled the lariat until it shortened enough to get him abreast of the tornado, which he mounted and rode all over Oklahoma, New Mexico and parts of Texas. Bill steered that tornado over a droughty part of Texas and there the tornado "*rained out from under him,*" saving the farmers below. Yes, Sir. And Pecos Bill? He simply slid down to his home county on a streak of lightning.

Old Pecos Bill fell in love, after that, and married a charmer named Sweet Sue who was determined to wear the chaps in the family. Bill ordered her never to ride his bucking horse, Widow Maker, but Sue was determined to do just that. And she did, worse luck, because the horse threw her so high she "liked never to come down" as Pecos Bill put it. And when she did, she lit on her bustle and bounced sky-high again, came down, bounced up and down - up and down - and this went on for days. Bill let her do it until she promised not to disobey him again and then he lassoed her and pulled her to safety. They lived happily ever after.

But some say that it didn't work out that way, that poor Sweet Sue couldn't stop bouncing and they had to shoot her to keep her from starving to death.

Now you take Paul Bunyan. There was a man. He lumbered in Michigan, Wisconsin, and North Dakota and you can believe these stories that follow because Professor Walter Blair of the University of Chicago, a good friend of Paul Bunyan and his biographer, has warranted them true (more or less).

It seems that old Paul was faced with a humongous forest that had to be downed in a hurry. So he got him a long steel blade, about a quarter of a mile in length, filed teeth on it, put a handle on both ends, put fifty men on one handle while he took the other and they commenced to saw through that entire forest. They finished the job .... a full section of trees or, if you don't know it, 640 acres, in just one week. Paul said he could have done the job before breakfast if the men on the other end had only worked a little harder.

And one time Paul had his foreman, Pokey Gunderson, take a huge boom of logs down the Mississippi River to St. Louis. But Pokey forgot where he was supposed to go and ended up in New Orleans. Well, old Paul was mad as all get out. But he soon set things right. He took his giant ox, Babe, fed her six blocks of salt, then took her to the Mississippi where she drank so much water she caused the Mississippi to flow backward and float those logs right back up the St. Louis where they belonged.

There are some things that Americans don't know. One of them is why you don't see tree stumps in North Dakota today. It's because old Paul took a sledge hammer and whacked every danged stump so hard he drove them four feet underground. And now they can plow and farm North Dakota because Paul cleared the land for them.

America has plenty of such heroes. You bet we do. Men like John Henry who was black as tar and weighed thirty-six pounds at birth. No mother's milk for John Henry. No, Sir! He demanded a menu and ordered four hog jowls, a kettle of black-eyed pears, three ham bones and a kettle of fried catfish.

As you might guess, John Henry grew up right fast to become the greatest steel-driving man in the world. And it was steel-driving that finished him. He got in a steel-driving contest with a new invention .... a steam-powered driving machine. Over a million dollars was bet on who could drive the most steel posts in one week. Well, John Henry won but the effort so exhausted him that he died. What a man!

Or you can consider Mike Fink. Some readers may recall his great qualities. Mike had the same problem with new inventions, "thingumajigs," he called them. You see, Mike was a keelboat operator. Keelboats used oarsmen to propel their keelboats up and down the river, hauling freight. Well, when the steamboat came along with its newfangled sternwheeled driving power, Mike began to lose business. Mike challenged that steamboat to a race. In the course of it, Mike collided with the boat and his keelboat sank. His men swam to shore but that finished Mike's days of keelboating.

After the accident, Mike took to the mountains and fur-trading and trapping. Folks doubted his ability along this line but Mike shouted, "I'm a ring-tailed roarer. Whoopee. And Bang-all, my gun has a trigger that takes to my finger like a nursing babe to its mama. Whoop! I can out-shoot and out-trap any man anywhere. Cock-a-doodle do!" That was Mike Fink for you.

And Mike could and did do just what his brag said he'd do.

Now you take Davy Crockett who, one day, noticed how cold it was even though it was July in Tennessee. What was wrong? Old Davy went outside and noticed that the sun wasn't moving, that it had got stuck on its axis and couldn't budge an inch! So Davy hopped a stationary sunbeam and climbed up the immobilized beam to the sun, poured a couple of tons of oil at the base of the sun, whereupon the sun worked itself loose. Then Davy skeedaddled down the sunbeam before the sun could move it. They say that Davy put a fresh chunk of sunlight in his pocket to show his fellow United States Congressmen, then lit his pipe with a chunk of sun and went on about his business.

One thing is certain, if it hadn't been for Davy moving that sun off dead center, this would be a mighty cold world to live in.

And could they brag! Their braggadocio was not only violent and daring but downright poetic. Just listen to old Davy Crockett tell the U.S. Congress a thing or three back in the days when he was a U.S. Congressman.

Davy Piles It On Thick

"Mr. Speaker.

"Who -- Who -- Whoop -- Bow -- Wow -- Wow -- Yough. I say, Mr. Speaker; I've had a speech in soak this six months, and it has swelled me like a drowned horse; if I don't deliver it I shall burst and smash the windows. The gentleman from Massachusetts (Mr. Everett) talks of summing up the merits of the question, but I'll sum up my own. In one word I'm a screamer, and have got the roughest racking horse, the prettiest sister, the surest rifle and the ugliest dog in the district. I'm a leetle the savagest critur you ever _did see._ My father can whip any man in Kentucky, and I can lick my father. I can outspeak any man on this floor, and give him two hours start. I can run faster, dive deeper, stay longer under, and come out drier, than any _chap_ this side the big _Swamp._ I can outlook a panther and outstare a flash of lightning, tote a steamboat on my back and play at rough and tumble with a lion, and an occasional kick from a _zebra._ To sum up all in one word _I'm a horse._ Goliath was a pretty hard colt but I could choke him. I can take the rag off - frighten the old folks - astonish the natives - and beat the Dutch all to smash - make nothing of sleeping under a blanket of snow - and don't mind being frozen more than a rotten apple."

That was old Davy Crockett at his big talk best. Now take a look at Mike Fink and his big talk. He was not a man you'd want to pick a fight with. No, Sir! Old Mike was every bit as good as his brag. Just listen to him!

Mike Fink's Brag

"Hurray for me, you scapegoats! I'm a land-screamer -- I'm a water-dog -- I'm a snapping-turkle -- I can lick five times my own weight in wildcats. I can use up Injens by the cord. I can swallow bears whole, raw or cooked. I can out-run, out-dance, out-jump, out-dive, out-drink, out-holler, and out-lick, any white thing in the shape o' human that's ever put foot within two thousand miles o' the big Massassip. Whoop! holler, you varmints! -- holler fur the Snapping Turkle! or I'll jump straight down yer throats, quicker than a streak o' greased lightening can down a bear's! ... I'm in fur a fight, I'll go my death on a fight, and a fight I must have, one that'll tar up the arth all around and look kankarifferous, or else I'll have to be salted down to save me from spiling, as sure nor Massassip alligators make fly traps o' thar infernal ugly jawrs."

Now don't get the idea that only the men were rip-roarin' screamers. The women, too, were just as tough, or sometimes, tougher. Here's an example of the big doin's of Sal Fink, Mike Fink's wife. She was a real doer, a rumscrumptious shemale tougher than crocodile hide. She had to be to qualify as Mike Fink's wife. Here she is.

She fought a duel once with a thunderbolt, an' came off without a single scratch, while at the fust fire she split the thunderbolt all to flinders, an' gave the pieces to Uncle Sam's artillerymen, to touch off their canon with. When a gal about six years old, she used to play see-saw on the Mississippi snags, and arter she war done she would snap 'em off, an' so cleared a large district of the rive. She used to ride down the river on an alligator's back, standen upright, an' dancing *Yankee Doodle,* and could leave all the steamers behind.

And Sal Fink was by no means the only barbed-wire female on the frontier. Most were like her. Here's Colonel Coon's wife, Judy, who was some punkin of a woman. She was the kind we needed to settle and civilize the frontier.

Colonel Coon's Wife Judy
It's most likely my readers has all heered of Colonel Coon's wife Judy. She wore a bearskin petticoat, an alligator's hide for an overcoat, an eagle's nest for a hat, with a wild-cat's tail for a feather. When she was fourteen years old, she wrung off a snapping turtle's neck and made a comb of its shell, which she wears to this day. When she was sixteen years old she run down a four-year-old colt, and chased a bear three miles through the snow, because she wanted his hair to make a toothbrush. She out-screamed a catamount, on

a wager, when she was just come of age; and sucked forty rattlesnake eggs to give her a sweet breath, the night she was married.

Hoifjeld

American Legion

". . . But the worst part of his thinking he's a refrigerator is that he sleeps with his mouth open and the light keeps me awake."

Reprinted by permission, The American Legion Magazine

Our senior citizens today have lived through a time of invention and innovation that makes Davy Crockett and Mike Fink and John Henry appear to be easy-going fellows. Such changes as the automobile, telephone, modern plumbing, air travel, atomic power, modern medicine, all this would have exfluncticated those earlier heroes. What a tall age we have lived in!

But the American gusto at telling tall tales never ends. Remember Lowell Thomas, that great newscaster and world-traveler? Well, he told some dandies. In his travels, he ran into an area of Missouri so dry that the fish in this particular river were stirring up a dangerous quantity of dust! Imagine that! The fire department had to come down and spray water all over that stream to reduce the dust to manageable proportions.

And that was the very same hot summer that a newspaperman reported seeing a dog chase a cat and both were walking. Now that is HOT!

Feeling too hot? Well, let us switch to winter, in Wisconsin, where the farmers said it was so cold that their cows gave ice cream. Devastating for the farmers? Not a bit of it. Using American innovativeness, they fed their cows cocoa beans and got chocolate ice cream. And frozen strawberries and raspberries mixed in the feed gave strawberry and raspberry ice cream. Those farmers set up roadside stands and sold every quart they produced at premium prices, too. Once again, American ingenuity turned adversity into a blessing.

In Minnesota that same year, the power went out in early evening. Farmers lit candles and for a while they had light until the flames froze, then they had to be broken off and thrown outside. Unfortunately, the hens thought it was a new and attractive feed, gobbled up those frozen flames so that when the farmers went out to collect eggs next morning, they discovered that every dadblamed egg was hard-boiled!

If you think that was strange, consider an experience of Mark Twain who told of a day at sea so cold that the shadow of the captain froze to the deck of his ship. The poor fellow couldn't move until his men got pry bars and worked his shadow loose from the deck.

The very same winter, Lowell Thomas related that there were 16,368,287 frozen automobile radiators. It was so cold, Mr. Thomas testified, that the fog froze into solid chunks of ice causing uncounted numbers of automobile and truck accidents as they smashed into the frozen chunks of fog. They had to get bulldozers to push the fog chunks off the road so that the cars and trucks could pass safely through the roads.

Tall heroes and tall doin's go together like a horse and carriage (or should that be hard roads and automobiles!). And here we'll put just a few more of those tall doin's that Americans have been reporting ever since the nation began. One thing is sure. . . . these stories illustrate the American imagination when it gets down to coping, to handling life's rigors such as heat, cold, wind, bugs, and the like. The truth is that since we must live with these hardships of life, well, we might as well joke and tell stories about them.

Some parts of Nebraska are not blessed with benign weather. Near Omaha, it got so hot one year that all their popcorn popped in the field, then shot up in a huge white cloud that looked just like snow. In fact, herds of cattle saw the billowing white, thought it _was_ snow and froze to death. Seems kind of nutty but it must be true because they say that in the town hall near the freeze, there is an affidavit attesting to the truth of the story.

But let us move on to cooler times. We simply must do that because the keys on the typewriter recording the above facts got so hot that the editor could touch them no longer.

Consider Michigan where, in Detroit, people must talk to one another through scarves when outside, or the words freeze in the air, fall to the ground where they must be gathered, taken inside and thawed out so as to know what each said to the other.

And those words must be collected because if they blow onto the street, car tires will be cut into ribbons by the words, especially if there has been an argument with sharp words!

Mosquitoes get mighty pesky in Michigan and Minnesota, especially Minnesota where they have eight legs, with stingers on each one. The stinger at the head is six inches long and deadly as all get out. One sting and you're a dead man in one hour. But if the six leg

291

stingers get you along with the beak, well, you are a goner in ten minutes, after turning six shades of green.

But in Chicago, the mosquitoes are a different breed entirely. They are suspicious and refuse to take your blood unless you have a certificate of clean blood out where they can see it.

Speaking of Chicago, the spring of 1991 was the wettest they have had in all the history of that great city. It was so very wet that three hundred and six babies were born with webbed toes!

And there are thousands of American stories that are just as big "whoppers," "windies," or "blanket-stretchers" as those above. They mark the American as a master story-teller who always uses humor to ease the way on the job, in the home, or at leisure. We older Americans understand the need for laughter and the stories that bring it on.

And it is true that our generation has left some of the best stories, the most wonderful humorous tales that the world has ever heard.

So here's to our laughing seniors, whose humorous tall tales and other forms of humor are the equal of any American humor of the past.

Long may they laugh!

ACKNOWLEDGMENT

We are indebted to Laurie Bartolini, Pat Blinn, Marie Ellen Halcli, Jenny Holmberg, Classie Murray, Chris Wagner and Julie Wullner of the Reference Department and Janna Mohan and Jean Ann Long of the Interlibrary Loan Department of the Lincoln Library, Springfield, Illinois; and Vicky Zemaitis and Larry Weyrich, Reference Department and Sondra Hastings, Interlibrary Loan Department, Illinois State Library; Springfield, Illinois; and to Mary Ellen McElligott of Springfield, Illinois, our proof reader.

BIBLIOGRAPHY

A Little Book of Yankee Humor. Yankee Books, Camden, ME

American Legion Magazine. Daniel S. Wheeler, Editor-in-Chief. Indianapolis, IN

As I Look Back, Oscar M. Ridge. 1937. Doubleday & Co. Garden City, NY

Burlington Liar's Club, John Soeth, President. Burlington, WI

Carolina Chats. Carl Goerch. 1944. Edwards & Broughton Co., Raleigh, NC**

Cartoons by William H. Boserman, Garnett, KS

Cartoons by Dave Carpenter, Emmetsburg, IA

Cartoons by Dan Earlywine, Chatham, IL

Cartoons by James Estes, Amarillo, TX

Cartoons by Larry Harris, LaJolla, CA

Cartoons by Norman Hoifield, Fort Lee, NJ

Cartoons by Lo Linkert, Port Coquitlam, B.C. Canada

Cartoons by Eldon Pletcher, Slidell, LA

Cover of book reprinted by permission of Copyright © 1961 Curtis Publishing Co.

Dick Wick Hall, *Stories From The Salome Sun.* Published by Northlands Press, Flagstaff, AZ

Down Home, Carl Goerch. 1943. Published by Edwards & Broughton Co., Raleigh, NC**

Illinois Farm Bureau. 1991. Don Phillips, Editor. Bloomington, Il

It's A Funny World, Gurney Williams. 1941. Crowell-Collier Publishing Co.

Just For The Fun Of It, Carl Goerch. 1954. Edwards & Broughton Co., Raleigh, NC**

Martha J. Beckman (Louise Marty), Granada Hills, CA

On A Slow Train, I & M Ottenheimer. 1905

On a Slow Train Through Arkansas. Thomas W. Jackson.

One Moment, Sir by Marione R. Nickles. Copyright © 1954, 1955, 1956 by The Curtis Publishing Company. Copyright © 1957, 1985 by E. P. Dutton & Co., Inc. Used by permission of the publisher, Dutton, an imprint of New American Library, a division of Penguin Books USA Inc.

Playbook Handbook, Wm. Alan Brooks, Editor. 1942. Knickerbocker Publishers, NY

Reggie The Retiree, (Wesley N. Haines), Ft. Myers, FL 33919

Saturday Evening Post, Indianapolis, IN

Sixth Over Sexteen, J. M. Elgart. Grayson Publishing Corp.

Slams of Life, J. P. McEvoy. 1919. P. F. Volland Co., Chicago, IL

Stories Told In The Kitchen, Kendall Morse. North Country Press, Belfast, ME 04915

Stop Or I'll Scream, Gurney Williams. 1945. Crowell-Collier Publishing Co.

Tall Tales Of The Devil's Apron, H. M. Sutherland. One Mountain Press, Johnson City, TN. Reprinted with permission of Rose E. Sutherland.

**Excerpts from *"Carolina Chats. 1944", "Down Home. 1943",* and *"Just For The Fun Of It. 1954",* written by Carl Goerch, used with the permission of the Estate of Carl Goerch.

Here is a list of the current books of superb humor published by the Lincoln-Herndon Press, Inc.

The humor in these books will delight you, brighten your conversation, make your life more fun, and healthier, because "Laughter Is The Best Medicine."

*Grandpa's Rib-Ticklers & Knee-Slappers	$8.95
*Josh Billings-- America's Phunniest Phellow	$7.95
Davy Crockett -- Legendary Frontier Hero	$7.95
Cowboy Life on the Sidetrack	$7.95
A Treasury of Science Jokes	$8.95
The Great American Liar -- Tall Tales	$9.95
The Cowboy Humor of A.H. Lewis	$9.95
The Fat Mascot. . . 22 Funny Baseball Stories & More	$7.95
A Treasury of Farm & Ranch Humor	$10.95
Mr. Dooley. . .We Need Him Now! The Irish-American Humorist	$8.95
A Treasury of Military Humor	$10.95
Here's Charley Weaver, Mamma and Mt. Idy	$9.95
A Treasury of Hunting and Fishing Humor	$10.95
A Treasury of Senior Humor	$10.95

* These books are also available in hardback.

Order From:

Lincoln-Herndon Press, Inc.
818 South Dirksen Parkway
Springfield, Illinois 62703